America in Decline

Other works by Raymond Lotta

And Mao Makes 5

*The Soviet Union: Socialist or Social-Imperialist?
Part II* (debate with Albert Szymanski)

America in Decline

*An Analysis of the Developments
Toward War and Revolution,
In the U.S. and Worldwide,
in the 1980s*

Volume One

By
Raymond Lotta
with Frank Shannon

BANNER PRESS • CHICAGO

Library of Congress Cataloging in Publication Data

Lotta, Raymond
    America in decline.

        Includes index.
        1. Economic history--20th century--Collected works.
2. Imperialism--History--20th century--Collected works.
3. United States--Foreign economic relations--Collected
works. I. Shannon, Frank, 1947-   . II. Title.
HC54.L63 1984   330.973'0927   83-22294
ISBN 0-916650-12-X (v. 1.)
ISBN 0-916650-13-8 (pbk. : v. 1)

Printed in U.S.A.

Published by:
Banner Press, P.O. Box 6469, Chicago, IL 60680

Contents

Tables and Figures

Tables

Figures

Acknowledgements

America in Decline is the product of several years research and theoretical struggle. Many individuals contributed to that process — sharing data, making specific criticisms and suggestions, and encouraging its completion. But it would be impossible to conceive of this work without the assistance of Bob Avakian, Chairman of the Revolutionary Communist Party, USA. It is to him that we owe the greatest intellectual debt. In the face of a fashionable dismissal of Lenin's conceptual framework of imperialism and disorientation in many quarters as a result of the loss of proletarian power in China in 1976, Avakian has not only stood for Marxist-Leninist principle, but advanced it through analyses of the class struggle in China and of the shifting world situation. We have learned from him and from his example of combining theoretical rigor with historical sweep. He has given us continuing guidance in the preparation of *America in Decline* and has developed fundamental theses which inform this work.

Once the inner connection is grasped, all theoretical belief in the permanent necessity of existing conditions breaks down before their collapse in practice.

— Marx to Kugelmann, 1868

America in Decline

Preface

For years, movements and struggles have pounded at U.S. imperialism. In fact, right within the "belly of the beast," during the period of the 1960s and early 1970s, the mass revolutionary upsurges of Black people and other oppressed nationalities and the antiwar struggles swept the country with an extraordinary ferocity never before seen in U.S. history. While there was an ebb in those struggles and social upheaval has not yet assumed seismic proportions, today the underlying crisis in the world is far more profound.

Yet comprehension of the laws and mechanisms of imperialist crisis, of the historical momentum behind the current crisis, and where it is heading have seriously lagged. Indeed, such an analysis has been most conspicuous by its absence. It is to this task that *America in Decline* is addressed. This work examines the forces shaping U.S. imperialism, the reasons for its enormous strength in the postwar period, the causes of its decline, and the historic significance of the developing international situation.

History's most powerful empire was erected on the ashes of World War 2. Puffed up and confident, the U.S. imperialists coined a phrase to describe the new state of affairs: "The American Century." They tried to portray their savage international exploitation and plunder as the "natural" order of things. And, for large sections of the American people, such plunder came into sharp relief only when mass resistance, especially armed revolutions, broke out in the U.S. empire, or when some other imperialist confronted the U.S.

For all its imperial arrogance, the American colossus would not have its century. The very advantages and real strengths the U.S.

derived from the settlement of World War 2 not only made possible
a period of marked expansion, but also contained the seeds of
severe economic crisis. The defense and extension of empire gave
rise to resistance from the world's people and to conflicts with
rivals. These nearly four decades of United States dominance are
now turning into their explosive opposite. Listen to the somber
prediction made by the Middle East chief of a major U.S. bank: "It
was easy in the pre-Vietnam days to look at an area on the map and
say, 'that's ours' and feel pretty good about investing there. That's
no longer the case, as Iran has made so terribly clear. American investment overseas is going to happen at a reduced rate until we can
redefine our world. . . ."[1]

The year 1968 can be viewed as a turning point; certain events
were bellwethers of America in decline. The Vietnamese launched
their nationwide Tet offensive. The dollar-gold standard had its
first real trial of strength, a fact hardly unrelated to Vietnam. Later
that year the Soviets invaded Czechoslovakia. The Soviet revisionists, who seized power in the mid-1950s and began the process
of restoring capitalism, emerged in the 1970s as imperialist rivals
increasingly forced to mount, and capable of mounting, a challenge
to the worldwide interests of U.S. imperialism. As the 1980s opened,
the economic and political crisis gripping both the U.S.-led and
Soviet-led blocs and the interimperialist rivalry with which that
crisis interacted were approaching the boiling point. In the following typically grim prognosis, *Business Week* bemoaned the uncer-
tainty facing the world economy: "For the first time in nearly forty
years, forecasts can no longer be based primarily on financial and
economic criteria. The international arena has so deteriorated in
the last year that political factors — and the potential for military
conflict — are as important in predicting world economies as are inflation, growth, unemployment, or foreign exchange."[2] The imperialists are readying to hurl entire continents at one another. The
brutal yet inescapable fact is that world war not only looms on the
horizon, but is an integral and necessary feature of capitalism in the
imperialist epoch.

As this preface is being written, it is possible to look back on a
brief two years in which the pace of events in the "deteriorating"
international arena noticeably quickened: near economic collapses

---

[1] Quoted in *Business Week,* 12 March 1979, p. 74.

[2] *Business Week,* 31 December 1979, p. 110.

in Mexico and Poland; insurgencies in Central America; wars in the South Atlantic, Africa, the Persian Gulf, and the Middle East; and massive weapons systems build-ups on land, at sea, and in space by both imperialist blocs. In the Third World, the combined effects of world economic crisis and political conflict have resulted in vast migrations of humanity — out of Haiti, Nigeria, the Horn of Africa, Southeast Asia. . .the list goes on. In the seven major imperialist countries of the U.S.-led bloc, twenty-two million are officially unemployed, while in the "wealthiest" country itself fifty percent of Black youth cannot find work.

Against this backdrop, the bankruptcy and inanity of mainstream economics stand out the more. In a survey of the difficulties wracking the economies of the Western countries during the 1970s, the London-based financial journal, *The Economist*, examined the track record of contemporary bourgeois economic theory: "It has been a bad decade for economics."[3] Indeed it was. Forecasters were habitually off in their predictions, public officials reversed themselves on policy prescriptions, and research institutes found themselves grasping at straws. When it came to explaining the 1974-1975 global downturn, a watershed in post-World War 2 economic history, the Organization for Economic Cooperation and Development (which acts to coordinate economic policy among the Western powers) produced this authoritative observation: "the most important feature was an unusual bunching of unfortunate disturbances unlikely to be repeated on the same scale, the impact of which was compounded by some avoidable errors in economic policy."[4]

Such thinking reflected the conventional wisdom of the postwar period: the notion that satisfactory levels of output and employment could be sustained through the right mix of fiscal and monetary measures. But this wisdom, once seemingly validated by a sustained and dynamic expansion of unprecedented dimensions, was shattered by the continued deepening of crisis. The annual economic summits which commenced in the wake of the mid-'70s downturn saw reflationary strategies replaced by deflationary measures, inflationary pressures yielding to stagnation, and attempts at monetary stabilization leading to major financial disturbances. One specialist quipped in connection with fashionable

---

[3] *The Economist,* 29 December 1979 - 4 January 1980, p. 41.

[4] Paul McCracken, et al., *Towards Full Employment and Price Stability* (Paris: Organization for Economic Cooperation and Development, 1977), p. 103.

monetarism: "we have a quantity theory of no one knows what."[5] As the 1980s opened, Nobel laureates were haggling over whether "depression" or "recession" was the right term to describe the current state of the world economy.

It is certainly not for want of technical sophistication that bourgeois economics cannot explain crisis. If anything, the formal elegance of its computer-nourished models seems to correlate with their essential emptiness. The problem could be likened to the practice of alchemy — some highly complex and developed procedures and methods, but lacking any scientific foundation. This is not to deny the value of computers; it is simply to observe that the class position and interest of those who seek to rationalize and defend a rotting system make it impossible for them to grasp the world as it is, and as it is developing. To be sure, the scholars and experts have not all been Pollyannish. Running counterpoint to the antiseptic micro- and macro-theories of capitalist rationality and adaptability has been a kind of doomsday thinking, which found an early and celebrated expression in the Club of Rome's 1972 *The Limits to Growth*. This was a modern Malthusianism: predictions of a cataclysmic collapse of the world economy due to overpopulation and resource exhaustion. There has also been a revival of "long-wave" theory, which postulates a prolonged slowdown. If the learned hands do not know exactly what should be done, they do know the capitalist system is pushing against certain limits — even as they seek to theoretically explain this with a conjurer's trickery.

America in Decline owes its existence to a renascence of Marxist theory stimulated by the revolutionary upsurges of the 1960s. Many activists, inspired by the national liberation struggles in the Third World and the Cultural Revolution in China, turned to Marxism, both to develop a systematic understanding of what was happening in the world and to establish the theoretical line of sight of the struggle to transform it. The Cultural Revolution embodied a living critique and produced a body of ideas which challenged what had come to be regarded as socialism and socialist theory, namely the Soviet Union and a "Marxism" which, in method and outlook, had been effectively gutted of rebellion and revolution. In their polemics with the Soviets, Mao and the Chinese revolutionaries defended the principles of armed struggle and the dictatorship of the proletariat. They undertook the formidable task of making an

---

[5] *The Economist,* 29 December 1979 - 4 January 1980, p. 41.

analysis of the dynamics of classes and class struggle in socialist society, and they generated a politics – the theory of continuing revolution – and a political economy of the socialist transition period. But while the Chinese revolutionaries posited an assessment of the international situation in the early 1970s, based on the likely outbreak of interimperialist world war unless prevented by revolution, they did not develop a comprehensive analysis of the political economy of imperialism in the postwar period.

The foundation for such an analysis had been laid several decades earlier in Lenin's *Imperialism, The Highest Stage of Capitalism,* which represented the major breakthrough in Marxist political economy since *Capital.* Not only did it systematize an understanding of the major developments in the capitalist mode of production since Marx wrote his masterwork, but it provided the framework for a revolutionary internationalist politics in the imperialist era. However, as Lenin himself reminded his readers, this was only an outline. Unfortunately, the theoretical work begun by Lenin was not carried forward by the international communist movement. In fact, in the formulations of "general crisis" associated with the Comintern, which continue to exert a deleterious influence on Marxist political economy, Marx and Lenin's methodology was largely abandoned. Given an impoverished tradition which, in effect, served as an immunization against reality and could only counsel faith in the "coming collapse," it was not surprising that various noncommunist schools of Marxist economic thought developed and to some degree flourished during different phases of the postwar period.

In coming to grips with the dynamics of imperialism since the end of World War 2, it has been necessary on our part to settle accounts with these schools. Neo-Marxists subjected the basic laws of accumulation discovered by Marx to major criticism. Many brands of "Third Worldist" thought (which in fact incorporated central tenets of neo-Marxism) saw in the very sharp contradictions between the metropoles and the oppressed periphery the basic motor of capitalist accumulation which could run almost endlessly. And particularly as the inadequacies of these other conceptions became more manifest, there were those who argued for a "return to *Capital*," mainly restricting themselves to exegetical glosses or "proofs" of Marx's theorems. Each school has in a fashion attempted to tackle the real problems of analysis posed by world developments, but none has been capable of grasping the dialectics of imperialism and proletarian revolution in any thoroughgoing and scientific way. The neo-Marxists focused on a single aspect of the postwar period, the sustained boom, without grasping its contradictory coordinates. While the "Third Worldists" correctly laid great stress on the role of the colonies in the process of imperialist accumulation, they raised one aspect of imperialism to the basic exclusion of all others. While correctly insisting upon Marxist rigor, many of those advocating a return to the categories of *Capital* functionally denied the specificity of imperialism. None of these approaches could explain the complexity and direction of world events, much less support a revolutionary and internationalist politics.

A conceptual starting point of this work is that the world economy must be treated as an integral whole. In a word, if we want to understand why there is starvation in the Sahel, why there are modern skyscrapers in São Paulo, why there is youth rebellion in the West or a momentary ebbing of revolutionary struggles in the 1970s, and why imperialism is headed toward world war, we must look first to the international environment of capitalism. One crucial feature of that environment is the existence of an imperialist power which arose out of the reversal of socialism and which still makes use of many of the forms and structures developed under socialism — that is, Soviet social-imperialism. We refer to the Soviet Union — and to its bloc — as social-imperialist because of its history as a socialist state and the peculiar ideological camouflage of its depredations. While the purpose of this work is not to analyze that particularity and its historical underpinnings as such, the basic laws which we analyze apply to both imperialist blocs, and a full presentation of their significance and operation is impossible without reference to the social-imperialist formations.

Much of the preparation of *America in Decline* involved close textual study of Marx in light of Lenin's work on imperialism, and of Lenin in light of major international developments since he elaborated his analysis. The continued development of imperialism and the accumulation of vast new experience (including that of socialist revolution) require and make possible further systematization, both of the particularities of the postwar period and of the inner driving forces of imperialism as a stage of world history. But this can only be undertaken by building on the conclusions of Marx and Lenin, and on the basis of their methodology and outlook. In this context, Mao's important philosophical contribution on dialectics and on the relationship between the objective and subjective factors and the conscious dynamic role of man becomes most relevant:

the purpose of making such an analysis is to accelerate the trend of history.

This work is no mere academic exercise. If it can be said to be making up for lost time, it is only because we are in a race against time. We are approaching one of those brief but decisive periods of exceptional historical and social tension, when the routines of normal life are shattered, when the possibilities for revolution are heightened. This has particular significance in a country like the United States which has been responsible for the suffering and deaths of hundreds of millions throughout the world. The very bulwark of imperialism in the postwar period will soon be plunged into great disorder. At the same time, revolutionary struggles in all parts of the world will bear tremendously on the situation and course of events in the U.S., and it is the inevitable conclusion of our analysis that maximizing revolutionary gains for the international proletariat as a whole must be the fundamental point of departure in all countries — a basic truth which takes on magnified significance in such decisive periods. What is attempted and accomplished — and here we speak of revolutionary initiatives — will reverberate powerfully through the future of human history.

* * * *

When *America in Decline* was originally conceived, our plan was to produce a single-volume study. In the years since, it has evolved into a more ambitious project and will appear in several volumes to be released successively. This first volume contains three introductory essays: a theoretical introduction, an historical introduction, and a critical introduction. Chapter 1 of this first volume sets forth the basic theory, arguments, and analytic approach of the work. It covers ground which the reader may find difficult to negotiate. But this chapter provides the necessary framework for grappling with the main themes of the work as a whole. Chapter 2 sketches the rise of U.S. imperialism through the first two world wars. Chapter 3 contains a critique of the traditional view of imperialist crisis promulgated by the international communist movement. The next series of volumes treats the reorganization of the world economy following World War 2; the forging of the U.S.-led imperialist bloc and its development through the postwar period; the significance of a socialist camp and its transformation into a rival imperialist bloc; and the Third World as a "gold-mine" and "mine-field" for imperialism. These studies will be followed by a detailed examination of the mechanisms and dynamics of imperialist accumulation and by analysis of the particularities of the political economy of U.S. imperialism, including the role of the state, banking and credit, and agriculture. The work will conclude with a mapping of the current world crisis and an assessment of the prospects and forces for revolution in the 1980s.

Chicago
October 1983   Raymond Lotta

1

Political Economy
in the
Epoch of Imperialism
and
Proletarian Revolution

Were the laws governing natural and historical phenomena simply reducible to or identical with external appearances, scientific inquiry would itself be unnecessary. When many of the classical bourgeois political and economic theorists took as their point of departure the discrete individual and the market (which ostensibly maximized and reconciled conflicting self-interests), they were not merely constructing an apologia, but fastening on and absolutizing certain surface features of a social order whose logic they regarded as natural and eternal. Karl Marx pierced this veil of appearance, revealing the underlying production relations of capitalist society, their historical evolution, and why they necessarily assumed particular external forms.

The Marxist science of political economy studies the production relations of society: ownership of the means of production, interconnections among people in the labor process, and distribution of the social product. It is not things, but relations among people that this science investigates, and in a society divided into classes these relations are ultimately manifested in class relations. Such a study, however, cannot be pursued narrowly — limited to factories or other similar production units or even, especially in this era, to countries, taken as self-contained entities. Nor can one system (of production relations) be taken statically, severed from the historical development of the productive forces. Political economy must confront dynamic systems in their international relationships and their processes of change.

In chronicling the bloody genesis of capital and showing that capitalist production pivots on the exploitation of wage-labor, Marx demonstrated how the particular motion of this mode of production lays the material foundations for a higher social order, producing the very agent of the old order's destruction and society's transformation, a social force whose emancipation will require the abolition of all forms of exploitation:

> [N]o credit is due to me for discovering either the existence of classes in modern society or the struggle between them. Long before me bourgeois historians had described the historical development of this class struggle and bourgeois economists the economic anatomy of the classes. What I did that was new was to demonstrate: (1) that the *existence of classes* is merely linked to *particular historical phases in the development of production*, (2) that class struggle necessarily leads to the *dictatorship of the proletariat*, (3) that this dictatorship itself only constitutes the transition to the *abolition of all classes* and to a *classless society.* [1]

As against religious and idealist views of history, of supermen and supernatural forces, of unchanging human nature and doctrine (or pure happenstance), Marxism attaches analytic primacy to the material substructure of society from which arise the institutions, ideas, passions, and social and political movements of particular epochs. Within the structure of a social formation, it is the economic sphere, or the unity and struggle of the forces and relations of production, which principally determines the complexion and motion of that formation. What is engaged here, however, is not a one-dimensional and mechanistic rendering of "ultimate" causes, but a materialist and dialectical understanding of how, in the crucible of humanity's productive activity and class struggle, social transformation takes place, and what the various links and different levels of mediation of this "life-process of society" are. [2] Specifically, with respect to the political economy of capitalism, we are dealing with a complex process: the working out of the contradiction between socialized production and private appropria-

---

[1] "Marx to Joseph Weydemeyer in New York" (5 March 1852), in Karl Marx and Frederick Engels, *Selected Correspondence* (Moscow: Progress Publishers, 1975), p. 64.

[2] Marx, *Capital,* I, p. 84. All references to the three volumes of *Capital* are to the hardcover Progress Publishers edition, Moscow, 1971.

tion; its interpenetration with the other contradictions flowing from or incorporated in this process; the interrelation among the spheres of production, exchange, and distribution, with the sphere of production dominant overall and ultimately determinant; and, finally, the continual movement, disruption, and transformation (of commodities into money and vice versa, of human labor into mechanized labor, of many capitals into fewer capitals, of expansion into crisis, etc.) through which this mode of production and its contradictions are reproduced on a higher level.

Marxism posits a dynamic of history based on the real material and social forces operating in human society. To contend that there are objective factors which account for movement and change is not, however, tantamount to positing a predictable progression of events: the specific pathway leading to — and the resulting configuration of — the present-day world was certainly not the only one possible. Wars won could have been lost, revolutions defeated could have triumphed, and vice versa. Nor is the Marxist dynamic of history predicated on smooth or unilinear progress. The disintegration of old production relations and the emergence of new ones is a continuing process of forward leaps and retrogression, a process suffused with complicated class struggles. Things develop, whether in nature or society, through the struggle of opposites and through spiral-like motion marked by profound discontinuities. Capitalism, then, must be understood as a mode of production which is subject to and develops according to laws specific to that mode of production. Yet it does not hew to a predetermined course of development. It must be studied in its historical concreteness and contingency, and the choices made and made good by the battalions of human actors are important elements of that concreteness and contingency. What is certain, however, is that capitalism's fundamental contradiction grows more intense and is repeatedly and more explosively posed for resolution. The advance to a higher social order, for which the material conditions are created by capitalism, can only be effected through ever more conscious struggle and transformation.

Capitalism has developed to a higher stage, its final stage, the outcome of the very laws of accumulation discovered by Marx. As Lenin concluded:

Imperialism emerged as the development and direct continuation of the fundamental characteristics of capitalism in general. But capitalism only became capitalist imperialism at a definite and very high

stage of its development, when certain of its fundamental characteristics began to change into their opposites, when the features of the
epoch of transition from capitalism to a higher social and economic
system had taken shape and revealed themselves all along the line.[3]

These features and their profound historic significance were the
object of Lenin's analysis. New structural relations, whose material
basis in the advanced countries lay in the growth of monopoly,
emerged out of the general environment of capitalism, competition, and commodity production. But in attempting to surmount
the environment into which it is locked, monopoly creates more
acute antagonism and conflict. The era of imperialism, Lenin emphasized, is a violent threshold to something higher:

> Capitalism in its imperialist stage leads right up to the most com-
> prehensive socialization of production; it, so to speak, drags the
> capitalists, against their will and consciousness, into some sort of a
> new social order, a transitional one from complete free competition
> to complete socialization. . . .
>
> The extent to which monopolist capital has intensified all the
> contradictions of capitalism is generally known. . . . This inten-
> sification of contradictions constitutes the most powerful driving
> force of the transitional period of history. . . .[4]

The purpose of this introductory chapter is to examine the laws
of motion of the imperialist system and to show how they heighten
revolutionary possibilities. It is, of necessity, a defense and extension of Lenin's analysis of imperialism, which remains the essential
framework for understanding the diverse trends of this epoch. But
just as imperialism arose on the foundation of capitalism, so, too,
did Leninism arise on the foundation of a certain science — Marxism. It is necessary to grasp what is universal to the capitalist mode
of production in order to uncover the laws particular to its imperialist stage of development. The chapter thus has two major
tasks. The first is to establish that the inner laws of capital as
discovered and expounded by Marx remain the heart of accumula-

---

[3] V.I. Lenin, *Imperialism, The Highest Stage of Capitalism* (Peking: Foreign
Languages Press, 1975), p. 104; also in Lenin, *Collected Works (LCW)* (Moscow: Progress Publishers), Vol. 22, p. 265. Hereafter references to *Imperialism* will be given first
to the Peking edition, followed in parentheses by the parallel citation to the *Collected
Works*. All *Collected Works* references are to 1977 printings.

[4] *Imperialism*, pp. 25, 150 (*LCW*, 22, pp. 205, 300).

tion in the imperialist era. The second is to uphold and to extend Lenin's work and to elucidate the particular dynamics that govern the process of world accumulation in this epoch. We begin by examining the properties of capital identified by Marx.

I

Common to every social formation is the labor process. Society is an organized means within and through which human beings produce (and reproduce) their requirements of life — in a word, they work, and in doing so at once meet and alter these requirements; they are themselves changed. Production constitutes the essential interchange of human beings with nature; but production, this struggle with nature, exists in dialectical unity with the relations, and the struggle, among people:

> In production, men not only act on nature but also on one another. They produce only by cooperating in a certain way and mutually exchanging their activities. In order to produce, they enter into definite connections and relations with one another and only within these social connections and relations does their action on nature, does production, take place.[5]

Capitalism is merely a concrete, historical stage of human society corresponding to a certain level of development of the productive forces (that is, the materials and techniques fashioned by human labor and the capabilities of that labor itself) which require "definite connections and relations." Capitalist society, understood as a productive process and a web of social and class relations, turns on commodity production: production not for direct and immediate use or consumption, but for exchange organized and controlled by individuals or groups of individuals.[6]

In all societies some mechanism must regulate and determine distribution of the means of production and labor in order to produce and utilize a social surplus. In capitalist society, the products

---

[5] Marx, *Wage-Labor and Capital*, in Marx and Engels, *Selected Works (MESW)* (Moscow: Progress Publishers, 1973), 1, p. 159.

[6] In what follows we draw on the exposition of Owen Natha, "Commodities, Capitalism, Class Divisions — and their Abolition with the Achievement of Communism," in *The Communist*, Vol. 1, No. 1 (October 1976), pp. 3-22.

of concrete labor, or use values (the material substratum of all wealth), simultaneously present themselves as values: they possess a determinate amount of abstract labor, of society's total expenditure of labor — that is, the application of labor power in general, abstracted from its particular form — according to which they may exchange in definite proportion and on the basis of which social labor itself is allocated. This is the law of value:

> Every child knows that a nation which ceased to work, I will not say for a year, but even for a few weeks, would perish. Every child knows, too, that the volume of products corresponding to the different needs require different and quantitatively determined amounts of the total labor of society. That this *necessity* of the *distribution* of social labor in definite proportions cannot possibly be done away with by a *particular form* of social production but can only change the *mode* of *its appearance*, is self-evident. . . . And the form in which this proportional distribution of labor asserts itself, in a social system where the interconnection of social labor manifests itself through the *private exchange* of individual products of labor, is precisely the *exchange value* of these products.[7]

In capitalist society, human labor and its products are not *consciously* allocated; social production is not subject to the *direct* calculation of labor time. This occurs *indirectly* through exchange and the mediation of value relations. Under capitalism, independently organized labor processes are dominated by the pursuit of profit. Discrete capitals or blocs of capital decide what and how much to produce, and control the fruits of socialized labor. Yet each particular labor process is objectively linked to and dependent on others. The law of value unites these fragments into a social whole. Through the lure of profit and the signaling of prices (which are ultimately regulated by the expenditure of living labor), a specific social division of labor coheres and asserts itself. The direct measurement of value does not enter into the actual calculations of the capitalists; they deal with monetary phenomena, specifically the difference between cost price and selling price. It could be no other way given the private organization of the labor process. In exchange, specifically through money, individual concrete labor is directly

---

[7] "Marx to Ludwig Kugelmann in Hanover" (11 July 1868), *Selected Correspondence*, p. 196.

represented as its opposite, social abstract labor.[8] *Value is the manifestation of social labor peculiar to commodity-producing society; the law of value, most especially the production and capitalization of surplus value, is the connecting and directing force of capitalist society.*

Capital is indeed guided by an "invisible hand," though not in the fashion presumed by Adam Smith. The individual capitals of society interact with each other as units of the total social capital; what appears as the product of the capitalists' free will in fact expresses the inner pressure of a social mechanism. As Marx explained: "The essence of bourgeois society consists precisely in this, that a priori there is no conscious social regulation of production."[9] Capitalist economic laws operate behind the backs of individual capitals. Competition, that harmonizing wand in the world of bourgeois political economy, is actually an internecine battle. Further, these laws are realized through and in the midst of ceaseless flux:

> [T]he law of the value of commodities ultimately determines how much of its disposable working time society can expend on each particular class of commodities. But this constant tendency to equilibrium, of the various spheres of production, is exercised, only in the shape of a reaction against the constant upsetting of this equilibrium.[10]

Elsewhere, discussing value/price deviations, Marx noted that the "total movement of this disorder is its order."[11] Moreover, this mode of production is founded on and rent by antagonistic class conflict.

In sum, then, capitalism neither functions according to nor is comprehensible on the basis of some immanent equilibrium. Its regulatory processes generate disequilibrium and conflict, and operate through disequilibrium and conflict. Capitalism is a contradictory and antagonistic unity.

---

[8] Commodities acquire a definite measure of their value in money — value assumes the external form of price in the realm of circulation — and in becoming manifestations of social, abstract (general) labor, commodities can act as such, i.e., they can be exchanged for all other commodities in proportion to their value. See Marx, *Theories of Surplus Value*, III (Moscow: Progress Publishers, 1969, 1968, and 1971 editions for Parts I, II, and III respectively), pp. 130-36. The objective existence of abstract labor allows money to function as a measure of value.

[9] "Marx to Kugelmann," *Selected Correspondence*, p. 197.

[10] *Capital*, I, p. 336.

[11] Marx, *Wage-Labor and Capital*, MESW, 1, p. 157.

The commodity is the germ of the social relations of capitalism. Capitalism grows out of and represents the highest development of — in fact, it generalizes — commodity production. Central to such generalized commodity production is the transformation of labor power into a commodity. The exchange of this unique commodity against capital is the most fundamental exchange in capitalist society; within it lies the origin of surplus value, of profit. "The essential difference between the various economic forms of society, between, for instance, a society based on slave labor, and one based on wage-labor," Marx wrote, "lies only in the mode in which this surplus labor is in each case extracted from the actual producer, the laborer."[12]

The violent separation of the immediate producers from the means of production constituted the social basis of capitalism's rapid development in parts of Europe. The various poor and vagabond laws of the sixteenth and seventeenth centuries and the land enclosure acts, which helped prepare the way for the industrial revolution in Great Britain, were prominent institutional expressions of the formation and disciplining of an "outlaw" class of proletarians. This separation lies at the core of the capital relation: "[the] severance of the conditions of production, on the one hand, from the producers, on the other . . . forms the conception of capital."[13] Capitalism's historical conditions of existence, Marx argued,

> are by no means given with the mere circulation of money and commodities. It can spring into life, only when the owner of the means of production and subsistence meets in the market with the free laborer selling his labor power. And this one historical condition comprises a world's history. Capital, therefore, announces from its first appearance a new epoch in the process of social production.[14]

As an individual, the wage laborer is free from personal and customary servitude or obligation; he or she is not property, as is the slave in that mode of production. But the wage laborer is barred from access to and control over means of production, and forced, therefore, to sell the only property at his or her disposal, labor

[12] *Capital*, I, p. 209.
[13] *Capital*, III, p. 246.
[14] *Capital*, I, p. 167.

power (the capacity to work), in order to receive wages with which to live. The laborer becomes a wage-slave, a slave not to particular capitals, but to capital in general. "The Roman slave was held by fetters: the wage laborer is bound to his owner by invisible threads. The appearance of independence is kept up by means of a constant change of employers, and by the *fictio juris* of a contract."[15] The proletarian is "freed" from ownership of means of production and "free" to work or to starve. Monopolization of the means of production by the capitalist class and the existence of free wage-labor allow the capitalist to combine means of production and labor power fluidly and flexibly (in this or that line of investment, in this or that locale, in response to this or that market condition) in the pursuit of profit.

The category abstract labor is not an arbitrary construct or a logical common denominator. It reflects the historical displacement of artisans and craftsmen by propertyless and mobile laborers and the separation of labor from the land: "Indifference towards specific labors corresponds to a form of society in which individuals can with ease transfer from one labor to another, and where the specific kind is a matter of chance for them, hence of indifference."[16] Abstract labor thus reflects the objective transformation of the labor process, its socialization and homogenization. The material reality of equivalent labor, of labor as value, is bound up with the transformation of labor power into a commodity.

The separation of the producers from the means of production estranges them from the products of their labor and the very process through which those products are produced. Labor, as Marx penetratingly described it, becomes "alienated from itself" — on the one hand, there is the laborer and, on the other, there is the laborer's physical and mental powers, to be bought and sold.[17] Not only is there this separation of the individual from his or her activity — in that the capitalist controls it — but this productive activity itself is transformed into the material conditions for the continued and expanded enslavement of wage-labor, for the reproduction of

[15] *Capital,* I, p. 538.

[16] Marx, *Grundrisse,* translated with a foreword by Martin Nicolaus (London: Penguin, 1973), p. 104. On the material and social basis of abstract labor, see Lucio Colletti, "Bernstein and the Marxism of the Second International," in *From Rousseau to Lenin* (London: New Left Books, 1972), pp. 76-88.

[17] *Theories of Surplus Value,* III, p. 259.

the capital relation, a class relation of exploitation. The proletariat is confronted and ruled by its own creations.

With the generalization of commodity production, the whole of social life is at once stamped with exchange relations, incorporated into the cash nexus, and mystified:

> [A] definite social relation between men . . . assumes, in their eyes, the fantastic form of a relation between things. In order, therefore, to find an analogy, we must have recourse to the mist-enveloped regions of the religious world. In that world the productions of the human brain appear as independent beings endowed with life, and entering into relation both with one another and the human race. So it is in the world of commodities with the products of men's hands. This I call the Fetishism which attaches itself to the products of labor, so soon as they are produced as commodities, and which is therefore inseparable from the production of commodities.[18]

Under commodity production, relations between people in production and social relations between people in general are disguised as relations between things, between products, between commodities. People appear to each other as the owners of this or that commodity and the fact that they are part of a broader social division of labor only becomes clear when they exchange commodities in the market (through which individual labor manifests its social character and is validated). Social labor is not treated as such; it is not directly and consciously deployed by society as a whole. That labor is the bond between people in society, indeed the very basis for society, is hidden because labor is carried out by socially fragmented (privately organized) groups of individuals. Hence, any given part of social labor is not immediately recognized as just that — part of the aggregate labor of society — nor is it stamped as social labor except in the exchange of commodities.[19] In sum, as a result of

---

[18] *Capital,* I, p. 77.

[19] Fluctuations in prices are the signal that too much or too little social labor has been expended in particular spheres of production. In response to these market signals, social labor is reallocated. Changes in supply and demand produce fluctuations of commodity prices around commodity values. If a particular commodity is overproduced, its price will fall below its value and the producers in that line of production will fail to receive the full value of their commodities. If, on the other hand, demand for a particular commodity is greater than its supply, then the producers will receive more value in the form of money than the socially necessary labor contained in their commodities. The market prices of commodities will deviate from the direct monetary expression of their value. But the sum total of prices is tied to the sum total of values.

this spontaneous development of the social division of labor and the mediating role of the exchange process and money, labor times are indirectly compared and social labor indirectly distributed.

The historically progressive role of capitalism (apart from creating a world market) lay in concentrating and transforming limited and scattered means of production into social means of production worked by — and only workable by — a collectivity of individuals. Capitalism transformed production from a series of individual acts, in which tools and instruments were mainly used by and adapted to the labor of single or small groups of individuals, into a series of social acts, in which individual products become much more fully social products with the development of more advanced means of production. In lower stages of society people did at times work together in large aggregations; in ancient society labor was combined into one process in mining and construction of "public works," and large-scale agriculture was an occasional feature of both ancient and medieval society. In essence, production always is social, since particular activities are part of the objective division of labor. But by dramatically scaling previous natural and technical barriers, capitalism raised the objectively social nature of production to a qualitatively new level; it created socialized labor based on the combination and interaction of mass labor with the machine system. Under capitalism labor became directly social *within the process of production itself.* [20]

The energy and acquired knowledge and skill of various kinds of labor were formed into a cooperative mode of activity and articulated into a complex division of labor to produce a social product. Capitalism stimulated scientific discovery and it became possible to apply science on a far-ranging scale to the productive process. Perfection of the factory system and the subsequent mechanization of labor operations converted the individual laborer into what Marx called "an organ of the collective laborer [to] perform one of its subordinate functions." [21] The collective laborer is the embodiment of this profoundly social process of production: the mining of ore, the casting of steel, the design and manufacture of a machine tool are, by themselves and in connection with each other, highly

[20] See Engels, *Anti-Dühring* (Moscow: Progress Publishers, 1969), pp. 318-19; *Capital*, III, pp. 104, 266.

[21] *Capital*, I, p. 476.

socialized and interdependent processes. But this living social organism must adapt and subordinate itself to the imperatives of capital and its organization of production.

The fundamental contradiction of capitalist society is between socialized production and private appropriation. The means of production are produced by socialized labor and can only be made use of by socialized labor. But capitalism, owing to the monopolization of wealth and of the means of producing wealth by the capitalist class which controls labor power, stands in the way of the direct social organization of production — and of distribution, which depends on production — of the material requirements of life. In capitalist society, the productive process is a complex aggregation of highly entwined and interdependent elements. Yet, the individual elements forming this totality are discrete, if increasingly collective, units of capital, which exist in opposition to each other and which are driven, on pain of extinction and on the basis of this property relation of private ownership, to outflank and outstrip each other. In capitalist society, social development takes place and societal interests are met through the interaction of contending capitals — but the internal contradictions of this social matrix continually impinge upon and undermine it.

As the most highly developed, most general form of commodity production, production under capitalism finds expression in the operation of blind forces: the tendency to expand the social productivity of labor as though there were no limits, and the collision of this expansion with the actual limits imposed by capitalist relations. And so, within the U.S. auto industry, for example, one can observe intensified competition leading to the near bankruptcy of one of the "Big 3," the potential shock waves from which would be staggering. In terms of intersectoral relations, one can observe the disparity, for instance, between Soviet heavy industry and agriculture, which has reached crisis proportions in recent years and which is placing enormous strains on that economy. On an international plane, the steel industry of the Western bloc is saddled with excess capacity, its markets saturated. Certain oppressed countries, like Mexico and Brazil, where industrialization has been most extensive and rapid, now face the prospect of economic collapse and political upheaval. Looking at the world economy as a whole, the years 1948-1971 witnessed unprecedented expansion — the average annual rate of industrial growth was virtually twice the average annual rate during the entire period 1700-1971.[22] Yet, today, capitalism is engulfed by its most serious crisis ever and stands poised for a world war of mutual conquest beside which the destruction and the fifty million killed during the last one will pale in comparison.[23]

The greater the development of socialized production, the more it undermines the basis of capitalism's existence and brings into sharper and sharper antagonism the basic contradiction between socialized production and private appropriation. In its historical development, this contradiction has characterized and shaped the entire capitalist epoch — and this is so in an intensified and more all-encompassing way in the epoch of imperialism and proletarian revolution.

Capitalism has laid the foundations for the world as a whole to advance to an entirely new stage of human history, to overcome the scarcity which is the ultimate source of antagonistic social conflict. But it has done so through exploitation, plunder, and by greatly distorting distribution and rational allocation of the world's resources. Only when worldwide proletarian revolution puts an end to *all* the social relations of capital will the era of communism begin. It is this revolution that strikes at and rips up the roots of exploitation, oppression, and social inequality; only with the achievement of communism can society rationally confront and transform nature — and itself.

[22] W.W. Rostow, *The World Economy: History and Prospects* (Austin: Univ. of Texas Press, 1978), pp. 48-49, 659-62 (where the sources for this index of world industrial production are cited along with a discussion of methodology). The aggregate growth rate includes the Soviet bloc and Third World in the post-World War 2 period. The growth rates for the earlier periods are based on the most comprehensive data available for world totals.

[23] Indeed, the scale and speed of technical and scientific advance in this century know no parallel in human history. It has been estimated that the entire body of human knowledge roughly doubled from the mid-1950s to the mid-1970s; 90 percent of all scientists and engineers ever professionally trained are now alive (Rostow, *World Economy*, p. 630). Yet twice already in this century the major effort of industrial countries has been parlayed into the development and manufacture of weapons — the sum spent on the development of the first atomic bomb was more than had been spent on all the scientific research and development carried out since the beginning of human civilization (J.D. Bernal, *Science in History*, Volume 3 [Cambridge: MIT Press, 1971], p. 834).

II

The aim and motive of capitalist production is not use values as such, but production of surplus value, production of commodities containing more labor than has been paid for by the capitalist. The secret behind the extraction of surplus value lies in the surplus (unpaid) labor appropriated by the capitalist. As Marx laid bare, what the laborers bring to the market and sell to the capitalist is not in fact labor but the temporary use of themselves as a working power, that is, their *labor power*. The value of their labor power is equivalent to the labor time (value) embodied in their means of subsistence — their physiological and social needs must be met so they can offer themselves for sale on a continuing basis — and the cost of rearing a new generation of workers. Ultimately, wages correspond to these reproduction costs. Again, with the replacement of natural production by commodity production relations, reality is masked: in the realm of circulation, a relation of equality appears to exist, i.e., wages are received in return for work. In fact, in exchange for wages (representing the value of their reproduction costs) workers perform labor in excess of what these wages represent; they produce the equivalent of their wages *and* an increment above and beyond the cost of their necessities of life.

Capitalist accumulation is the accumulation of surplus value, the reconversion of surplus value into capital (into additional means of production and labor power) with which to produce more surplus value. The capitalist strives neither to amass use values for himself nor simply to form a money hoard, but to carry on this process of accumulation as an end in itself. Production of surplus value is not a matter of choice or desire; it is an inner necessity. From this necessity flows the objectively operating tendency of capital to constantly reduce the labor time necessary for the production of commodities.

As will be recalled, only on the basis of capitalist production does the commodity become the general form taken by the products of social labor. With the advent of capitalism an important and crucial development takes shape: the ingredients now entering into the productive process itself do so as commodities, and the entire production process becomes one of capital circulation. Marx explains:

> We are no longer faced with the individual commodity, the individual product. The individual commodity, the individual prod-

uct, manifests itself not only as a real product but also as a commodity, as a *part* both really and conceptually of production as a whole. Each individual commodity represents a definite portion of capital and of the surplus value created by it.[24]

A commodity requires for its production only a certain amount of labor time (socially necessary labor time), and the different producers face a certain compulsion. To begin with, they must sell their entire output as commodities. Further, if they are to retrieve what they have expended for means of production and labor power and realize the surplus labor performed by wage workers, that is, if they are to convert their commodities into money (and more money than they began with, besides), then they must produce according to certain norms. These norms are established through the interaction of competing capitals and enforced by the requirement that capital seek out the highest rate of return. The existence of a market for means of production and labor power presents the individual capitalist with a simultaneous opportunity and threat: he can move from one sphere of production to another in search of higher profits, yet other capitals can enter his line of production and undermine his position. The capitalist cannot resume and expand commodity production, cannot complete and begin anew the circuit of capital, unless he produces at the socially determined level of efficiency. Failing this, he could not sell his commodities — they would be overpriced — or he would be forced to sell at a loss, compelled to modernize or go bankrupt. Hence the labor (or part of the labor) performed and embodied in the new commodities would not be socially recognized.

When all (or practically all) the elements of the productive process are commodities or, to put it differently, when a labor market and a market for means of production come into being, commodity producers become integrated into a single process in which genuinely social conditions of production emerge. These phenomena are very much linked with the historical gathering together of scattered, isolated elements of production and social structure and their qualitative transformation into national markets and social formations. The rise of capitalism was also, historically, the rise of the modern nation and nation-state.

---

[24] *Theories of Surplus Value*, III, pp. 112-13; see also John Weeks, *Capital and Exploitation* (Princeton: Princeton Univ. Press, 1981), pp. 29-38, on the monetization of production inputs under capitalism, in relation to the discussion that follows.

Contrast all of this with commodity production under feudalism. Then, a surplus was produced beyond the consumption needs of the direct producers. The surplus not consumed by the lords was thrown into commodity exchange. However, precapitalist commodity producers were not compelled to produce and dispose of this surplus product on a constantly changing (and widening) scale of productive efficiency; due to the relative insularity of feudal producers, they did not face the same danger the capitalist does of being wiped out by competition.[25]

Not only were such producers more isolated from each other, but their material conditions of production did not generally conform to the laws of commodity production. A large portion of feudal exchange consisted of luxuries. The form of the circulation of commodities then taking place, C-M-C, involved the transformation of commodities into money, and the change of money back again into commodities, that is, selling in order to buy. The capitalist, on the other hand, must purchase the vast bulk of his means of production (he cannot himself supply all the materials, fuel, components, transport facilities, spare parts, and machinery that he requires) and make good on these expensive investments in plant, equipment, etc. Of course, precapitalist commodity producers were confronted by all manner of necessity. They might be wiped out by natural disaster, pillage, recurrent peasant rebellions, or the political pressure of peers (leaving aside pressure from a more advanced, capitalist mode of production), and, in order to function, they could not simply produce at any level — nor, obviously, could they fail to produce. But they were not preponderantly subject to the pressures of economic competition, though competition with other commodity producers existed in some forms. And despite the increasingly significant influence exerted by the law of value in exchange, not until labor power itself was transformed into a commodity did the law of value regulate the allocation of social labor.

Capitalist commodity producers are interdependent in a qualitatively different way than were those producing for exchange in the precapitalist epoch. First, capitalist producers themselves form

---

[25] See Lenin's early writings, particularly "A Characterization of Economic Romanticism," *LCW*, 2, p. 164, and "The Development of Capitalism in Russia," *LCW*, 3, p. 66, for noteworthy discussion of the inherently expansionary drive of capitalism relative to precapitalist modes of production.

a market for each other's commodities, both for means of production and (along with workers and other strata) for means of consumption.[26] Second, they jointly contribute to the establishment of
and are mutually constrained by standards of socially necessary
labor time, as reflected in the existence of specific productive
norms which must be observed on pain of ruin. These commodity
producers are separate yet linked to each other by the law of value.
What is involved is an historically specific form of commodity circulation: M-C-M′, the transformation of money into commodities,
and the change of commodities back again into money (of a greater
magnitude than at the beginning of the process). Or, in short, buying in order to sell.

Shattering the "eternal" verities of bourgeois political economy, Marx revealed the conditional and transitory character of the
capitalist mode of production. Value is inextricably bound up with
commodity production and commodity production in turn is
bound up with the historical appearance and persistence of definite
social relations: "articles of utility become commodities, only because they are products of the labor of private individuals or groups
of individuals who carry on their work independently of each
other."[27] Mankind must and always will create use values (wealth
in the general sense) or else there could be no society and no human
life. But, as opposed to the production of use values, commodity
production and the production of value — that is, that form of social
organization in which labor time and relations between differing
labor times are revealed indirectly through the value form (as expressed in monetary units of account) — only correspond to a certain historical stage in the development of production.

This puts the preceding discussion in some perspective. Exchange of equivalents, which is one aspect of the law of value, is
based on the objective existence of socially necessary labor time.
This is predicated on the generalization of commodity production,
including the crucial transformation of labor power into a commodity. But this transformation separates property from labor and
enables the capitalist to appropriate without equivalent the labor of
others (and its product). Indeed, capitalist property prevents the

---

[26] Even workers' consumption is, in an overall sense, subsumed by capitalist demand since their consumption depends on their employment and wages (their articles of consumption must also in the main be purchased as commodities) and this
depends on the capitalists' demand for labor power.

[27] *Capital*, I, p. 77.

wage laborer from appropriating his own product.[28] Labor power is socially useful (and employable) only insofar as it is capable of producing surplus value and meeting the demands of profitability. It is allocated and paid for in accordance with the law of value. In capitalist society, what gets produced is determined not by the social utility of particular products or activities, but by the profits generated by their production. Efficiency and technical progress are measured in terms of their contribution to profitability. The average social profit rate on invested funds (about which more will be said shortly) sets the norm for enterprise performance and viability. These phenomena are aspects of the commanding role of the law of value in social production.

In capitalist society, the labor process — purposive activity through which human beings make use of and transform nature — is subordinate to the value-creation process. Indeed, as Marx emphasized, value formation is at once a process of value augmentation. The very measure of value, socially necessary labor time, is established in the context and on the basis of the capitalist pursuit of profit. The urge to produce more with less labor, that is, to reduce socially necessary labor time, is the requirement of maximizing profit with a minimum of capital. The law of value, then, is not a neutral arbiter of efficiency; its dominance rests on exploitative social relations. Socially necessary labor time is determined with reference to and exists in dialectical unity with appropriation of surplus (unpaid) labor.[29] Put differently, where the law of value dominates production and exchange, compelling the cheapening of commodities, the production of surplus value dominates. Where value and profit form the starting and end point of social production, waste, crisis, and destruction must result. In a genuinely socialist economy, the value-creation process is subordinate to the socialist labor process and the conscious activity of the masses, exchange value is subordinate to use value, and economy of time is subordinate to and governed by revolutionary, proletarian politics.[30] When the pro-

---

[28] See *Capital,* I, p. 547.

[29] For a relevant discussion of this, see Charles Bettelheim, *Economic Calculation and Forms of Property* (New York: Monthly Review Press, 1975), Chapter 1, Part 3.

[30] These points are developed in two important works written by the revolutionary forces in China prior to the revisionist coup of 1976. See George Wang, translator and editor, *Fundamentals of Political Economy* (White Plains, NY: M.E. Sharpe, 1977), Chapter 15, and Writing Group of the Kirin Provincial Revolutionary Committee, "Socialist Construction and Class Struggle in the Field of Economics, Critique of Sun Yeh-Fang's Revisionist Economic Theory," *Peking Review,* No. 16 (17 April 1970).

letariat rules, social labor is consciously allocated and organized in accordance with the interests of world proletarian revolution.

The full development of commodity production signals the full development of the regulating role of the law of value and relations of competition among private commodity producers. How is competition, which is at the heart of the capital relation, even under imperialism, to be understood? Marx explained:

> Conceptually, *competition* is nothing other than the inner *nature of capital*, its essential character, appearing in and realized as the reciprocal interaction of many capitals with one another, the inner tendency as external necessity.
>   . . . [C]ompetition is nothing more than the way in which the many capitals force the inherent determinants of capital upon one another and upon themselves. Hence not a single category of the bourgeois economy, not even the most basic, e.g. the determination of value, becomes real through free competition alone. . . .[31]

The essential thrust of Marx's comment is that while the laws of accumulation operate through competition, which implies the mobility of capital, competition itself is neither an abstract "organizing" principle, nor some independently existing mechanism; it is the form in which the productive process of capital expresses the separateness yet codeterminantness of individual capitals: *"Free competition* is the relation of capital to itself as another capital, i.e. the real conduct of capital as capital."[32] Each unit of capital puts the others to the test in the marketplace; none can stand still and none can be secure in its position. The possibility of gaining advantage (on the basis of intensified exploitation and more productive

---

[31] *Grundrisse,* pp. 414, 651; see also the critique of bourgeois notions of competition in Weeks, *Capital and Exploitation,* pp. 152-54 and 163-66, which is drawn on here.

[32] *Grundrisse,* p. 650. It was the anarchic thrust of a more productive mode (rising capital) which tore down the barriers to mobility represented by guild associations, state regulation, tariffs, and, most especially, labor that was locked into social obligation and tied to the land during the feudal era. Competition then came fully into its own. To establish and extend the dominance of capital over labor, however – and here we might recall the role of politics, as exemplified by the coercive enclosure acts and poor laws mentioned earlier – the bourgeoisie needed to secure state power, hence the need for political revolution against feudal rule. Significantly, the industrial revolution in Great Britain occurred *after* the bourgeois political revolution of the seventeenth century. Mao Tsetung emphasized this historical sequence in the context of a broader discussion of how revolutionary transformations of the superstructure and production relations stimulate the development of productive forces. See Mao Tsetung, *A Critique of Soviet Economics,* translated by Moss Roberts (New York: Monthly Review Press, 1977), pp. 65-67.

technique) becomes the necessity to do so (on the basis of private appropriation). With improved methods of production not yet generally adopted, the individual capitalist can garner extra profit by underselling his competitors and yet selling his commodities at or above their individual value until the more advanced methods become generalized.

Competition is therefore the mechanism by which socially necessary labor time is established and continually modified. In search of higher profit, capital, based on its mobility, will also flow into and out of particular industries (drawing labor power, which is also mobile, to it) in such a way as to equalize rates of profit among industries of greater or lesser proportion of means of production to labor power, thereby establishing a general rate of profit.[33] This process serves to distribute capital in varying proportions to different spheres and to transform values into prices of production (cost price plus average profit), around which market prices gravitate. This aspect of the law of value, then, is also enforced through competition.

Competition is not a function of the degree of atomization of capital, but of the existence of the capital relation, and its intensity is not a function of how many individual capitals may exist. It is not to be identified with particular market practices, e.g., open price competition, or with individual market conditions, e.g., the existence of more than one firm in a specific product market. Fundamentally, competition involves struggle over the expansion and appropriation of surplus value and it grows more, not less, intense in the imperialist epoch.

Wherever there is private organization of the labor process and private appropriation of surplus value, capital emerges as many capitals:

---

[33] An average rate of profit generalized throughout the economy as a whole and its different branches of production is just that, an average around which particular capitals operate and which is itself in continual flux. The significance of the equalization process is that the profits of individual capitalists are not equal to the surplus value extracted directly from their work forces; they stand in proportion to their share of the total social capital invested. (This distribution of profits works itself out through the price mechanism.) Similarly, within a given industry, the more efficient producers capture a larger share of total surplus value. Hence, capitalist commodity producers are also linked through the redistribution of surplus value. In the imperialist epoch, the redistribution of surplus value is conditioned both by the dominance of monopoly and by international relations of economic and political domination.

> Capital exists and can only exist as many capitals, and its self-determination therefore appears as their reciprocal interaction with one another....
>
> Since value forms the foundation of capital, and since it therefore necessarily exists only through exchange for *counter-value*, it thus necessarily repels itself from itself. A *universal capital*, one without alien capitals confronting it, with which it exchanges...is therefore a non-thing.[34]

Capitalist production is a multiplicity of interdependent labor processes. But from the beginning labor is not directly social. These are independently organized labor processes; only through exchange do they form into a profoundly social division of labor. In capitalist society — a society regulated by commodity production and the law of value and the production of surplus value — things, i.e., means of production and labor power, must first undergo preliminary transformation into capital. Products (use values) enter into the productive process and emerge out of it as commodities, and the value embodied in them can be realized only upon sale. It is this "commodity environment" that makes it impossible for capital not to "repel itself from itself," impossible not to exist as many capitals.

The material basis for and seeds of competition in class society lie in the existence of independent sites of accumulation (separable production units or associations of such units), different branches of production, regional and sectoral differences (between agriculture and industry and between town and country), and different centers of decision-making (departments and ministries) in an interdependent and integrated economic formation. The determining role of the law of value and the expand-or-die urge of capital will invariably find expression in the opening of new fields of production and the more intensive development of old ones — with new capitals forming and old ones splitting on the basis of colliding claims to surplus value produced throughout society.

Capitalist accumulation is rooted in the appropriation of unpaid labor, which hinges on the buying and selling of labor power. But the compulsion to accumulate derives from the existence of many capitals. The reciprocal interaction of these many capitals forces the continual revolutionizing of the productive forces as a matter of internal necessity and self-preservation. Thus does capital unleash, through this contradictory form, the power of socialized produc-

---

[34] *Grundrisse*, pp. 414, 421n.

tion. The "inner nature of capital" to which Marx refers is precisely the contradiction between socialized production and private appropriation. This explains capitalism's unprecedented dynamism relative to previous modes of production:

> [T]he development of capitalist production makes it constantly necessary to keep increasing the amount of the capital laid out in a given industrial undertaking, and competition makes the immanent laws of capitalist production to be felt by each individual capitalist, as external coercive laws. It compels him to keep constantly extending his capital, in order to preserve it, but extend it he cannot, except by means of progressive accumulation.[35]

As Marx made clear, the process of capital accumulation is not the conscious expansion of value by the capitalists, but the *self-expansion* of value. The capitalist is not a capitalist because of what he *wants* to do, but for what he *must* do. There is an objective movement through which existing value must increase its value; this movement is governed by laws to which the capitalist is subject and subordinate, and of which he is merely an agent:

> As capitalist, he is only capital personified. His soul is the soul of capital. But capital has one single life impulse, the tendency to create value and surplus value, to make its constant factor, the means of production, absorb the greatest possible amount of surplus labor.
>
> Capital is dead labor, that, vampire-like, only lives by sucking living labor, and lives the more, the more labor it sucks.[36]

It is the capitalist, then, who is the instrument of technical progress, who is subject to the law of the reduction of production costs. And it is the means of production that employ living labor, not vice versa. Capital is value which generates surplus value. *Capital is both a social relation and a process whose essence is the domination of labor power by alien, antagonistic interests, a social relation and a process whose inner dynamic is to constantly reproduce and extend itself.*

The concentration of means of production in the hands of individual capitals enables them to apply as combined labor power the energies and capabilities of free wage workers. These workers are integrated into a highly organized and scientific regime of produc-

---

[35] *Capital,* I, p. 555.
[36] *Capital,* I, p. 224.

tion. The conditions of labor monolithically confront the direct producers in the form of strict and hierarchical control and authority.
On the other hand, the means of production are dispersed among
many capitals, and in the social economy overall quite the opposite
of such control and authority reigns: anarchy. In capitalist society
there exists a twofold division of labor:

> While within the workshop, the iron law of proportionality subjects
> definite numbers of workmen to definite functions, in the society
> outside the workshop, chance and caprice have full play in distri-
> buting the producers and their means of production among the var-
> ious branches of industry.... Division of labor within the work-
> shop implies the undisputed authority of the capitalist over men,
> that are but parts of a mechanism that belongs to him. The division
> of labor within the society brings into contact independent com-
> modity producers, who acknowledge no other authority but that of
> competition, of the coercion exerted by the pressure of their mutual
> interests.... [I]n a society with capitalist production, anarchy in the
> social division of labor and despotism in that of the workshop are
> mutual conditions, the one of the other.... [37]

No matter how highly concentrated and organized production
may be at a given ownership level (the workshop referred to in the
passage above must be understood more broadly as a unit of
capital), such "undisputed authority" cannot inform the total process of social production, although this is more systematically attempted in the imperialist epoch, particularly in the form of
capitalist planning. Commodity production remains private and independent in two senses: (1) appropriation of surplus value is
private to a class which effectively monopolizes the chief means of
production; and (2) this class is fragmented into independent and
discrete blocs of capital, even where these blocs of capital may be
juridically associated and institutionally embedded together, even
in state property forms.

This raises an important point. Private ownership of the means
of production refers to a specific production relation in which the
mass of producers are separated from the instruments and products of their labor. But the very fact that these are social means of
production — again, utilizable only by collective labor — leads to
the emergence of new practices and property forms which better

[37] *Capital,* I, pp. 336-37.

correspond to the needs of advancing development of the productive forces, but still rest on capitalist relations. In other words, capitalist property need not assume the form of personal and individual or juridically private capitalist property.

In fact, in the epoch of imperialism bourgeois relations increasingly assume more social forms, e.g., highly integrated private or state monopolistic aggregations of capital at the commanding heights of the advanced capitalist economies, while ownership itself grows increasingly collective. In his discussion of the banking and credit system, Marx analyzed some of the tendencies towards more directly social forms and practices of capital: "This social character of capital is first promoted and wholly realized through the full development of the credit and banking system.... It places all the available and even potential capital of society that is not already actively employed at the disposal of the industrial and commercial capitalists so that neither the lenders nor users of this capital are its real owners or producers."[38] And credit itself becomes an instrument to develop more collective forms of capitalist property, something which Marx noted in connection with the enormous expansion of the scale of production and the formation of joint-stock companies:

> The capital, which in itself rests on a social mode of production and presupposes a social concentration of means of production and labor power, is here directly endowed with the form of social capital (capital of directly associated individuals) as distinct from private capital, and its undertakings assume the form of social undertakings as distinct from private undertakings. It is the abolition of capital as private property within the framework of capitalist production itself.[39]

Engels also took note of such early attempts by the capitalist class — in the face of economic crisis and the sheer magnitude of certain undertakings — to directly treat the productive forces as social productive forces with the establishment of state-owned railways and other industries: "But the transformation, either into joint-stock companies (and trusts) or into state ownership, does not do away with the capitalistic nature of the productive forces.... The modern state, no matter what its form, is essentially a capitalist

---

[38] *Capital,* III, p. 607.
[39] *Capital,* III, pp. 436-37.

machine, the state of the capitalists, the ideal personification of the total national capital."[40]

It was not possible for Marx or Engels to predict just how far these phenomena would develop, nor to foresee the particular forms they would assume, but these profound insights regarding "social" capital point to the fact that, within and between such forms of "social" enterprise, commodities will continue to circulate on the basis of their exchange value, or with ultimate reference to the expansion of exchange value.[41]

The existence of a structure of independent capitalist commodity producers, no matter what the degree of centralization, means that production as a whole cannot be socially organized and rationally planned. Hence the social interrelations of production assert themselves through the blind interaction and conflict of particular capitals or blocs of capital. Each produces in the expectation that the market will clear its commodities. What is produced and in what share is determined through exchange, by the ability (or inability) of individual capitals to convert the labor incorporated in privately produced commodities into the general, money form of value. The division of labor in society develops spontaneously, anarchically: "under capitalist production the proportionality of the individual branches of production springs as a continual process from disproportionality, because the cohesion of the aggregate production imposes itself as a blind law upon the agents of production, and not as a law which, being understood and hence controlled by their common mind, brings the productive process under their joint control."[42] In other words, *individual units or blocs of capital are obedient to the social conditions of production and to capital as a whole, but they do not function as a coordinated whole.* Not only do social laws assert themselves behind the backs of particular capi-

---

[40] Engels, *Anti-Dühring,* p. 330.

[41] In a genuinely socialist economy, labor power no longer exists as a commodity and the law of value no longer occupies the dominant position in the organization of social production. But, as implied, commodity and value categories (the existence of abstract and socially necessary labor, etc.) have a material basis. Mao Tsetung's pioneering analysis must be noted in this connection. Mao argued that commodity exchange relationships exist within the socialist state sector itself, even though no transfer of ownership accompanies the exchange of products. For a discussion of this, see Bob Avakian, *Mao Tsetung's Immortal Contributions* (Chicago: RCP Publications, 1979), Chapter 3; and Wang, ed., *Fundamentals of Political Economy,* Chapters 14-16, 18.

[42] *Capital,* III, p. 257.

tals, they do so in the form of constantly changing and violently re-constituted norms and averages.

Such anarchy stems not from lack of foresight nor even from the absence of attempts to calculate and plan, but from the objective nature of private appropriation. In the modern corporation, for instance, investment, output, and price decisions taken by divisional units are administratively coordinated to meet centralized profit targets, and planning serves to integrate a complex supply-and-allocation system, to prescribe norms and priorities, and to forecast market developments. In fact, the competitive battle of each against all is facilitated precisely by the extensive application of advanced production technique, by rigorous and "despotic" organization at the corporate level, and, increasingly, by more comprehensive and sophisticated planning at the state level.

Under imperialism, market relations become increasingly *internalized* within large units of capital, between such units, and within the state. For instance, the head office of a multinational corporation organizes exchange between its subsidiaries. The prices charged its overseas divisions for components amount to planned value transfers within the universe of the corporation. Cartels and joint ventures link different corporations. The total social capital may in fact be reproduced and commodity relations extended through the medium of a plan (rather than through the operation of private markets) in a state monopoly capitalist formation. Or, to express it differently, the market may chiefly exist within and operate through a plan, as it does in the Soviet Union. The state seeks to minimize the risk inherent in separate production decisions — the discrete unit of capital does not know whether the labor process it organizes is socially necessary until its commodities are sold — by planning the sale of commodities in advance. Exchange takes place between fragments of the total capital, among units of production and centers of control which belong formally to the state.

Capitalist planning, however, proceeds in the midst of and intensifies the overall anarchy of social production. The more that particular (or allied) units of capital and the state, representing different fractions of the total capital, attempt to plan and coordinate investments in particular spheres and to develop the most efficacious forms to realize surplus value, the more explosive the internal contradictions of capital as a whole become over the course of a cycle of development, as the expansion of profits, which such planning serves, runs up against the limits posed by the actual capitalist relations of production. In short, the regulating role of the law of value impinges on planning, determining its goals, methods and outcome.[43]

Neither the "invisible hand" of the competitive marketplace nor the "far-sightedness" of capitalist planning can override the logic of self-expansion by discrete capitals. It is the inner urging of capital to produce to the limits set by the productive forces and to break beyond existing bounds, without regard to capital's specific limits as capital, that conditions both disproportionalities between individual spheres of production and generalized crises of over-production. Anarchy is not a matter of random capital flows which balance out over the long run. By its very nature, capitalism is marked by the uneven reproduction of capital. Capitalism, wrote Lenin,

> is in no position to go on repeating the same processes of production on the former scale, under unchanging conditions (as was the case under precapitalist regimes), and. . .it inevitably leads to an un-limited growth of production which overflows the old, narrow limits of earlier economic units. With the unevenness of develop-ment inherent in capitalism, one branch of production outstrips the others and strives to transcend the bounds of the old field of economic relations.[44]

There are two manifestations, two forms of motion, of the con-tradiction between socialized production and private appropria-

---

[43] In a highly centralized capitalist economy like the Soviet Union, where exten-sive planning is undertaken, the allocation of investment and loan capital is fundamentally determined by the criterion of profitability. One striking result (or manifestation) of this is the existence of extreme sectoral disproportionalities at the same time that capital is exported abroad. This is not to say there can be no im-balance and unevenness in a genuinely socialist economy. However, their character will be different and they will not arise from the struggle for surplus value. That plan-ning is far more comprehensive in the Soviet Union than in the Western bloc does not reflect the existence of a more highly developed or qualitatively different stage of monopoly capitalism. Rather, this is a function of Soviet social-imperialism's par-ticular evolution (a reversal of socialist relations of production, which involves main-taining many forms of these relations) and the exigencies of this formation in the par-ticular global context in which it must operate. On capitalist planning, see the valuable essay by Paolo Giussani, "Sur le concept de capitalisme monopoliste d'Etat," in *Communisme*, 25-26 (1976-77). On the nature of state monopoly capitalism in the Soviet Union, see Raymond Lotta, "Realities of Social-Imperialism versus Dogmas of Cynical Realism: The Dynamics of the Soviet Capital Formation," in *The Soviet Union: Socialist or Social-Imperialist? Part 2, The Question is Joined: Ray-mond Lotta vs. Albert Szymanski* (Chicago: RCP Publications, 1983).

[44] "The Development of Capitalism in Russia," *LCW*, 3, p. 591.

tion: (1) the contradiction between the organized character of production in individual enterprises (or at higher and more integrated levels of ownership) and anarchy in social production overall; and (2) the contradiction in class relations between the bourgeoisie and the proletariat. According to Engels:

> The capitalistic mode of production moves in these two forms of the antagonism immanent to it from its very origin. It is never able to get out of that "vicious circle" which Fourier had already discovered. What Fourier could not, indeed, see in his time is that this circle is gradually narrowing; that the movement becomes more and more a spiral, and must come to an end, like the movement of the planets, by collision with the center. It is the compelling force of anarchy in the production of society at large that more and more completely turns the great majority of men into proletarians; and it is the masses of the proletariat again who will finally put an end to anarchy in production. It is the compelling force of anarchy in social production that turns the limitless perfectibility of machinery under modern industry into a compulsory law by which every individual industrial capitalist must perfect his machinery more and more, under penalty of ruin.[45]

The theoretical and political implications of this passage from *Anti-Dühring* necessitate further interpretation and elaboration. First, the fundamental contradiction of capitalism constitutes the material foundation for these two forms of motion. It does not, however, have a separate form of motion unto itself: the accumulation process involves both forms of motion. And these two forms of motion, or contradictions — between the proletariat and the bourgeoisie and between individual organization and social anarchy (the struggle among capitals) — not only arise from this material foundation, but continually interact with and transform it. Although qualitatively new, nonexploitative production relations do not develop spontaneously — and cannot develop without the revolutionary seizure of political power by the proletariat — existing relations are not static. The structure of socialized production and private appropriation undergoes continual change, including major leaps through crises and wars, which is to say that the fundamental contradiction works itself out through these two forms of motion.

The most fundamental law of the capitalist mode of production is the production of surplus value, and the most fundamental pro-

---

[45] Engels, *Anti-Dühring*, p. 324.

duction relation of capitalism is the relation of capital to labor. Capital is both a relation and process of exploitation. But capital exists and can only exist as many capitals. Thus, the exploitation of wage-labor, which is the basis of the creation and appropriation of surplus value, is mediated by the blind interaction of many capitals. It is the anarchic relations among capitalist producers, and not the mere existence of propertyless proletarians or the class contradiction as such, which drive these producers to exploit the working class on an ever more intensive and extensive scale. Were not capitalist commodity producers separated from each other and yet linked by the operation of the law of value, they would not face the same compulsion to more widely and deeply exploit the proletariat internationally — the class contradiction between bourgeoisie and proletariat could thus be mitigated. *Movement compelled by anarchy is the principal form of motion of the contradiction between socialized production and private appropriation.* The struggle between the proletariat and the bourgeoisie interacts with changes in production relations and the class contradiction interacts with relations and contradictions among capitals. But the anarchy of capitalist production brings about those fundamental changes in the material sphere which set the context for the class struggle.[46]

It is precisely the force of anarchy, deriving from the very nature of capital, which accounts for a distinctive movement of accumulation. In *Capital*, Marx wrote:

> The battle of competition is fought by cheapening of commodities.
> The cheapness of commodities depends, *ceteris paribus*, on the productiveness of labor, and this again on the scale of production. . . .
> One capitalist always kills many. Hand in hand with this centralization, or this expropriation of many capitalists by few, develop, on an ever extending scale, the cooperative form of the labor process, the conscious technical application of science, the methodical cultivation of the soil, the transformation of the instruments of labor

[46] See Bob Avakian, "Fundamental and Principal Contradictions on a World Scale," *Revolutionary Worker*, No. 172 (17 September 1982), p. 15. Many variants of Marxism reverse the relationship between the two forms of motion. Some "Third Worldists" argue that, in the absence of popular revolt there, imperialism can limitlessly expand into the oppressed periphery. Other theorists argue that so long as workers' wage demands can be held in check in the advanced countries, capitalist production will remain profitable. Either way, accumulation can presumably continue in the imperialist countries without confronting its own barriers as capital — as expressed in crisis and the need to redivide the world — unless and until the people (somewhere) finally decide to oppose or to stop it.

into instruments of labor only usable in common, the economizing of all means of production by their use as the means of production of combined, socialized labor, the entanglement of all peoples in the net of the world market, and with this, the international character of the capitalistic regime. [47]

The social anarchy of production (involving the competitive interaction and uneven development of "many capitals") forces individual capitals to increase profit by effectively raising the rate of exploitation (the proportion of unpaid to paid labor). This inner compulsion of capital to expand is expressed in the progressive development of the social productivity of labor. There are, then, *laws of motion* of the capitalist mode of production through which the productive forces grow more socialized (with the rapid development of cooperative forms of the labor process and the systematic application of science) and through which new spheres and branches of production on a world scale are penetrated by capitalist relations, leading to a more complex and international division of labor.

The competitive battle results in the *law of the centralization and concentration of capital.* Weaker capitals are absorbed by their more powerful rivals and the new capital formed is thereby centralized into larger units. Particular units of capital also grow more concentrated as a result of the accumulation of surplus value they directly produce. All this becomes especially pronounced with the emergence of imperialism, and it continues to operate in the imperialist countries at the private and state monopoly level. The enormous concentration of capital and the general requirements of the total national capital provide the material basis for the kind of planning phenomena described earlier. At the same time, the continuous increase in productivity, essential to and an outgrowth of successful accumulation, is principally achieved by means of the progressive replacement of living labor by dead labor (machines, etc.); more of the capitalists' total outlays are tied up in means of production which do not of themselves produce surplus value. Hence, the *law of the tendency of the rate of profit to fall,* the coordinates of which become profoundly international in the imperialist epoch. [48]

These laws are *tendential* in nature, which is to say that they do not operate mechanically. Such laws themselves involve contradic-

[47] *Capital,* I, pp. 586, 714-15.

[48] The process of mechanization linked with the force and pulse of accumulation also produces a distinct *law of population* leading to the formation of an "industrial reserve army." The significance and modifications of this law will be discussed later.

tion; they are linked to countertendencies and modified by historical circumstances. Their influence is exerted unevenly and their rhythm is spasmodic; all this is part of the dynamism, disorder, and explosiveness of capitalism.[49] Engels made this point in describing the operation of economic laws in general:

> [N]one of them has any reality except as approximation, tendency, average, and not as *immediate* reality. This is due partly to the fact that their action clashes with the simultaneous action of other laws, but partly to their own nature as concepts.[50]

But these laws do in fact express a certain dynamic of capitalist development, revealing both the specificity of and limits to this mode of production. In this sense, "tendency" has a broader meaning.

This understanding also informed the trenchant analysis Marx made in the famous chapter from the first volume of *Capital*, entitled "The Historical Tendency of Capitalist Accumulation." Here is to be found Marx's stirring description of the movement of the fundamental contradiction of capitalism, which produces not only the material conditions for a more advanced form of social organization — the only form of organization which can resolve the contradictions engendered by capitalism — but capitalism's gravediggers as well:

> The monopoly of capital becomes a fetter upon the mode of production, which has sprung up and flourished along with, and under it. Centralization of the means of production and socialization of labor at last reach a point where they become incompatible with their capitalist integument. This integument is burst asunder. The knell of

[49] Marx pointed out that the law of centralization and concentration is countered by the very privateness of capital: "Accumulation and the concentration accompanying it are . . . not only scattered over many points, but the increase of each functioning capital is thwarted by the formation of new and the subdivision of old capitals. Accumulation, therefore, presents itself on the one hand as increasing concentration of the means of production, and of the command over labor; on the other, as repulsion of many individual capitals one from another" (*Capital*, I, p. 586). Again, capital exists as "many capitals." Moreover, the trend towards centralization is not uniform, it intensifies during certain phases of the accumulation cycle and operates at different rates in different sectors. Nevertheless, this law imparts an overall directionality to the development of the capitalist mode of production and this has real consequences for the needs and structure of accumulation.

[50] "Engels to Conrad Schmidt in Zurich" (12 March 1895), *Selected Correspondence*, p. 457.

capitalist private property sounds. The expropriators are expropriated.[51]

This was neither a forecast of automatic collapse nor a teleological view of history as the fulfillment of a preexisting or transcendent goal. It was a scientific statement that capitalism is an historical means for developing the productive forces, but that this very development must necessarily come into increasingly sharp conflict with the means by which such development is achieved, with the social relations of capital. Capitalism had its historical beginnings and will meet its historical end, though as it turns out its destruction will be an even more tortuous world-historic process than its genesis.

Marx lived to witness and champion the first momentarily successful assault against bourgeois state power by an aroused proletariat, the creation of the Paris Commune. But he did not live to see capitalism reach its final stage of imperialism, the era of worldwide proletarian revolution. Lenin applied Marxism to the new era exactly to explain the significance and repercussions of this new stage of development, and to reveal how the laws of accumulation discovered by Marx operate within the new imperialist framework. What is involved here is the spiral-like development of the fundamental contradiction, from one stage to another, until its final resolution — Engels' metaphor of a "circle that is gradually narrowing" — and the emergence of a new process.

The concept of spiral-like motion is central to dialectics and to Marxist-Leninist political economy. It signifies movement that is neither circular and repetitive nor simply quantitative and linear. Rather, it expresses the complex motion of processes determined by a fundamental contradiction but involving or incorporating a number of other contradictions, the interpenetration of these, and the transformation of things into their opposites — hence retrogression (and not simply advances), discontinuities, and leaps. This understanding stands opposed to traditional notions of evolutionary development and progress as well as to cyclic conceptions of history.

The forward motion of the accumulation process arises through cycles. The circulation of capital itself, whose formula is M-C-M', is described by Marx as "the restless never-ending process of profit-

---

[51] *Capital*, I, p. 715.

making," or the "circular movement of capital," of which he says: "This process as a whole constitutes therefore the process of moving in circuits."[52] Crises recur cyclically. But this circular and "never-ending" movement of capital, this cyclical recurrence, is also the process of accumulation of capital, and the process of movement from competitive to monopoly capitalism. The laws of accumulation operate through intertwined circuits and cycles, but they do not return endlessly to their starting point. And in the imperialist era, the cycle of accumulation in a particular country is conditioned by and subordinate to a larger spiral movement rooted in the operation of these laws of accumulation internationally.

What is actually happening is that capitalism is moving toward its final end, though not in an evolutionary (or automatic) way towards an absolute limit, nor all at once. The fundamental contradiction, as well as many of the contradictions to which it gives rise (or incorporates), intensifies, jolting society with ever more destructive crises and, in a heightened way in the imperialist epoch, wars. These are not exogenous or accidental phenomena – and this is where the question of tendency takes on profound importance – but are internal to this mode of production. These very dislocations create more favorable conditions for the resolution of this contradiction in the political sphere, the only sphere where it can be resolved. Lenin defined the imperialist era as precisely one of violent transition and transformation, of revolutionary upheaval and advance, which is also proceeding in a wave-like or spiral fashion. To repeat Engels' lucid formulation: "It is the compelling force of anarchy in the production of society at large that more and

---

[52] *Capital,* I, p. 151; II, pp. 53, 50. An individual capital passes through three stages of movement and transformation, assuming three distinct and necessary forms. The first stage and form, that of money capital, involves the purchase of means of production and labor power, preparing the conditions for production, and ending in the transformation of money capital into productive capital. The second stage is the production process itself. Here capital functions as productive capital — surplus value is created and embodied in new commodities. These commodities are ready for sale and assume the functional form of commodity capital. The third stage is the sale of these commodities, and the function of commodity capital is to realize the value of the capital advanced and the increment of surplus value in money form. Hence, two of these stages, that of money capital and commodity capital, lie in the sphere of circulation and one, that of productive capital, lies in the sphere of production. Each phase describes what Marx calls a circuit. The reconstitution of the value of a capital through the cycle of production and circulation (several cycles of production and circulation being required for the value contained in machinery and buildings) is the turnover of capital.

more completely turns the great majority of men into proletarians; and it is the masses of the proletariat again who will finally put an end to anarchy in production."

III

Under capitalism, the spontaneous development of the social division of labor precludes any kind of equilibrated growth. Reproduction of the aggregate social capital is a highly integrated and interdependent process, both in terms of its technical requirements and value formation. The value relations inhering in this social capital set the terms for the functioning of the individual parts it comprises. But these individual parts stand in uneven and sharply contradictory relation to each other: the turnover time of capital (reflecting the relative weight of fixed capital in total capital outlays) differs among industries;[53] technical innovation proceeds spasmodically within industries and across industrial lines; and the competitive strengths of particular capitals vis-à-vis each other are unequal and shift over time. At the level of price, the lack of synchrony between the development of individual fractions of capital and the needs of the total capital may not be apparent; even a sector producing a high profit may not meet the overall requirements of expanded reproduction.

The canard of bourgeois political economy that production simply follows demand and could never possibly exceed it implicitly assumes, Marx pointed out, that each capitalist "produces as if he were fulfilling orders placed by society."[54] More specifically: "In capitalist society . . . where social reason always asserts itself only *post festum* great disturbances may and must constantly occur."[55] But such disturbances express something more profound about accumulation than simply its varied pace and intensity.

Capitalist accumulation is a dialectical process of the destruction and restructuring of capital. Capital must constantly reorganize its conditions and relations of production; it must continually over-

---

[53] Fixed capital refers to plant, equipment, and infrastructural investment, whose material existence is fixed and a part of whose value is tied up in the production process through a whole series of turnover periods, unlike raw materials, whose entire value circulates at the end of each turnover period.

[54] *Theories of Surplus Value*, III, p. 121.

[55] *Capital*, II, p. 319.

come its self-generated barriers, barriers that at certain critical turning points can only be massively and destructively shifted to higher levels. It is movement compelled by anarchy which both leads to expansion and undermines it. Yet it is movement through anarchy that violently recomposes capital. Running through this destruction/reorganization dialectic is a longer-term trend which results in the intensification of the contradictions of accumulation.

The necessity to reorganize is rooted in the tendency of the rate of profit to fall. Capital is driven, in search of profit, to produce as though there were no limit to its expansion; yet "it only tolerates production commensurate with the *profitable* employment of existing capital."[56] Capitalist production is the production of use values and exchange values, but it is the latter, specifically the production of surplus value, which regulates and dominates production. The fundamental limit to the expansion of capital is to be found in the labor process as a value-creation process. In short, accumulation is regulated by the rate of profit. The internal contradiction of accumulation is that the very means capital uses to intensify the exploitation of wage-labor tend to depress the rate of profit. Put differently, there is a conflict between the expansion of production and the expansion of surplus value. In a way, capitalism is a victim of its own vigor: "The rate of profit does not fall because labor becomes less productive, but because it becomes more productive. Both the rise in the rate of surplus value and the fall in the rate of profit are but specific forms through which growing productivity of labor is expressed under capitalism."[57] From an historical standpoint, this law at once expresses the great stimulus afforded the development of the productive forces under capitalism and its self-limiting character.

Accumulation is not simply the reproduction and replacement of existing technique and machinery; it is the transformation of the whole system of production in technical and value terms. The overall cheapening of commodities is fundamentally predicated on mechanization, on an increasing amount of constant capital per worker employed, on an "increase in productive power" which, as Marx emphasizes, "must be paid for by capital itself."[58] Due to the

---

[56] *Theories of Surplus Value,* III, p. 122 (emphasis added).

[57] *Capital,* III, p. 240.

[58] *Grundrisse,* p. 776. The use value of a machine relates to its practical functions in production and its ability to increase the productivity of labor power. But a machine

increase in labor productivity (and the consequent overall decrease
in the value of the necessities to maintain and reproduce the
workers' labor power), a greater portion of the living labor contained in commodities is composed of unpaid labor. But an ever-
decreasing proportion of living labor is materialized in commodities in relation to the dead labor embodied in the raw materials
they contain and the means of labor (machinery, etc.) consumed by
them. With the advance of capitalist production, demand for labor
power (which alone produces value and surplus value) declines
relatively. Therefore, even though the proportion of unpaid to paid
labor increases (with each individual worker becoming more productive of surplus value), there is proportionately less surplus labor
time for the capitalist to appropriate – the sum of paid and unpaid
labor declines in relation to the constant capital advanced. Thus,
the capitalists' total costs increase proportionately more than does
the mass of surplus value, and their rate of profit declines, since this
rate is the mass of surplus value divided by the total invested
capital (constant as well as variable).[59]

Again, the amount of living labor expended per unit value of constant capital stock declines; an ever greater amount of capital is required to employ the same number of workers, even though the
growth in capacity will lead to an absolute increase in the volume of
employment. The rising organic composition, an underlying trend of
capital, is at the heart of the tendency of the rate of profit to fall. The

produces no value. It contains a certain amount of value, of stored labor time corresponding to the time required to produce it, which it transfers, bit by bit, to the fin-
ished commodity. Raw materials transfer their value all at once. Fixed capital and
raw materials are constant capital – unvarying in the magnitude of their value.
Labor power is a unique commodity in that its consumption is simultaneously the
production of value. Hence, what is expended for wages is called variable capital.
The organic composition of capital measures in value terms the proportion of means
of production to employed labor.

[59] A simple mathematical example will make this clear. If, at one stage, the capitalist spends $100 on machinery, raw materials, etc., and an equal amount on wages,
and, out of the process of production, $100 worth of surplus value is created and
appropriated by the capitalist, then his rate of profit equals 50 percent. Let constant
capital be indicated by c, variable capital by v and surplus value by s. Then, in this
example, $c=100, s=100, v=100$; the rate of profit $= s/(c+v) = 100/(100+100) = 100/200$
$= 50$ percent. But if in expanding production the capitalist spends $300 in constant
capital and $150 in variable capital, then – given the same rate of exploitation, the
same amount of surplus value extracted relative to variable capital – the rate of profit will fall to 33⅓ percent, as this equation shows: $s/(c+v) = 150/(300+150) = 150/450$
$= 33⅓$ percent.

rate of profit is influenced, then, by the rate of surplus value and the relation of dead to living labor; it is also influenced by the turnover time of capital and the relation of unproductive to productive labor (labor which produces surplus value).

In this way the contradictions inherent in the existence of many capitals become more apparent. If the capitalists had their druthers, they would avoid introducing a new method of production if they knew it were going to lower their rate of profit. But choice, as we have seen, is not the issue: competition compels the adoption of more advanced techniques suited to the battle of cheapening commodities. On the other hand, individual capitals operating under this compulsion and seeking to raise their individual rate of profit by improving productivity (and selling their commodities below the prevailing market price but above their individual price of production) cannot anticipate the aggregate consequences of their individual investment decisions, that is, the transformation of overall value relations (as competition levels out different rates of profit) and the ultimate undermining (through the anarchic interactions of the individual units of capital) of the general conditions of production and circulation.

However, this law, Marx emphasized, acts as a tendency whose effects become "strikingly pronounced" only under certain circumstances and, in general, only after extended periods. He noted:

> [T]he same influences which produce a tendency in the general rate of profit to fall, also call forth countereffects which hamper, retard, and partly paralyze this fall. . . .
>
> Alongside the fall in the rate of profit mass of capitals grows, and hand in hand with this there occurs a depreciation of existing capitals which checks the fall and gives an accelerating motion to the accumulation of capital values.
>
> Alongside the development of productivity there develops a higher composition of capital, i.e., the relative decrease of the ratio of variable to constant capital.
>
> These different influences may at one time operate predominantly side by side in space, and at another succeed each other in time.[60]

Marx categorized the principal counteracting influences which moderate the effects of the fall in the rate of profit: (1) "increasing

---

[60] *Capital,* III, pp. 239, 249.

the intensity of exploitation" through the intensification of work, prolongation of the working day, and the technical innovations of particular capitalists; (2) "depression of wages below the value of labor power"; (3) "cheapening of elements of constant capital," through technical advances, which also prevent the value of constant capital from rising at the same rate as the material volume of the means of production, and through cost savings deriving from the more efficient utilization of raw materials, waste, etc.; (4) "relative overpopulation," which furnishes a pool of cheap labor, especially to new industries; and (5) "foreign trade," which, on the one hand, brings all these other factors into play from outside the national circuit of capital and, on the other, yields monopolistic advantage and higher profits through trade with and investment in colonies.[61]

Capital seeks to harness and channel these counteracting tendencies in order to reorganize conditions for its profitable expansion, basic to which is the further concentration of capital as particular capitals strive to compensate for the fallen rate of profit by increasing their total mass of profit. Some capitals combine with or are swallowed by others, thereby altering the terms of competition. New organizational forms evolve to enhance efficiency and enlarge the scale of production. Markets are penetrated and extended, and new fields of production opened up. Reorganization is facilitated by mechanisms like the credit system and state intervention.

If increases in the rate of surplus value exert an upward influence on the rate of profit, it is just as true that this can *only* check or retard its fall. While labor productivity generally increases in proportion to employed capital, the amount of labor combined with it still relatively declines. Output per worker employed is mainly raised through greater inputs of materials and machines per unit of output. While increases in productivity may, for instance, cheapen the individual elements which make up a machine, the growth of social productivity hinges on the continual expansion of the aggregate stock of fixed capital and the transformation of the technical basis of the labor process. In other words, there are *more* machines and *more complex* machines (containing new elements). Indeed, the labor process grows ever more detailed and "perfect," splitting into interconnected subprocesses or stages of production

---

[61] See *Capital*, III, Chapter 14. This last factor — and even more so foreign investment — with all its ramifications for the maintenance of profitability, is of momentous importance in the imperialist era.

which become more mechanized and automated.[62] The tendency of the rate of profit to fall asserts itself, and capital must spend proportionately more to increase its mass of profit.

The existence and operation of this law is bound up with an historically determined mode of production based on the exploitation of wage-labor. It expresses the contradictory (and ultimately impossible) drive of capital, impelled by the force of anarchy, to free itself from its very basis.[63] But the tendency of the rate of profit to fall must be grasped as just that, a dynamic and dialectical law, as opposed to a mechanistic trend. It is not the case that in any given slice of time the rate of profit must (or should be expected to) be falling. The tendency asserts itself in the long run, over the duration of a particular trajectory of capital transformation and as an immanent barrier to accumulation, posing itself ever more formidably in the historical motion of capital. It is a far cry from Marx's conceptualization of this law to deduce as a corollary a secular petering out of growth or a chronic slowdown.

This law does not prejudge the precise course or rate of accumulation, which is subject to a multitude of concrete historical and political determinations. Rather, it defines the profoundly contradictory nature of accumulation — evidenced in the clash between this tendency and its countertendencies — and sets objective parameters to the accumulation process, all as a manifestation of underlying value relations. But, again, this can only be understood in terms of contradiction and motion: these parameters represent barriers which must and can only be overcome through major convulsions which shake out and reorganize capital as a whole. Understanding this law helps us understand why Marx never posited a separate theory of crisis; or, what is the same thing, it tells us why accumulation is necessarily punctuated by crisis.

The internal limits against which the self-expansion of capital collides are the product of its anarchic motion:

---

[62] See *Theories of Surplus Value,* III, p. 366. Roman Rosdolsky in *The Making of Marx's Capital* (London: Pluto Press, 1977), pp. 398-411, summarizes Marx's arguments as to why a rising rate of exploitation cannot permanently offset the tendential decline in the rate of profit. An important analysis and exposition of the relevant Marxian categories can be found in the work of Anwar Shaikh. See, for instance, his "Political economy and capitalism: notes on Dobb's theory of crisis," *Cambridge Journal of Economics,* No. 2 (June 1978), where Shaikh discusses the measurement of profit in relation to capital flow and capital stock.

[63] See *Grundrisse,* pp. 543, 706.

> [T]he capitalist mode of production involves a tendency towards absolute development of the productive forces, regardless of the value and surplus value it contains, and regardless of the social conditions under which capitalist production takes place; while, on the other hand, its aim is to preserve the value of the existing capital and promote its self-expansion to the highest limit . . . . [64]

Its contradictory methods and aims induce extreme disproportionalities and disturbances — capitalism breaks down under the weight of the productive forces whose development it has greatly fostered. Crisis is, then, nothing more nor less than the concentration point of overaccumulating capital, of capital which can no longer profitably reorganize itself in the context of its existing structure and composition, a framework which must be thoroughly recast. Capitalist crisis is *overproduction* crisis:

> Overproduction of capital is never anything more than overproduction of means of production — of means of labor and necessities of life — which may serve as capital, i.e., may serve to exploit labor at a given degree of exploitation; a fall in the intensity of exploitation below a certain point, however, calls forth disturbances, and stoppages in the capitalist production process, crises, and destruction of capital.
>
> . . . [T]oo many means of labor and necessities of life are produced at times to permit of their serving as means for the exploitation of laborers at a certain rate of profit. [65]

Thus, it is not an absolute overproduction of capital that characterizes capitalist crisis. There is overproduction of capital relative to the existing conditions of profitability and yet, at the same time and for the same reason, there is a capital shortage — the existing framework of accumulation does not generate profits adequate to fuel and underwrite expansion at a qualitatively higher level (which would transform overall value relations and conditions of profitability). [66] The essential feature of capitalist crisis is overproduction of capital, but this crisis presents itself *both as a shortfall and surfeit of capital.*

With respect to the development of crisis, the significance of the

[64] *Capital*, III, p. 249.

[65] *Capital*, III, pp. 255-56, 258.

[66] See Paul Mattick, *Marx and Keynes* (Boston: Porter Sargent, 1969), p. 68.

tendency of the rate of profit to fall does not lie in some preexisting threshold beyond which the capitalists more or less sit on their capital, unwilling to invest; it is more a matter of what this forces the capitalists to do in order to raise their rate and mass of profit and to preserve their mass of capital. In fact, as crisis unfolds, capitalists saddled with unprofitable investments, which elicit ever-diminishing reinvestment, will steer capital into more lucrative (if speculative) ventures which generate their own momentum. Crisis is an eruption of the dynamic, contradictory tendencies of accumulation. Capital is not gradually dragged down along a slope of declining profitability; rather, capital explodes as a consequence of its anarchic attempts to maintain itself as self-expanding value. There is, as it were, no predetermined scenario of crisis, no automatic triggering mechanism nor inexorable pattern according to which crisis unfolds. Crisis may first appear in any of the contradictory aspects or spheres of the total social capital. Moreover, political and social factors interact with the economic laws which have been described to invest each crisis with a certain uniqueness,

During "normal" periods of accumulation, individual capitals must strive to maintain themselves and their profitability in interaction and conflict with each other, and this is strewn with difficulty and disruption. Crisis represents a leap in the process. In essence, the whole system of reproduction is undermined: major dislocations and breaks in the circuits of capital lead to the interruption of accumulation on a grand scale and the struggle among capitals involves higher stakes and reaches a higher pitch. To comprehend crisis is to grasp that the tendential fall in the rate of profit asserts itself in the context of, and intensifies the underlying anarchy of, capitalist accumulation.

Accumulation does not, as noted, simply grind to a halt because profits are pinched. Certain capitals strive for major capital intensification and feverishly produce, as though there were no limit, as a means of compensating for falling profits. But the pressures and costs of technical change are sources of perturbation — in the form of premature renewal and obsolescence of fixed capital — and diminish the flexibility of individual capitals when this becomes an imperative. To be sure, these phenomena are endemic to accumulation at all times. But now they impinge pervasively and, given what happens to key units of the total capital, do so more abruptly on the day-to-day operation of capital. Those capitals unable to modernize at the same pace find themselves unable to realize the full value of their investment as it is rendered increasingly obsolete by more efficient capitals. Yet for these more efficient capitals there is a desperate need to recoup enormously expensive investments (buttressed by the accumulation of debt) in the midst of volatile market conditions. Exactly because capital develops unevenly, different sectors and capitals are affected to a greater or lesser degree by declining profitability and react differently, due to specific competitive pressures and their specific capabilities. But these are, after all, elements of the aggregate capital. What comes into sharper relief is how the very interknittedness of reproduction turns in on itself.

Until now our discussion has focused on the expansion and transformation of values. But for accumulation to proceed successfully, very definite material conditions must also be fulfilled. This is another aspect of the contradiction between use value and exchange value, which is inherent in the commodity form and an integral element in the breakdown of accumulation. A model of "ideal" reproduction would assume that the particular components of the total capital cheapen their outputs (which in turn constitute vital inputs for other capitals) at an increasing and relatively even rate. But capital is not distributed according to the needs of planned and proportionate growth: some sectors are undercapitalized, causing bottlenecks, while technological innovation and renovation do not proceed uniformly. If all units of capital did in fact advance uniformly, it would be far easier to overcome the tendential decline in the rate of profit. When steel mills, for instance, are not modernized, the ability of steel-consuming sectors to minimize costs and push forward accumulation is impaired. Again, the total capital contains and is composed of highly differentiated elements. Particular capitals of differing efficiency are distributed among sectors which differ widely in dynamism. Some sectors embody production processes which materially and technically lend themselves to high-technology investments, while others rely more on intense forms of (super)exploitation. As capital bolts and invades different investment spheres, unevenness is accentuated and the distribution of capital becomes more skewed, with whole industries rotting. Certain capitals are eventually bankrupted in the heat of competition, dropping entirely out of the circuits of capital and causing severe ruptures in the reproductive process (since they no longer furnish specific use values). In crisis, the existing distribution of the total capital impedes further advance.

The overaccumulation of capital finds concentrated expression in the overproduction of commodities. Some capitals speed up workers to raise productivity and lay off others to cut costs. The mass of commodities thus produced must be sold — but there is no guarantee of this. Feverish efforts to increase the mass of profit in the face of sharpening competition only intensify the contradiction between production and consumption. At the same time, those capitalists who curtail new investment on account of falling profits reduce demand for means of production (forcing cutbacks and lay-offs in those branches of social production producing capital goods) and means of subsistence (since fewer workers can be profitably employed). Insufficient demand results from and is grounded in insufficient profitability; yet the swelling glut of unsold commodities is not only the outward appearance of crisis, it gravely exacerbates it. The accumulation funds of those capitals which cannot realize the value of their commodity output decline further and the given price relations governing reproduction now undergo more violent fluctuation.

It is in the financial realm where the contradictions of accumulation become entwined and, through this realm, transmitted with jarring effect. Reference was made earlier to the increasingly "social" character of capital. The network of credit enables particular capitals to draw on a centralized pool of surplus value and to produce beyond the limits set by their own accumulated funds, and it speeds up the turnover of capital since the producing capitalist need not await formal money payment (in exchange for his previously produced commodities) in order to start a new cycle of production — all of which permits the more extensive development of the productive forces in general. In effect, an elongated chain of indebtedness, premised on continuous production and profitability, is established. But this chain snaps in different places as over-extended creditors press strapped debtors (who very likely have creditor relationships with others) for settlement of debts. Everyone must sell and liquidate to pay back; there is a rush for means of payment and a premium placed on real money assets. Here the inability to realize commodity values portends disaster, and the struggle over the apportionment of surplus value into interest, rent, and enterprise profit sharpens, with each capital trying to cut its losses. In addition, financial strains grow as speculative stockpiling, merger, etc., increasingly take the place of real investment. The credit system, which facilitates expansion and reorganization far beyond what would be possible in its absence, now serves, almost in falling-domino fashion, to amplify and generalize crisis.

If crisis reveals the inability of capital to overcome its barriers, it also shows itself to be the most powerful means for temporarily breaking through them. If crisis is a sharp interruption in the process of capitalist accumulation, it is also a radical upheaval — internal to the motion of capital — which generates the requisite conditions for a qualitative thrust forward in accumulation. Crisis, then, is neither external nor dysfunctional to accumulation, it is integral to this process and the principal mechanism of its adjustment and regeneration:

> The crises are always but momentary and forcible solutions of the existing contradictions. They are violent eruptions which for a time restore the disturbed equilibrium.[67]

In another context, Marx spoke of the divorce of purchase from sale, commodity from money, use value from exchange value, and pointed out that such contradictions existing in bourgeois production "are reconciled by a process of adjustment which, at the same time, however, manifests itself as crises, violent fusion of disconnected factors operating independently of one another and yet correlated. . . ."[68] Competition takes on a different hue as each capital, to preserve its quality as capital, seeks to force the others to withdraw from a narrowing field of production. The "operating fraternity" that previously shared in the loot of expansion now breaks apart into a brawl among "hostile brothers," each trying to shove losses onto the other.[69] In crisis the competitive struggle becomes the instrument of a violent and massive restructuring of capital; hence, the "purgative" role of crisis which paves the way for further accumulation.

Integral to this purgative role, crisis transforms the existing value relations of capital and the relations among capitals in the accelerated trend of centralization. The more concentrated capitals emerging out of this process are positioned to decisively reorganize the conditions of production. Thus, not simply larger, but newer and more efficient capitals are formed. The dislocations that occur on a large social scale in crisis interact with changes in relations among the larger and more critical capitals to render the whole mass of capital more profitable. How is such restructuring effected and how is it effective? Fundamentally, reorganization takes place

---

[67] *Capital*, III, p. 249.
[68] *Theories of Surplus Value*, III, p. 120.
[69] *Capital*, III, p. 253.

on the basis of the destruction of a portion of the total capital. The role and mechanisms of this destruction of capital (and capital values) and its renovation require further elaboration.

An increase in the productive force of labor devalues or destroys existing values since the same use values can be produced more cheaply. A machine, for instance, whose cost of production has declined (or which is replaced by a more efficient one) is worth less, and part of its value, reflecting previous conditions of its production, is thus destroyed. Investment in the form of accelerated replacement of fixed capital has just this effect. In crisis, destruction of capital is widespread and destabilizing. However, such destruction does not mainly occur through a real increase in the productive force of labor, but rather by means of a decrease in the existing value of raw materials, machines, and labor power.[70] The competitive scramble for a shrinking market leads to a fall in commodity prices, and since part of the commodities produced can only be cleared on the market through a contraction of prices, the capital they represent is depreciated, as if it had been produced more cheaply. Stocks, bonds, and other securities suffer the same fate; their market value depreciates on account of price declines and speculative collapses.

During crisis, centralization occurs largely as a consequence of the elimination of particular capitals (as opposed to the kind of merger and consolidation activity of booms). Those capitals under immense creditor pressure are forced to sell off assets (from idle machine tools to raw materials contracts) cheap. Those that are unable to realize their commodity values at a level permitting reproduction go bankrupt, and their assets, or at least some usable portion of them, are thrown onto the market. Depreciation makes possible the absorption of capitals that have ceased to function as capital, and this creates a more favorable basis for accumulation for those who do survive: "A large part of the nominal capital of the society, i.e., of the *exchange value* of the existing capital, is once for all destroyed, although this very destruction, since it does not affect the use value, may very much expedite the new reproduction."[71]

Because of the drop in prices, the means of production bought up in the welter of liquidation embody less exchange value than previously existed but represent the same use value. When produc-

---

[70] See *Grundrisse*, pp. 445-46.

[71] *Theories of Surplus Value*, II, p. 496.

tion resumes — and eventually crisis clears away excess commodity stocks — a given mass of surplus value will be larger relative to total capital since the same stock of means of production has been redistributed at lower cost to the stronger capitals, and this raises the rate of profit of those capitals.[72] Marx emphasized the role played by the transfer of assets from bankrupted capitals, ruined by the sudden devaluation of commodities and depreciation of capital: "large enterprises frequently do not flourish until they pass into other hands, i.e., after their first proprietors have been bankrupted, and their successors, who buy them cheaply, therefore begin from the outset with a smaller outlay of capital."[73]

But capital does not only become more centralized. On the one hand, the most inefficient and obsolete capital is discarded entirely; on the other, reduction of the total number of capitals carrying on production facilitates "economies of scale," that is, growth in the size of the unit of production to achieve a lower cost per unit of output. Plant and equipment investment previously held back can potentially be carried out more widely and profitably. In short, the technical level and efficiency of the total capital is raised. The renewal of fixed capital, in turn, provides a major impetus to expansion. As these elements come into play, the field of production can and must be widened still further, which involves further specialization of the division of labor, penetration of surrounding precapitalist formations, and expansion of foreign trade and investment. Linked with this crisis/recovery dialectic, the reconstitution of the reserve army of labor through enforced idleness during crisis enables capital to both depress wages and to impose a more intense regime of accumulation via speed-up, tighter discipline, etc., and this in turn enhances profitability and recovery.[74] In crisis, pervasive depreciation of capital promotes centralization of capital and enhances its profitability. On this basis it becomes possible to reorganize and technologically transform the conditions of production. The resultant capital is more concentrated and is reproduced on a higher technical basis; the commodities now entering into the reproductive process as elements of constant and variable capital are cheapened.

[72] See Mattick, *Marx and Keynes*, pp. 70-71.

[73] *Capital*, III, p. 114.

[74] The role of the reserve army of labor, however, though not without its contemporary international significance, is more central to the crisis resolution mechanism of the preimperialist era.

To sum up, major disturbances at the level of production, exchange, and distribution alter the relations among capitals and between capital and labor. Surplus commodity stocks are absorbed. Disproportionalities wracking social production and difficulties in the realm of circulation are momentarily suppressed. Based on the establishment of new value and price relations, capital is distributed in new proportions to the various spheres of social production. This temporarily facilitates the more harmonious and profitable reproduction of the total capital. At the same time, the bankruptcy of debt-ridden capitals and the depreciation of financial assets and securities shake out the financial superstructure; the lower interest rates ultimately emerging out of crisis relieve pressure on the surviving capitals. The credit chain broken during crisis can thus be reestablished, with production resuming and confidence between creditors and debtors restored.

It is precisely the process of destruction of exchange values and inefficient capitals which unleashes the massive restructuring of capital towards greater profitability, which creates a new framework for accumulation, including more complex and socialized mechanisms of reorganization:

> The ensuing stagnation of production would have prepared — within capitalistic limits — a subsequent expansion of production.
>
> And thus the cycle would run its course anew. Part of the capital, depreciated by its functional stagnation, would recover its old value. For the rest, the same vicious circle would be described once more under expanded conditions of production, with an expanded market *and* increased productive forces. . . . [75]

> Hence overproduction: i.e., the sudden *recall* of all these necessary moments of production founded on capital; hence general devaluation in consequence of forgetting them. Capital, at the same time, [is] thereby faced with the task of launching its attempt anew from a higher level of the development of productive forces, with each time greater collapse *as capital*. [76]

Crisis, therefore, is not only, as mentioned earlier, an integral part of the accumulation process, it is the *decisive* moment in that process exactly because it is within and through crisis that the contra-

---

[75] *Capital,* III, p. 255.
[76] *Grundrisse,* p. 416.

dictions of accumulation are concentrated and forcibly — if temporarily — resolved.[77] Capitalism undergoes great leaps owing to the contradiction fundamental and peculiar to it, between socialized production and private appropriation. Specifically, the "compelling force of anarchy" leads to breakdown, through which capital is violently recomposed.

The objective tendencies and requirements of capital do not exist apart from and are certainly influenced by the conflict between the working class and the capitalist class. Exactly how a specific crisis unfolds and is resolved is not a given. More to the point, it is precisely in such periods of crisis that the class struggle generally sharpens most: history and possibility, as well as the contradictions of accumulation, are condensed in these moments. But barring its revolutionary overthrow, capital will reconstitute itself according to its own logic. In advancing from a lower to a higher level of socialization a basic law is, nevertheless, at work: the means whereby the capitalists get out of crisis only lay the basis for more profound crises in the future. In one of the most powerful passages of the *Grundrisse,* Marx described the motion of this process:

> The growing incompatibility between the productive development of society and its hitherto existing relations of production expresses itself in bitter contradictions, crises, spasms. The violent destruction of capital not by relations external to it, but rather as a condition of its self-preservation, is the most striking form in which advice is given it to be gone and to give room to a higher state of social production.... Hence the highest development of productive power together with the greatest expansion of existing wealth will coincide with depreciation of capital, degradation of the laborer, and a most straitened exhaustion of his vital powers. These contradictions lead to explosions, cataclysms, crises, in which by momentaneous suspension of labor and annihilation of a great portion of capital the latter is violently reduced to the point where it can go on.... Yet, these regularly recurring catastrophes lead to their repetition on a higher scale, and finally to its violent overthrow.[78]

Thus we return to the concept of spiral development. The "regularly recurring catastrophes" to which Marx referred were the crisis phase of the acute periodic process of accumulation, as-

---

[77] A similar point is made with respect to the cycle in Ben Fine and Laurence Harris, *Rereading Capital* (London: MacMillan, 1979), p. 80.

[78] *Grundrisse,* pp. 749-50.

suming at first a five-year pattern and later emerging as a ten-year industrial and trade cycle, which was typical of the most developed capitalist country, Great Britain, in the early and mid-nineteenth century. These breakneck leaps and explosions were the essential framework through which capital became more concentrated, paving the way for more serious crisis and preparing the conditions for its "violent overthrow." Through this process — although Marx could not foresee it — capitalism developed to a higher stage, imperialism, inseparable from the very laws of motion he discovered. Under imperialism accumulation began to take place on a world scale. The fundamental contradiction of capitalism became the fundamental contradiction of a single, if extremely complex, world process involving the motion and interpenetration of many other contradictions. Far from being attenuated or overcome, capitalism's basic contradictions were intensified. The first world war and the revolution Lenin successfully led were striking confirmation, harbingers, of an era in which the "knell of private property" would indeed sound. We now turn to the dynamics of this era.

IV

Lenin set out precisely to explain the complex causes of both the continued growth of capitalism and the sharpening of its contradictions in the imperialist era — to identify the economic roots of modern war and modern politics. Introducing his study of imperialism, Lenin described the work as presenting "a *composite picture* of the world capitalist system in its international relationships."[79] Throughout, he pointed to changes within and between the advanced and the oppressed countries, which transformed capitalism into a world system of colonial oppression, and to processes of development which inevitably lead to convulsions within the whole of world capitalism. Clearly, Lenin was not simply concerned with changes in the structure of the advanced countries or even mainly with the relations between the advanced and backward countries, although these he deemed of great importance. His object of analysis and starting point was the system in its global totality.

In *Imperialism, The Highest Stage of Capitalism*, Lenin analyzed the profound changes which had taken place in the structure and

---

[79] *Imperialism*, p. 3 (*LCW*, 22, p. 189).

functioning of capitalism by synthesizing a mass of data on the development of capitalism in the late nineteenth century. An important benchmark in that development was the prolonged crisis which began in 1873 and deeply affected the major capitalist countries. This crisis vastly increased the tendency toward concentration; in Germany, for instance, the highly developed system of trusts and cartels first emerged in the ensuing years of economic slowdown. The boom at the end of the nineteenth century and the crisis of 1900 still further accelerated the trend toward concentration and centralization, leaving in their wake a financial and industrial system dominated by a few strategically situated, giant agglomerations of capital.[80]

By the last third of the nineteenth century, Western European feudalism had been overcome and capitalism was spreading its reach to the farthest stretches of unconquered land in the world. In great measure because of this, the system could develop relatively peacefully at home (although not without breaks in growth). Indeed, this stabilization of capitalism was linked precisely with the savagery of its expansion into regions it newly or more thoroughly penetrated. At the close of the nineteenth century, what has come to be known as the Third World[81] was transformed from a subsidiary market and outlet for capital of the advanced countries into an indispensable component of their prosperity. Internationaliza-

---

[80] The period between 1873 and 1896 has often been referred to as the "Great Depression," or, more accurately, as the "Great Price Depression." These were indeed years of plummeting prices, due mainly to agrarian crisis in many parts of the world and rising labor productivity propelled by massive technical advance. Further, investment opportunities were pinched and overproduction difficulties felt in some of the advanced countries. However, while average annual growth rates in real output slowed considerably in Great Britain and France, the U.S. and Germany were able to sustain growth at levels approaching those of the preceding twenty years. This was not a period of global economic crisis of the order of the world depression of the 1930s or of the current world crisis. Nor was it a period of revolutionary upheaval in these countries.

[81] We use the term Third World because it has become widely accepted as a kind of shorthand for the peoples and countries of Asia, Africa, and Latin America. But its use in this book has no connection with the use of this term by the revisionist rulers of China. They employ it to obscure class relations within these countries and between them and imperialism, and frequently accompany its use with equally unscientific divisions between the "second world" (lesser imperialist and capitalist states) and the "first world" (the two superpowers), which obscure the imperialist and reactionary character of these states and promote alliance with the U.S. bloc against the Soviet bloc. In describing the Third World countries, we use the terms (neo)colonial, dependent, and oppressed interchangeably.

tion of investment of productive capital transformed the world market. On a political level, Great Britain's military, colonial, and economic preeminence was challenged by rival empire-builders. Free trade was being eclipsed by an aggressive and bellicose protectionism. A veritable paroxysm of colonial conquests culminated in the complete partition of the world by and among the great powers. The great powers had imposed their power over every corner of the globe. Lenin summarized the leap that had occurred:

> On the threshold of the twentieth century we see the formation of a new type of monopoly: firstly, monopolist capitalist combines in all capitalistically developed countries; secondly, the monopolist position of a few very rich countries, in which the accumulation of capital has reached gigantic proportions.[82]

This emergence of monopoly, inward and outward, as it were, at a deeper level expressed that "narrowing circle" to which Engels referred. Capitalism was pressing against the limits of private ownership and facing ever more formidable barriers in the international arena. The compelling force of anarchy had propelled socialization of the productive forces to a whole new level of domestic concentration and centralization. This same compelling force pushed these powers outward, where they collided with the less powerful, old-style colonial powers, let loose their cannon on nascent national movements, and lashed out at each other.[83] The contours of modern capitalism could be discerned: capitalism was in violent transition to something higher.

The emergence of imperialism, then, was nothing less than the fundamental development of capitalism into a separate and distinct phase. The imperialist era is an era of war and revolution determined by an ensemble of historically constituted and interrelated phenomena. With the caveat that such definitions tend to simplify the complexity of nature or society, Lenin enumerated imperialism's most basic features, recognizing as well that no single aspect of imperialism defined its essence:

> Imperialism is capitalism in that stage of development in which the dominance of monopolies and finance capital has established itself;

---

[82] *Imperialism*, pp. 72-73 (*LCW*, 22, p. 241).

[83] The Anglo-Boer and Spanish-American Wars and the subsequent Russo-Japanese War of the late nineteenth and early twentieth centuries were the first significant imperialist conflicts.

in which the export of capital has acquired pronounced importance; in which the division of the world among the international trusts has begun; in which the division of all territories of the globe among the biggest capitalist powers has been completed.[84]

Imperialism is the product of the interaction of the laws of capital (in their historical concreteness) in the advanced countries with other historical processes taking place in the world. It is not just the simple unfolding or logical extension of the laws of motion of capital. For instance, while the dominance of capitalism was established during the time Lenin wrote, it was not the case that the world was fully capitalized. Precapitalist modes of production were subordinated to and integrated into the world capitalist system — this was an exceptionally important particularity of the genesis and development of the imperialist epoch. Lenin's whole view cut against teleological accounts of imperialism's origins and its mechanisms. He examined real, concrete historical development, and the salient fact to which he drew attention was that by 1900 the capitalist mode of production was rapidly enmeshing the world as a whole in its contradictions and bringing the various elements of the world economy into new relations with each other.

Marxism has always stressed both the relation between capitalism and the world market and the relation between international events and developments in specific countries. Marxists emphasize the international character of capitalist production and exchange and argue that this becomes even greater with the further development of capitalism. As early as *The German Ideology* and *The Poverty of Philosophy*, Marx and Engels underscored how growth in international trade made it possible to speak of a real world history, and how such diverse phenomena as inventions in Europe and crop yields in the Americas reacted upon domestic developments in different countries.[85] In the *Grundrisse*, Marx pointed to the universalizing thrust of capital: "The tendency to create the *world market* is directly given in the concept of capital itself."[86] "The modern history of capital," Marx wrote in *Capital*, "dates from the creation in the sixteenth century of a world-embracing commerce and a

[84] *Imperialism,* p. 106 (*LCW,* 22, pp. 266-67).

[85] See, for example, Marx and Engels, *The German Ideology* in Marx and Engels, *Collected Works (MECW)* (New York: International Publishers), 5, pp. 50-51; Marx, *The Poverty of Philosophy, MECW,* 6, p. 167.

[86] *Grundrisse,* p. 408.

world-embracing market," and he sardonically assessed the allegedly idyllic beginnings of capital, its so-called primitive accumulation: "The discovery of gold and silver in America, the extirpation, enslavement and entombment in mines of the aboriginal population, the beginning of the conquest and looting of the East Indies, the turning of Africa into a warren for the commercial hunting of black skins, signalized the rosy dawn of the era of capitalist production."[87]

These were the important international factors facilitating that forcible expropriation of the mass of producers in the "home country" which was referred to earlier as the social basis of the rise of capitalism.[88] The external economic activities of the rising European powers in the fifteenth and sixteenth centuries — particularly the brutal conquests and plunder conducted by the trading monopolies — played a crucial role in generating a surplus which nurtured the still tender shoots of the capitalist relations then developing in Europe. But unique to the trading and plundering activities of the West European merchants and states, as compared with previous empires, was that there existed a basis within the European economies to employ accumulated treasure as *capital*, to invest it in means of production and combine it with the labor power of propertyless proletarians. This also explains why these merchants could accumulate more rapidly than their trading partners in other parts of the world. On the other hand, while internal development of the forces and relations of production was the basis for the emergence of capitalism in Europe, the world market accelerated and mediated this process: it influenced not only the pace of development, but the actual configuration of emerging capitalism.

This was the period of mercantile capitalism, in which trading and usury activities predominated. The means of production remained primitive and scattered and there was as yet no capitalist international division of labor. In the eighteenth and nineteenth centuries, with the further spread and deepening of commodity relations, a capitalist world market was created under the dominance of industrial capital and spurred forward by free competi-

---

[87] *Capital*, I, pp. 145, 703.

[88] Marx also remarked that the "veiled slavery of the wage workers in Europe needed, for its pedestal, slavery pure and simple in the new world" (*Capital*, I, p. 711).

tion.[89] The international requirements of industrial capital brought the backward regions of the world under the domination of capital and caused their penetration by capitalist relations, a phenomenon no more "idyllic" than the mercantile thrust outward. A greater portion of the world's production became commodity production, serving the needs of expanding industrial capital:

> [T]he expansion of foreign trade, although the basis of the capitalist mode of production in its infancy, has become its own product, however, with the further progress of the capitalist mode of production, through the innate necessity of this mode of production, its need for an ever-expanding market. . . . [90]

> So soon. . .as the general conditions requisite for production by the modern industrial system have been established, this mode of production acquires an elasticity, a capacity for sudden extension by leaps and bounds that finds no hindrance except in the supply of raw material and in the disposal of the produce. . . . By ruining handicraft production in other countries, machinery forcibly converts them into fields for the supply of its raw material. . . . A new and international division of labor, a division suited to the requirements of the chief centers of modern industry springs up. . . . [91]

During the ascendancy of industrial capital, the world market was not so much a precondition for capitalist production as it was an extension of it, serving as an outlet for commodities and a source of raw materials. Between 1840 and 1850, foreign trade within

---

[89] Indeed, during different periods of capitalism's history a different layer of the bourgeoisie has been dominant and has invested the process of capitalist development, both on the national level and in the formation and functioning of the world market, with certain characteristics. In the feudal period, merchant capital emerged in the interstices between largely self-sufficient communities whose conditions of production and exchange were generally unknown to others. Merchant capitalists were not engaged in production proper; they operated in the sphere of commerce, buying cheap and selling dear in separate markets, combining trading activity with outright plunder. The ascendancy of industrial capital in the eighteenth and nineteenth centuries corresponded to the full development and integration of the three circuits of capital within national formations and the establishment of average prices and profits of production within national formations under the impetus of free competition. These industrial capitalists, who more or less owned and controlled their capital independently of others, were typically rooted in a particular branch of production or line of activity. In the imperialist epoch, finance capital becomes ascendant and imparts definite features to accumulation and the world market.

[90] *Capital*, III, p. 237.

[91] *Capital*, I, pp. 424-25.

Europe increased seventy percent. [92] At the same time, diffusion of industrial processes to the United States and throughout most of Western Europe, the growing food and raw material requirements of these countries, and the specific dynamics of the British cotton and textile industries led to increased trade with non-European nations. [93]

Extensive regions of the non-European world were drawn, although unevenly, into industrial capital's sphere of circulation. From a world-historic viewpoint, foreign capitalism played a revolutionary role in these areas: it battered at the precapitalist production relations and superstructures of these variegated societies and stimulated the development of commodity production and of bourgeois production relations, breaking these societies out of much of the insularity that had previously characterized them. Commerce between the advanced and backward countries came to play a more central role than the extortion and transmission of riches. The plunder of the sword, which had typified the mercantile era and which had helped destroy the feudal fetters of production in Europe, while far from ceasing, increasingly served the ever-expanding need for markets of industrial capital.

If, however, international connections were growing and drawing new territories into the vortex of the world economy, and if the mutual interaction between different societies made for a higher degree of interdependence, capitalist and precapitalist lands still confronted each other as basically separate societies, the development of each determined by its own internal dynamic, with the international context functioning secondarily as external condition. What, then, changed such that the terms of these interactions were transformed and the bourgeois mode of production became dominant on a world scale?

Here it is necessary to return to the long-term effects of the increasing socialization and, at the same time, heightened anarchy of capitalist production in its national framework, and the nature and terms of the struggle for international supremacy — which are entirely related phenomena. Toward the middle of the nineteenth century, capitalism in Western Europe was attaining a degree of de-

---

[92] Claudia von Braunmühl, "On the Analysis of the Bourgeois Nation State within the World Market Context," in John Holloway and Sol Picciotto, eds., *State and Capital* (Austin: Univ. of Texas Press, 1979), p. 207, note 34.

[93] For example, between 1846 and 1860, export of cotton and wool from India to England grew sixfold and over fourfold, respectively (*Capital*, I, p. 424, note 2).

velopment and maturation which intensified its contradictions. It had fundamentally conquered and transformed feudalism domestically — not completely or uniformly, but substantially — which, as will be recalled, was an essential means through which capital reorganized itself. (In Japan and Germany the full transition to capitalism was coextensive with and telescoped by the approach to the imperialist stage.) With the further growth of capitalism in the advanced countries, foreign trade assumed greater importance as a means of countervailing the tendential decline in the rate of profit internal to these countries. This expansion of trade accelerated the accumulation of capital and thus, as described earlier with respect to the general operation of the countertendencies to the falling rate of profit, ultimately compounded the difficulties of accumulation, necessitating still further expansion of trade. But the expansion of trade with the backward regions of the world was increasingly hampered by the limited capabilities of their precapitalist modes of production. Due to its relative stagnation, feudalism, for instance, could not expand production at a rate which could meet the growing trade requirements of capitalism.[94]

Something was happening within the very circuits of capital which interknit the world in a new way. Before imperialism, the economic integration of the world was principally a function of trade and monetary transactions. The circuit of commodity capital had been internationalized in Marx's time — we have already taken note of the exceptionally rapid growth of world trade. The circuit of money capital was also internationalized prior to the advent of im-

---

[94] Marx dealt with this phenomenon in his writings on British trade with India in the mid-nineteenth century. After the opening of trade in 1813, commerce with India tripled in a very short time. Further, India, which had previously been an exporting country, now became an importing one. By 1850 India accounted for more than one-eighth of Britain's export trade. However, Britain's cheap cotton manufactures had the effect of ruining indigenous industry, and in so doing actually undermined the basis for extended trade. In the four years ending in 1850, two-way trade between the two countries was less than in the four years ending in 1846. So important was the Indian market to British industry that it would be necessary, according to Marx, for British capital to create "fresh productive powers" in India (Marx, "The East India Company — Its History and Results," originally published in the *New York Daily Tribune*, 11 July 1853, in *MECW*, 12, pp. 148-56). Yet Marx was writing in a transitional period. The initially stimulating effect of European trade with Asian society was already ebbing; the trade requirements of precapitalist modes of production were wholly inadequate to the trade needs of industrial capital. The industrial development that eventually took place in India was fostered under the rule of imperialism and it would not repeat the socioeconomic trajectory of the advanced countries.

perialism; Marx himself spoke of gold as world money, and it was a necessary element in facilitating world trade.

With imperialism, however, the circuit of productive capital itself became effectively internationalized for the first time, creating the basis for a new unity of capital on a global plane. Profitable investment in the advanced countries was more limited and strained by an already high degree of development and concentration. There was an inner urge for capital, according to its national needs, to seek out and develop foreign outlets for capital as capital — value that generates surplus value — on a qualitatively greater scale. This was made possible by the fact that by the middle to late nineteenth century the means to export capital and make use of it in different parts of the world had developed in depth and breadth.[95] Capital's outward flow took a leap and it was extensively invested internationally in accordance with the law of value and profitability. Consequently, value transfers — and value formation itself — became internationalized. Previous modes of global integration were transformed by the dominance of this internationalized circuit of productive capital, and trade and monetary transactions stood in a new (subordinate) relationship to the export of capital. A recent analysis offers this useful description:

> In the course of the process of accumulation, of the extension, differentiation and intensification of the social division of labor, of the increasing establishment of international capital mobility and supranational interpenetration, the unity of the divided complexes of reproduction (i.e., national capitals), previously established selectively and essentially in the sphere of circulation, coheres increasingly to become a real, unified, global complex of reproduction.[96]

At the same time, the great capitalist powers were locking horns with each other over the distribution of colonial spoils. There was no further room for expansion into previously unconquered territories of the world, only for *redivision* of existing ones: "For the first time the world is completely divided up, so that in the future

---

[95] Major improvements in global communications and transportation, particularly submarine cable and the steamship, were key factors.

[96] von Braunmühl, "Bourgeois Nation State," p. 168. In making this important observation, the author does not, however, clearly distinguish between imperialist and preimperialist stages of capitalist development.

only redivision is possible, i.e., territories can only pass from one 'owner' to another, instead of passing as ownerless territory to an 'owner.' "[97] Lenin emphasized that the transition to the stage of monopoly capitalism is directly associated with intensification of the struggle for partition of the world, although he did not, as his critics — bourgeois and "Marxist" — often contend, posit a crude causal relation between the rise of monopoly and the partition struggle.[98] The statistics he cited underscore how this struggle sharpened with the development of the monopolist stage of West European capitalism: between 1876 and 1914 the colonial possessions of the six great capitalist powers (measured in land area) increased by over fifty percent. In absolute terms this orgy of foreign conquest was staggering. In Africa, to take perhaps the most striking example, only one-tenth of its total area had been colonized by 1876. By 1900, just twenty-five years later, fully nine-tenths of its total area was under foreign rule![99]

New structural relationships emerge in the imperialist era and

---

[97] *Imperialism*, p. 90 (*LCW*, 22, p. 254).

[98] Lenin's theory of imperialism is sometimes attacked for resting on (or manufacturing) a double coincidence: that certain internal and external developments, most notably the overripening of domestic capital, on the one hand, and the territorial division of the world, on the other, had historically converged, and that these developments occurred simultaneously in all the capitalist countries. This argument figures prominently in Bill Warren, *Imperialism: Pioneer of Capitalism* (London: Verso Editions, 1980). Now it could scarcely be argued that the major capitalist countries had each attained an identical level of internal development in the late nineteenth or early twentieth centuries. Germany, for instance, had reached a much higher degree of monopolization than had Great Britain (although World War 1 dramatically accelerated this process in Great Britain). Nor were the features of imperialism as they exist today present in every way in the advanced countries (several were not even fully imperialist). However, there was indeed such a   double coincidence, understood as a qualitative phenomenon of the world capitalist system. The particularities of the different countries were secondary to the general trends of domestic accumulation and to the general fact that foreign trade as a main avenue of expansion was reaching certain limits in the consumption and productive capacities of colonial markets. Capital export did acquire "pronounced importance." Moreover, while it would surely be foolish to argue that specific outflows of capital caused governments to secure specific portions of the globe, an international dynamic of economic expansion and political and economic rivalry was decisively shaping the entire development of capitalism and reacting back upon the major capitalist economies and their states, although with differences related to both their historical development and position within the world market. Capitalism had thus reached a stage of development *requiring* that it operate on a wider, international scale in a way it previously had not.

[99] *Imperialism*, pp. 95, 90 (*LCW*, 22, pp. 258, 254). Table 2.1 presents a comprehensive picture of colonial conquests during this period.

invest the accumulation process with specific and systemic distortions. Under imperialism, accumulation proceeds decisively through *monopoly,* specifically the dominance of international finance capital, which is the key activating and stimulating factor in the reproductive process. It proceeds on the basis of the *division of the world between oppressor and oppressed nations.* Colonial expansion and superprofits play a crucial role in the overall process of accumulation. And, in the imperialist era, accumulation proceeds through *rivalry* between different national capitals. If national capitals and formations are locked into a single international system, it is also the case that this system, though a coherent whole, is divided inescapably into national capitals and blocs of national capitals. These phenomena are not incidental but part of the form of existence of internationalized capitals. The laws of accumulation assert themselves in interpenetration with the division of the world and with political struggles in the world, including, very decisively, revolutionary struggles.

The political and economic transformations we have been examining were, in their historical development and dynamic interrelation, responsible for a qualitative change in world relations. It was not simply that the world market now encompassed more countries; this was no longer the same world market. With the rise of imperialism, an international dynamic subordinates and integrates different societies. Building on Lenin's systematization of the political economy of the epoch, Bob Avakian has given more precise meaning to this change in world relations and, in particular, to its significance for the international class struggle. Avakian's conclusions have profound methodological and political implications:

> [I]n an overall sense the development of the class (and national) struggle, the development of revolutionary situations, etc., in particular countries are more determined by developments in the world as a whole than by developments in the particular countries — determined not only as a condition of change (external cause) but as a basis of change (internal cause). . . . [T]his was not so before the advent of imperialism — or before bourgeois society (and to put it that way, the bourgeois epoch) became dominant in the world and changes in societies throughout the world became integrated in an overall way into a whole (single) process. . . . China, for example (or the U.S., or any other country) has its own particularity, its own particular contradiction; and in one context, the rest of the world (and struggle and change in it) is external (to China, or the U.S., etc.). But it is also true that, in another context, China, the U.S., and the rest of

the countries of the world form parts of the world (of human society) as a whole, with its internal contradiction and change, determined in an overall way by the fundamental contradiction of the bourgeois epoch, between socialized production/private appropriation.... [C]ouldn't it be said that each country in the world, and changes within it, have always been part of the world and world relations — and changes in them — or even that, going further, the world is after all part of the solar system, the solar system part of a galaxy, etc. But it can — and must — be said that the difference between the solar system and the world, for example, is of a *qualitatively* different type than the difference between one country and the world, *in the context we are considering things* — which is precisely the context *of changes in human society*; and the same for the relationship between different — more or less isolated — societies in the period before the dominance of the bourgeois epoch and then in the period of that dominance, because before, changes in particular societies were not part of a whole — single — world process in the way they are now.[100]

Avakian's insight is a central thesis of this work. With the rise of imperialism, the fundamental contradiction of the bourgeois epoch becomes the underlying contradiction of a single, overall world process of the advance from the bourgeois epoch to its replacement by the epoch of world communism. Through this process this contradiction grows more intense, in turn intensifying many of the subordinate contradictions and struggles in the world, while also bringing some new conflicts into being, particularly that between the socialist and imperialist systems. The other main contradictions which arise from this single fundamental contradiction are integrated into this process, as are still other contradictions that predate or existed previously outside bourgeois society.[101]

The monopolization and relative saturation of capital in the advanced countries and the concomitant internationalization of the entire circuit of capital promoted the subsumption of different societies into a single world process. In the colonies, it is now no longer merely a matter of old structures being broken and battered down, but transformation on the basis of subordination to and integration within the international flow of imperialist capital. A new production relation defines the interaction of the advanced and op-

---

[100] Avakian, "On the Philosophical Basis of Proletarian Internationalism," *Revolutionary Worker*, No. 96 (13 March 1981), p. 3.

[101] For example, consider the contradictions characteristic of the feudal system which still persist, though in modified form, in large parts of the world.

pressed nations. The division of the world among the major capitalist powers, and the struggles and conflicts to which this gave rise or heightened, represented a fundamental historical factor underlying this change in world relations. The network of international relations and connections, then, is at once the critical stimulus of accumulation and the principal set of barriers to accumulation, both economically and politically.

The world — and the changes in relations within the world determined by the fundamental contradiction of the bourgeois epoch — is the essential arena (and analytic framework) for understanding the forces and influences shaping politics and economics in the imperialist era. Yet the world, understood in terms of human society, is a structured totality made up of distinct levels, including national formations, blocs, and opposing systems, which are themselves internally contradictory and partake of their own specificity and effectivity. National particularities will, for instance, determine the strategy for revolution in any given country. But this is only relative: in an overall way international factors become the internal basis for change and development in particular countries, both as an ongoing determinant and especially during periods of international crisis. And, dialectically, struggles or events in individual countries will have far-reaching international significance, exactly because the unfolding of the fundamental contradiction on a world scale, while enormously complex and contingent, is a coherent and determining totality. The objective and analytical primacy of international relations and the existence of this single world process must, therefore, inform any serious analysis of the coordinates of imperialist accumulation and of revolutionary struggle.

V

The specificity of imperialist accumulation is concentrated in the structure and workings of finance capital. The concept refers both to a layer of the bourgeoisie and a characteristic mode of operation.[102] Lenin stressed two developments underlying the rise of finance

---

[102] We use the terms imperialism, monopoly capitalism, and finance capitalism synonymously; they refer to the same phenomena of this epoch. As Lenin stressed, imperialism is the monopoly stage of capitalist development. However, in order to clarify the argument and to emphasize certain aspects of the accumulation process, we vary the choice of terms in particular contexts.

capital in the late nineteenth century: the monopolization of banking and industry and the merger (or coalescence) of banking with industrial capital.

Owing to the increasing scale and complexity of production, it became necessary, in order to advance accumulation, to pool and centralize capital. The banks played an important role in this process by mobilizing huge reserves of money capital and providing the credits upon which large enterprises were dependent. The links between individual capitals increased, accumulation accelerated rapidly, and with this came further centralization and monopoly. Having acquired a significant stake in enterprises (in which, for instance, large amounts of their credit were tied up for extended periods as fixed capital), the banks sought to safeguard these investments by promoting trusts and cartels. This, however, required even greater financial injections, something which reacted back upon the banking system, encouraging centralization and even closer ties between industry and banking. At the same time, industrial monopolies penetrated into banking activities, replicating this process from the other side. "[F]inance capital is the bank capital of a few very big monopolist banks, merged," Lenin observed, "with the capital of the monopolist combines of industrialists...."[103] Based on this monopolization and commingling, certain strategically situated capitals could marshal and exclusively command huge amounts of money and investment capital, and in so doing control the whole process of production.

Monopoly does not signify that one capital has literally displaced all others. It simply means that a sufficient share of the total capital and production in any given branch or sector has fallen under the control of a few big enterprises and that such enterprises wrest or establish control over supply, processing, and marketing channels, enabling them, by dint of their position or monopolistic agreement, to restrict competition and appropriate a larger than average — a surplus (or monopoly) — profit. Free competition and the press of cost reduction no longer hold sway as in the premonopoly era; within certain bounds, coalitions of finance capital can fix output and prices to preserve and allocate market shares and high profits according to the weights of their respective capitals. Recognizing that the actions of any of the major finance capitalists would influence overall price levels and that each will re-

---

[103] *Imperialism*, p. 105 (*LCW*, 22, p. 266).

spond similarly to disturbances, monopoly attempts to minimize predatory competition that results in lower profits. Monopoly strives, therefore, to rationalize production and exchange, to stabilize earnings and cushion itself against cyclical fluctuations.

Imperialism, however, cannot free itself from its foundation of commodity production — the very cell of capitalist production — and competition. No matter how far it develops, no matter how socialized production (and the mechanisms of reorganization) becomes, imperialism cannot escape the compelling force of anarchy which drives individual capitals (or coalitions of capital) into antagonistic interaction on the basis of the exploitation of wage-labor. Lenin wrote:

> Imperialism, in fact, does not *and cannot transform* capitalism from top to bottom. Imperialism complicates and sharpens the contradictions of capitalism: it "ties up" monopoly with free competition, but *it cannot do away* with exchange, the market, competition, crisis, etc.
>
> Imperialism is moribund capitalism, capitalism which is dying but not dead. The essential feature of imperialism, by and large, is not monopolies pure and simple, but monopolies in conjunction with exchange, markets, competition, crises.... In fact, it is this combination of antagonistic principles, viz., competition and monopoly, that is the essence of imperialism, it is this that is making for the final crash, i.e., the socialist revolution. [104]

The competition to which Lenin refers is not mainly within the nonmonopoly sector or between monopoly and nonmonopoly but among these enormous imperialized blocks of capital. The contradiction between monopoly and competition is a powerful expression of the organization/anarchy contradiction. Monopoly cannot override the internal laws of capital; indeed, by modifying them, it makes for more acute anarchy at higher levels.

By the late nineteenth century, the process by which individual forms of capitalist property evolved into collective forms of capitalist property, that is, the predominance of joint-stockholding companies and embryonic forms of state capitalist property, had become a process of monopolization. Along with and as an expression of this, a stratum of the bourgeoisie, an oligarchy, made up of separate, yet interrelated, finance capitalists, came to occupy a

[104] "Comments on the Remarks Made by the Committee of the April All-Russia Conference," from "Materials Relating to the Revision of the Party Programme," *LCW*, 24, pp. 464-65.

dominant position. A new type of monopoly arose on the basis of highly socialized production.

Finance capital is not money capital, much less does it represent a new or separate circuit of capital. It works through bank, industrial, and commercial capital, which become monopolistically structured and integrated. Nor is finance capital institutionally reducible to a bank or corporation — although it involves a peculiar financial practice. It is not a question of banks controlling corporations or vice versa. Finance capital criss-crosses and links different corporate entities, industrial firms and banks, each of which increasingly combines features of the other. A Chase Manhattan Bank or a General Motors Corporation are organizational units in which finance capital is embedded and embodied and through which it operates. What emerges out of these monopolistic interconnections is a layer of the bourgeoisie composed of capitalists who, in the main, are neither industrialists nor bankers and whose horizons and loyalties are not defined by or limited to a particular firm or industry. In fact, they explicitly avoid being locked into such a position, although they have particular "base areas" of activity: in terms of their national base, particular oppressed countries, and with respect to specific industries and banks in any given country.

These finance capitalists do not mainly function according to the logic of the classical entrepreneur, i.e., how to make a cheaper car or run a more efficient bank. Although the operation of finance capital is ultimately rooted in the creation of surplus value in production, its activity pivots principally on financial relations and decisions: which enterprises, industries, or even countries to finance in order to increase financial control and weaken the control of adversaries.

This ramifying and interlacing has a crucial implication: profit maximization ceases to be principally determined, nor is it necessarily operative, at the firm level. The juridically autonomous firm is no longer the locus of decisive decision-making. The enterprise remains the *site of accumulation*; this is where capital is productively applied. But the enterprise or firm is not the paramount *unit of appropriation*. Enterprises and firms are at once chess pieces and battlegrounds on a larger board where the profit constraint asserts itself. Surplus value is ultimately appropriated — and this means the final control exercised over the mobilization and deployment of capital — at the level of the *financial group*.

The financial group is an essential category in the Marxist-

Leninist political economy of imperialist accumulation. In the Western bloc, these groups tend to be loosely knit and juridically private banking/industrial complexes whose command posts are core banking institutions or industrial corporations (one or the other of which may be more prominent and strategic in particular countries).[105] In the Soviet bloc, these groups are situated at the level of and are interwoven with the party and state structures, e.g., ministries, state banks, etc.

The actual composition of financial groups may be hazy and their inner networks are nothing if not labyrinthine; moreover, they interpenetrate one another (several financial groups can be represented in a single large industrial corporation). But financial groups are real entities. Finance capital divides into definite spheres of influence which are grounded in definite ownership interests. They are blocks of associated capital: coherent constellations of independently managed enterprises (as well as investments and interests) which are subject to common control and which act according to a group strategy (including designated profit structures, price mechanisms, and supply channels for their component enterprises).[106] The financial group is a particular institutional expression of monopoly, reflecting both the high degree of socialization of the productive forces and the parasitism of imperialism.

Under the regime of finance capital, the tendency toward a systemwide average rate of profit is modified, on the one hand, by the enormous scale of production which impedes the rapid transfer of capital into and out of investment spheres of high and low profitability and, on the other — and of far greater importance — by the obstacles and barriers thrown up by monopoly itself to the free

---

[105] In Japan many firms are linked through intercorporate stockholdings, ties to trading companies and banks, and regular gatherings of executives. In Sweden, stockholdings and family banking connections make it possible for a small number of family groups to wield control over the manufacturing sector. In Germany, a few key banks play a dominant role in the economy. Some of the literature on forms of corporate interlocks and financial control in the Western bloc is summarized in F.M. Scherer, *Industrial Market Structure and Economic Performance*, 2nd ed. (Chicago: Rand McNally, 1980), pp. 51-53. The subtlety and intricacy of financial groups and their sources of control in the U.S. emphasize that legal ownership of a firm or share capital and actual control over such property are not at all the same thing. This is perhaps best illustrated by the enormous stockholdings of financial intermediaries, e.g., bank deployment of corporate pension funds.

[106] A similar characterization of financial groups is posited by Henk Overbeek, in "Finance Capital and the Crisis in Britain," *Capital and Class*, No. 11 (Summer 1980), p. 103.

movement of capital. Capital continues to flow from low to high profit investments, but within particular bounds. This results in the formation of monopoly (or surplus) profits which are not so much constituted and marshaled at the industrial firm level as they are, again, at the level of the financial group.[107]

The linchpin of finance capital's functioning is the most extreme dissociation of capital ownership from its direct management, so that enterprises, branches of production, and particular countries are subordinated to its imperatives. Lenin wrote:

> It is characteristic of capitalism in general that the ownership of capital is separated from the application of capital to production, that money capital is separated from industrial or productive capital, and that the rentier who lives entirely on income obtained from money capital is separated from the entrepreneur and from all who are directly concerned in the management of capital. Imperialism, or the domination of finance capital, is that highest stage of capitalism at which this separation reaches vast proportions. The supremacy of finance capital over all other forms of capital means the predominance of the rentier and of the financial oligarchy; it means the singling out of a small number of financially "powerful" states from among all the rest.[108]

Particular circuits and sites of accumulation are expanded or drained, not in relation to their internal needs, but as part of a global logic, a global maximization of profits. Yet, this separation of finance capital from the productive employment of capital is not absolute. These financial groups confront each other economically and politically. As we have emphasized, they are built upon associations of large units of capital and their survival and successful expansion ultimately depend on the profitability of these underpinnings.

---

[107] This represents a mechanism through which surplus value is redistributed. The significance of monopoly profits will be treated extensively in a subsequent volume of this work. What must be emphasized here, however, is that precisely because capitalism is governed by the self-expansion (and competition) of capital, the equalization process is dominant. Monopoly profits are neither stable nor durable. They will in fact fall – not, however, as a result of the operation of classical competition, but as a result of the mechanisms associated with the internationalization of capital and imperialist rivalry. In the oppressed nations, sectoral and entrepreneurial disparities, reflecting the differentiation of imperialist and nonimperialist capital, have enormous relevance vis-à-vis the extreme forms of unevenness within these countries.

[108] *Imperialism*, p. 69 (*LCW*, 22, pp. 238-39).

By virtue of monopoly over the means of production and finance, and the interpenetration of the bank, industrial, and commercial forms of capital, finance capital extracts surplus value from different sites of accumulation, from different moments of the circuit of capital, and over different phases of the cycle. It converts discrete and scattered economic units into its tributaries and canals. Finance capital plays a special role in accumulation. It is primarily engaged in a process of *financial centralization* — merging surplus value from diverse sources into a highly centralized and fluid capital that can be readily shifted and flexibly applied. A hierarchy of extractions is thus embedded in the accumulation process in the form of financial charges, dividend payouts, technological royalties, international transfer prices, and other forms of monopoly pricing and gouging. What is involved is a dialectic of the centralization of capital out of and its reallocation into highly complex and overlapping circuits. And this is generally accomplished on the basis of control over a narrow, yet strategic, segment of any given enterprise or operation.[109]

Lenin furnished a cogent summary of the forces shaping the formation of finance capital and its special character:

> At a definite stage in the development of exchange, at a definite stage in the growth of large-scale production, namely, at the stage which was attained towards the turn of the century, exchange so internationalized economic relations and capital, and large-scale production assumed such proportions that monopoly began to replace free competition. Monopoly associations of entrepreneurs, trusts, instead of enterprises, "freely" competing with each other — at home and *in relations between the countries* — became typical. Finance capital took over as the typical "lord" of the world; it is *particularly mobile and flexible, particularly interknit at home and internationally, and*

---

[109] A critical, controlling mass of share capital, for instance, may actually amount to a small percentage of total stock outstanding. On the other hand, a particular financial group will not necessarily dominate or control every enterprise in which it invests. In the U.S.-led bloc of imperialist powers (and historically), the formal circulation of titles of ownership has been integral to the consolidation of such a critical mass of enterprise control. However, neither this nor the actual extent of private bank participation exhausts the question of financial control, particularly the disposal and deployment of money capital and credit. In the final analysis, the property rights of finance capital are bound up with its strategic relationships and interconnections, which enable it to effectively command the means of production and dispose of society's surplus product.

> *particularly impersonal and divorced from production proper;* it lends
> itself to concentration with particular ease.... [110]

The particular mobility and flexibility of finance capital, its inter-knittedness, and its separation from production are not mere elements of manipulation and control for their own sake, but express something essential about the nature of imperialist accumulation.

Financial operations and this process of financial centralization represent the necessary means to sustain satisfactory rates of accumulation of enormous aggregations of highly internationalized capitals. The ability to pump money capital into or out of particular sectors, to build up or tear down with grotesque efficiency, to subsidize entry into or losses in one national market with profits from another — all this is basic to counteracting declining profitability and the crisis tendencies of capital that are heightened with the forward motion of accumulation. More specifically, capitalism at this stage can only function through unprecedented leaps in concentration and centralization. Indeed, given the degree of socialization of the productive forces within the framework of private appropriation, *only finance capital* can, outside a complete and revolutionary rupture, organize and command the economies of the imperialist countries and those of the oppressed nations (the latter in a qualitatively different manner than at "home"). By channeling capital into profitable domains and achieving higher levels of integration, finance capital pushes forward the process of accumulation, but this is something which, in its international dimensions, ultimately turns into its opposite and undermines itself.

In opposition to this understanding, many contemporary "Marxist" (i.e., revisionist) analyses, especially those accounts issuing from within the Western-bloc countries, interpret finance capital's parasitism as a cancer in the body of capitalism impeding its proper functioning. Rather than analyzing finance capital as the top and leading part of the structure of capital in the imperialist countries and as an institutional embodiment of imperialism's mode of existence, such interpretations equate finance capital with sinister conspiracy, with "milking" and bilking out of spite and greed or neglect and indifference. Their bottom line is that a hand-

---

[110] "Preface to N. Bukharin's Pamphlet, *Imperialism and the World Economy,*" *LCW*, 22, pp. 104-5 (first emphasis in original, remaining emphasis added). Finance capital is particularly mobile and flexible at the same time that capital in general is *less* mobile due to high technical barriers and the encumbrances of monopoly.

ful of financiers are "ripping off" the small farmers, corner grocers, and even the steel mills, and are wreaking havoc with what would otherwise, or potentially, be a healthy economy (or a vigorous and healthy sector of it).[111] In point of fact, finance capital is an objective outgrowth of and response to the fetters and contradictions of capital. But over the long run it intensifies these contradictions and creates new fetters in the framework of a specific political division of the world. It is this dynamic and necessity, deriving from the basic unevenness and anarchic drive of capital, which results, for instance, in the gutting and "cannibalization" of certain productive sectors.

Although, historically speaking, "competitive" capitalism, especially since it became the ruling system, never existed in "pure" form, competition tended, during the premonopoly stage of capitalism, to attenuate the quirks or privileges of particular capitals. That is, no one capital could fundamentally pull ahead and stay ahead on any basis other than cost reduction and revolutionization of the productive process, and these advantages were usually quite transitory, given the relative ease of entry into and exit out of particular branches of production. Since in most industries firm size had not passed a critical threshold conferring market control upon the few, no single capital (or alliance of capitals) could in any fundamental sense determine the fate of others except by transforming the social conditions of production and objectively working towards new productive norms. When capital accretes into giant formations and monopolistic blocks, however, these units themselves and their strategies count for much more. Monopoly leads to and requires the exercise of domination and control; monopoly price and finance give freer play to mechanisms of advance and subordination other than cost reduction and technical transformation.[112] *Power relations* become much more central to this mode of operation, exerting a profound influence on accumulation.

Nevertheless, however mobile, flexible, and far removed from production proper, finance capital is still grounded in the real production of values and the exploitation of wage-labor. It does not float in the empyrean mists. Although finance capital operates prin-

---

[111] The strategic orientation accompanying this view is that of reform and capitalist reconstitution based on alliance with an "enlightened" segment of the bourgeoisie — in the name of "socialism," of course.

[112] Such mechanisms include control of raw materials, lines of credit, and patent rights, as well as product differentiation and promotional expenditure.

cipally in the domain of money capital, the alpha and omega of accumulation remains productive capital, and finance capital must concern itself first and foremost with its profitability. Finance capital is not a thing unto itself, but arises out of and rests upon the real structure of capital. At the same time, it reacts back upon and influences that structure. But finance capital is itself an expression of anarchy involving enormous, interrelated masses of capital, and it cannot nullify the expand-or-die character of capital. Moreover, while it is the most prominent and leading element of the reproductive process as a whole, representing a profound characteristic of the imperialist era, finance capital is exactly the pinnacle of a complex edifice and process. It is neither the totality of that edifice and process (which subsumes nonmonopoly, precapitalist modes of production, etc.) nor by any means the only new phenomenon of this stage of capitalist development, although, again, it interpenetrates with and presides over the other transformations.

VI

The historical maturation of capitalism led to certain structural changes — namely, the increasing concentration of the means of production and the coalescence of bank with industrial capital to form finance capital. This process also pushed capital beyond its national framework in a qualitatively greater way than before. Particular national units of imperialist capital are founded in a national market, but they cannot be confined to it — they are international at the same time. It is in the nature of capital to expand in search of higher profits. Yet the extraordinary dimensions that capital export reached only in the beginning of the twentieth century, and the fact that capital export plays a role in the overall process of accumulation far out of proportion to its actual share of total output or direct contribution to total profits, cannot be explained simply in terms of the natural processes of capital expansion.

Capital export is inseparable from the politico-strategic angling of various imperialist powers for position in the world market and from the struggle for colonies and spheres of influence. On the other hand, there is an underlying *compulsion* specific to the imperialist stage of development (although it may appear to individual capitals as the simple lure of higher expected rates of return) which propels capital export. Lenin's formulation that an ''enormous 'superabundance of capital' has arisen in the advanced countries"[113] remains a contentious one among Marxist scholars. None of the historical developments since Lenin wrote this have, however, rendered his insight any less crucial for understanding the dynamics of imperialist accumulation:

> As long as capitalism remains what it is, surplus capital will be utilized not for the purpose of raising the standard of living of the masses in a given country, for this would mean a decline in profits for the capitalists, but for the purpose of increasing profits by exporting capital abroad to the backward countries. In these backward countries profits are usually high, for capital is scarce, the price of land is relatively low, wages are low, raw materials are cheap. The possibility of exporting capital is created by the fact that a number of backward countries have already been drawn into world capitalist intercourse. . . . [114]

The first sentence from this passage is no mere tautology. Since the law of value commands production, the uses to which capital can be put are limited by the imperatives of profit — capital cannot be deployed rationally for all-around development or to meet societal need. Lenin is not suggesting, however, that imperialism necessarily leads to or pivots on absolute impoverishment in the advanced countries. In fact, he associates a social-chauvinist labor movement with the bribes parceled out to layers of the working class. To be sure, this bribery has grown considerably in the post-World War 2 period, extending to far broader strata since Lenin wrote; yet, then and today, these material privileges rest on the export of capital and the prerogatives of empire, not on "technological revolutions" or on the militance of working classes, and these bribes are related precisely to the political needs of empire.

The superabundance of capital relative to the home market is both a *tendency and an essential feature* of capitalism in the imperialist epoch. It is a tendency in the sense that there is no *absolute* surplus. Put differently, it is not the case that domestic outlets for investment completely dry up and that, therefore, capital literally overflows into the international arena suddenly and for the first time after a given stage of development has been reached. However, and this is the important point, capitalism does in fact reach a degree of internal maturation such that the export of capital

---

[113] *Imperialism*, p. 73 (*LCW*, 22, p. 241).

[114] *Imperialism*, p. 73 (*LCW*, 22, pp. 241-42).

acquires the pronounced importance to which Lenin referred, both quantitatively and qualitatively, while the profitability of domestic outlets for investment is conditioned by a specifically international mode of reproduction. The phenomenon of superabundance is often, and mistakenly, equated with an apparent sum of disposable money capital. But the concept embraces the structure and underlying value relations of capital in the advanced countries and the resultant complications of the reproductive process. More precisely, the motion of accumulation produces such a high concentration of capital, leads to such an intensification of its major contradictions, that it must rely on the more profitable and rapidly expanding areas of accumulation without which its contradictions would come to a head sooner — but as a result of which these contradictions are ultimately heightened.

When capital of such magnitude is employed productively it tends, given the structure of accumulation, to be of a very high organic composition and thus exerts downward pressure on the rate of profit. Further, the extended reproduction of this capital would contradict an essential goal of monopoly, that is, limiting the free movement of capital and deliberately restricting production in order to smooth out fluctuations and garner extra profit.[115] However, these aspects of the problem can neither be treated in isolation from each other nor, again, as absolute limits. Lenin did not undertake an analysis of all the mechanisms leading to superabundance, but it is significant that he described a situation in which "the accumulation of capital has reached gigantic proportions."[116] He did not consider the structure of capital narrowly in terms of its organic composition, although this becomes a greater fetter, nor did he deal narrowly with the limits to domestic realization. Rather, he conceptualized a stage of capitalist development marked by a high degree of socialization and concentration such that capital presses up against the shell of private ownership and outgrows its national framework.

Here we must return to a methodological point of departure. The emergence of imperialism cannot be deduced from the logic of capital per se. The laws of capital interacted with specific historical

---

[115] Such monopolistic practices are not the outcome of avarice or mere perquisites of size, but also reflect the requirements and urgings of highly concentrated capital.

[116] *Imperialism*, p. 73 (*LCW*, 22, p. 241).

conditions and international relations. Capitalism did not spread homogeneously throughout the world; capital has become "over-ripe" in the advanced countries, but the world was never — and is not now — uniformly capitalized. There were and are regions of the world to which capital can be profitably exported. Thus, the out-ward flow of capital is as much a function of a *pull* from without as it is of a *push* from within the imperialist economies. Investment flows are objectively conditioned by the uneven profitability of particular national circuits (especially the difference in profitability between the imperialist and oppressed countries). Indeed, such unevenness is itself a reflection of superabundance in the advanced countries. Capital, then, is superabundant at home relative to prof-itable investment opportunities abroad. Further, such investments figure prominently in the combat among capitals. Each financial group makes its decisions in opposition to others; where the oppor-tunities for capital export (and higher profits) exist, each capital must strive, on pain of extinction, to tap such possibilities since some other financial group might or already has. [117]

This push and pull, arising from uneven and unequal develop-ment, will, however, operate differently in different imperialist countries at different times. The actual magnitude of exportable (surplus) capital will vary in part according to particularities of domestic accumulation. In the decade and a half following World War 2, for instance, the West European imperialists steered invest-ment capital overwhelmingly into reconstruction of their war-torn economies and expansion of their domestic bases; only later were they driven to more directly and massively export capital. At the same time, profitable investment of surplus capital abroad will vary according to the international opportunities that may or may not be "open" to any one imperialist national capital (or group of such capitals). Many such opportunities were, for instance, closed off to defeated Germany at the end of World War 1.

The internationalization of capital, like the question of finance capital in general, is not a matter of particular institutional arrange-

---

[117] A remarkable study of the 2000 subsidiaries set up in 23 countries by 187 major U.S. corporations in the period 1948-67 discovered what was described as a "band-wagon" effect. Almost one-half of these foreign subsidiaries were established within three-year peak clusters. That is, investment initiatives taken by one firm were quickly matched by its rivals. See Frederick T. Knickerbocker, *Oligopolistic Reaction and Multinational Enterprise* (Boston: Division of Research, Graduate School of Business Administration, Harvard Univ. Press, 1973).

ments but of a mode of reproduction, captured well in Lenin's image of the "chain of operations of world finance capital."[118] Whether this concretely manifests itself as interest-bearing portfolio investments, profit-yielding branch plants of multinational corporations, or loans to governments is a matter of secondary importance. The primary issue is the export of value to generate surplus value abroad.[119]

While there are different domestic and overseas rates of profit, they are completely interrelated from the standpoint of the overall accumulation process. The profitable application of capital outside the home market, even as it means that more must ultimately be exported and reinvested, is inextricably bound up with the overall dynamic — and continuity — of imperialist accumulation; it is in-

---

[118] *Imperialism,* p. 103 (*LCW,* 22, p. 264).

[119] In the late nineteenth and early twentieth centuries, the main form of capital export was portfolio investment (holdings of foreign securities, both government and private, etc.). Direct foreign investment was centered mainly in agriculture, the extractive industries, commerce, and the requisite infrastructure. For a considerable period after World War 2, direct investments (especially in manufacturing) represented the more prevalent form of capital export. This has led some Marxist scholars to suggest that imperialism entered a new stage in the post-World War 2 period, symbolized by the transnational corporation and the general practice of branch planting. This was certainly a striking feature of the 1950s and, especially, of the 1960s. But the multiplication of international lending channels and the explosion of international debt, as seen in the growth of the Euromarkets, the increased role of the World Bank and the International Monetary Fund, and the monumental debt crisis of Third World countries, are no less striking and significant developments of the 1970s and early 1980s. It would be just as wrong to posit a new stage of imperialism based on these phenomena. The changes in the proportion of one form of capital export (the lending of money capital) to another (direct investment), both over the course of the postwar period and in relation to previous periods, are not without their significance. But these are, after all, simply differing *forms* of capital export through which surplus value is generated and extracted. Christian Palloix is a prominent representative of the view that the circuits of capital only became fully internationalized in the post-World War 2 period. He associates this development with the consolidation of the transnational firm; methodologically, Palloix equates the internationalization of the circuit of productive capital with direct shifting of industrial activities to a world level. See Christian Palloix, "The Self-Expansion of Capital on a World Scale," *The Review of Radical Political Economics,* Vol. 9, No. 2 (Summer 1977), pp. 1-28. By equating the two, Palloix functionally denies the integrating and controlling force of *finance capital.* Again, the key change that takes place in the imperialist era is investment of capital qua capital on a world scale. A similar critique of misconceptions of capital export is contained in Santosh K. Mehrotra and Patrick Clawson, "Soviet Economic Relations with India and Other Third World Countries," in *The Soviet Union: Socialist or Social-Imperialist? Essays Toward the Debate on the Nature of Soviet Society* (Chicago: RCP Publications, 1983), pp. 115-17.

separable from it. To try to conceive of the domestic imperialist economies as self-contained units into which some external additives are introduced or to propose "what if . . ." scenarios — i.e., what if everything invested abroad were invested at home — is to overlook the real and broad forces that compel capitalism to do certain things and that create an "international network of dependence and connections of finance capital."[120] At this stage of capitalist development, accumulation is an internationalized process of reproduction with a home base as opposed to a self-contained economy looking outward for new investment opportunities or outlets to absorb idle capital.[121] This is not to say that in the absence of massive capital exports for a particular period of time a capitalist economy would immediately collapse or that revolution would automatically take place. Rather, it is to say that monopoly capitalism's mode of existence and functioning require — and ultimately cannot do without — such overseas investments (although they may be highly disguised and involve complex interimperialist financial relationships).[122]

There is also an international political structure of capital, and overseas investments take on a strategic dimension as well. Capital

---

[120] *Imperialism*, p. 72 (*LCW*, 22, p. 240).

[121] It is sometimes objected by opponents of Lenin that the export of capital is self-defeating if these capital exports eventually generate greater earnings that are repatriated into the home country: "If the imperialists are winding up with more surplus capital than what they started with, then what's the purpose, why export capital in the first place?" But capital is not something that has to be burned up or gotten rid of in the abstract. It must be *profitably* utilized and in this era the international application and accumulation of capital is essential to such utilization, although this is not a linear and static process, but one which produces its own contradictions.

[122] In his writings on the character of World War 1 and the tasks of revolutionaries, Lenin pointed out that "defense of the fatherland" was no more justifiable in small imperialist countries like Switzerland than it was in the big imperialist countries, with which the Swiss bourgeoisie was intimately associated: "[T]he Swiss bourgeoisie has long been tied to imperialist interests by thousands of threads. It is of no concern whether this is implemented by a system of interrelationships and 'mutual participation' of the big banks through export of capital, or through the tourist trade, which thrives on the patronage of foreign millionaires, or through unscrupulous exploitation of disfranchised foreign workers, etc. . . . One's 'own' bourgeoisie is being depicted as an innocent lamb and the case-hardened bank directors of present-day Switzerland as heroic William Tells, and, furthermore, the secret agreements between Swiss and foreign banks and between Swiss and foreign diplomats are overlooked" ("On the Defense of the Fatherland Issue," *LCW*, 23, pp. 161-62). In the case of Denmark, Lenin speaks of its colonial holdings and privileged international trading position based on a symbiotic relationship with British imperialism ("Ten 'Socialist' Ministers!" *LCW*, 23, pp. 134-36).

export is linked with the modalities and turns of interimperialist rivalry; capital also flows in reaction to and with an eye towards other imperialist capitals and powers. Moreover, the very pursuit of rivalry requires international reserves. In order for any power to throw the requisite political, economic, and military resources into the fray without draining its national economy, it needs super-profits as a source of strength. In other words, superprofits are both an *object* of interimperialist rivalry and a *means* for prosecuting it. Again, the fact that the world is completely divided and can only be redivided is of great historical moment.

The consequences of these historical and structural phenomena are profound. *Capital can no longer be decisively reorganized within a national framework.* The continuous advance of accumulation depends on the expansion of capital globally, on its securing inter-national spheres of influence. This is actually internal to the way that monopoly capital functions. When the system enters into a crisis of overproduction, what is involved are the contradictions associated with the internationalization of capital. The export of capital is the essential mode of economic integration linking the various parts of the world economy.

VII

The imperialists must seek high profits abroad to stimulate and ac-tivate the entire mass of capital anchored in the imperialist coun-tries. The leading edge of this process is investment in the colonial and neocolonial countries. Now nowhere did Lenin argue or imply that capital — and perhaps the bulk of exported capital — will not also be invested in other imperialist countries; actually, he pro-duced data showing that it was. Such investment is undertaken not only because profits may frequently be obtained in other im-perialist countries which are higher than in the home country, but also because interimperialist rivalry may demand such invest-ment. Further, the relatively low level of development in the op-pressed nations might preclude certain investments. The issue here, however, is not the quantitative but the *qualitative* role of Third World investments in the overall process of accumulation, of what they enable the imperialists to do.

The superprofits that can be extracted from the backward and colonial countries constitute a fundamental and indispensable con-dition of the overall operation of imperialist capital. In addition, the backward regions furnish vital inputs into the reproductive process, notably raw materials. The cheapness of these raw materials (which serve as the raw materials of machinery, as auxiliary materials applied in machine operation, and as elements in the process of production) generally lowers the cost of constant capital and favorably affects the rate of profit, even if the rate of exploitation remains unaltered. Marx attached great importance to such phenomena in discussions of the role of world trade (although imperialism is not just this, since capital export now assumes a central place):

> Other conditions being equal, the rate of profit, therefore, falls and rises inversely to the price of raw material. This shows, among other things, how important the low price of raw material is for industrial countries, even if fluctuations in the price of raw materials are not accompanied by variations in the sales sphere of the product.... [E]conomists like Ricardo, who cling to general principles, do not recognize the influence of, say, world trade on the rate of profit.[123]

As the fixed capital of machinery and buildings attains ever more enormous dimensions in the imperialist era, this becomes an even greater factor.

The higher rates of return yielded by investments in the Third World, the extra value derived from the manifold unequal trade relations between the advanced and dependent social formations, and the material inputs originating from the Third World are crucial elements of imperialist accumulation. At the same time, these backward regions are precisely the areas of the world where capital can undertake the most significant transformations of production relations; indeed, the ability of imperialist capital to profitably extend itself there is a decisive condition of overall reorganization and expansion. Grasping the all-sided character and importance of imperialist penetration into the Third World represents a crucial line of demarcation between a scientific understanding of imperialist expansion and other views of imperialism.[124]

A theory of imperialist accumulation must recognize that finance capital plays the commanding role and generates the essential momentum in both the imperialist and the dependent coun-

---

[123] *Capital,* III, pp. 106-7.

[124] Various theories of imperialist domination of the Third World will be treated in a separate volume.

tries, and that overseas expansion and the international environment in general are, taken together, the pedestal of this process. As
already emphasized, finance capital is particularly disposed to concentrate surplus value from disparate sources. But what is the significance of this? What do these superprofits (and extra value issuing
from unequal exchange) and the overall centralization of surplus
value facilitate? How does all this qualitatively interact with the
domestic base of imperialist capital and the ability of this capital to
reproduce itself? *The heart of the matter is that by concentrating
surplus value, finance capital can, over the course of a particular trajectory of development, more effectively employ this surplus value and sustain a rate of accumulation that would not be possible were the same
surplus value scattered among a multiplicity of capitals (in the fashion of
the laissez-faire period).*

In vastly interdependent, advanced capitalist economies, highly
integrated units of finance capital play the strategic reproductive
role. When these top and decisive components of the total capital
are stimulated, the core sectors of these economies — which have
crucial linkages and extensive satellite relations with the rest of
these economies — are also, in turn, stimulated, keeping the mass
of national capital functioning. [125] At the same time, the capacity of
finance capital to centralize surplus value interconnects with and
further unleashes other essential mechanisms for reorganizing
capital, notably the state and the credit system, which function integrally in mitigating but ultimately exacerbating the contradictions of accumulation. Viewed globally, the stimulus offered by imperialist accumulation plays the principal role in shaping the
character and development of the economies in the oppressed nations, while the export of capital to,and the oppression of,these nations is inseparable from imperialist accumulation. This is not,
however, a static arrangement. Such mechanisms and processes
hinge on a particular division of the world and a structure of world
capital. Given the prominence and character of finance capital, the

---

[125] Consider the important role of raw materials investments in the Third World.
Such investments cheapen the cost of raw materials to the domestic components of
these highly integrated financial groups. At the same time, given their scale of production, these productive units tend to make more efficient use of such inputs than
could smaller enterprises. In short, they benefit disproportionately. On the other
hand, whether or not these benefits are passed on to other capitals in the form of
lower prices, the enhanced profitability of the core sectors will have ripple effects on
the rest of the economy: subcontracting to others for supplies, the stimulation of
retail trade (e.g., auto dealerships), and the multiplier effects of the consumption expenditures of their huge work forces.

laws of accumulation leading to crisis manifest themselves differently in the imperialist countries and the oppressed nations, respectively.

Finance capital reorganizes itself on the basis of an international mode of operation. The imperialists invest within and to advance integrated empires; they do not operate strictly according to the rate of profit in any given market, but according to a global logic of profit maximization bound up with interimperialist rivalry. Particular investments and even particular countries are but links in a single chain of imperialism's world operations, and such a global complex calls forth a high degree of integration, planning, and coordination in the spheres of investment, trade, and finance to facilitate the international transfer and allocation of capital. Nevertheless, there is a specific dialectic to this mode of accumulation: on the one hand, it is critically and inextricably bound up, in terms of its overall profitability, with the extensive and intensive exploitation of the masses in the oppressed countries; on the other hand, it is anchored to a strategic national base in the imperialist home country. The needs of imperialist accumulation are objectively rooted in the advanced countries, in the expansion and requirements of particular imperialist capitals. The bottom line of imperialist calculations and undertakings, of the perspective of finance capital, is how well all these international interconnections bolster the imperialist centers and bases of accumulation.

Imperialist chauvinism has definite material underpinnings. There exists a *basic division* in the imperialist-dominated world between *the imperialist countries*, where finance capital is rooted and controlled by the metropolitan bourgeoisies, *and the oppressed nations*, which are controlled by foreign finance capital. At the same time, capital which roams the world in search of higher profits *remains profoundly national* — this represents an essential feature and contradiction of the imperialist epoch. The imperialist character of any developed capitalist country is determined, on the one hand, by the internal structure and level of development of the national capital (monopolization and formation of finance capital, etc.) and its relative autonomy and control over the national circuit and, on the other, by the place it occupies in the division of the world into oppressor and oppressed nations and in the international division of labor. A country which does not export large sums of capital may conduct trade with and extend loans to others that do. A country which does not station troops in the oppressed nations may penetrate them under a broader military umbrella. Again, what must be examined are the specific terms of integration into the imperialist financial, political, and military networks and the benefits derived, directly or indirectly, from international plunder.

There is a difference between capital and imperialist capital. The backward countries of the world are not simply so many years or decades behind the advanced countries in their development; the process of capitalist development of 150 years ago is not being reenacted in these countries. This is a new era. The oppressed nations are highly variegated: the degree to which precapitalist relations continue to exist (especially in the countryside) differs from country to country, and the urban and industrial sectors are more significant in some than in others. But the key production relation and defining feature of these economies — even more important and determining than the proportion of peasants to workers or rural to urban population — is the extent and nature of their subordination and integration into the world dynamic on the basis of a structured relation of dependency. In fact, the relationship between imperialism and the oppressed nations *is itself a production relation.*

How is this to be understood? To begin with, the imperialists directly own many pivotal enterprises in the oppressed countries; they indirectly control others, especially in the crucial state sector, by means of credit and financial allocations and their political hold over the dependent states. Based on its extractions and mechanisms of control, finance capital also influences the magnitude of distributable social product and shapes its specific distribution — among the popular classes and among the ruling strata, all of whom are entwined with the circuits of imperialist capital. Finally, the generation of superprofits within these countries calls forth (indeed, depends on) more intense forms of exploitation and more open coercion in the productive process itself than are required in the advanced countries. Such an all-encompassing production relation is inseparable from and asserted through class relations. There exists a symbiotic relationship between the metropolitan capitals and the oligarchy of compradors (private and state) and the landholding strata of the oppressed nations. Nations are divided into classes and the colonial and neocolonial countries are concrete social formations with specific social relations and institutional structures reflected in the existence of dominant and dominated classes.[126] However, these social formations fit into a

---

[126] A social formation may be defined as a concrete unity of an economic base (which may comprise several modes of production with one, however, dominant) and its historically evolved superstructure.

larger structure of international capitalist production. The relationship between the oppressed nations and imperialism locks the national markets of these dependent countries into a specific place in the international division of labor, and superexploitation serves the expansion of imperialist capital.

This is not to say that imperialism simply holds down the oppressed countries, or that it just extracts wealth through unequal trade or naked plunder, although these certainly occur. Imperialist capital can, and in the long run must, develop the economies of these countries.[127] But it must develop them on an imperialist basis — in particular, on a basis favorable to the foreign capital — and in contradiction both to the welfare of the broad masses of these countries and to the development of a relatively articulated social formation. Even where capitalist relations have been extensively introduced into these countries, they are not on the road to independent capitalist development. A major consequence of this is the phenomenon of "lopsidedness" analyzed by Bob Avakian:

> What do I mean by this lopsidedness? Lenin, of course, insisted on the basic distinction between the handful of advanced imperialist exploiters and imperialist states and the great majority of the world's people in colonial and dependent situations. But the problem has developed in a more acute way in the sense that in a handful of advanced countries is concentrated — perhaps even in an absolute quantitative sense, but certainly qualitatively — the advanced productive forces in the world. . . . [I]n most of the world the productive forces are backward; such development of the productive forces as there is is under the domination of finance capital and imperialism internationally, which distorts and disarticulates these economies.[128]

Lopsidedness is certainly an apt and graphic description if we take a snapshot of the global distribution of resources and expenditures as the 1980s opened: while the "developing countries" contained 75 percent of the world's population, they accounted for only 21 percent of total Gross National Product, 25 percent of total export earnings, 23 percent of total energy consumption, but 81

---

[127] This applies to the Third World as a whole. Certain countries within it, however, have lain relatively fallow for particular periods since the existing order could not favorably utilize (exploit) their peoples and resources.

[128] Avakian, *Conquer the World? The International Proletariat Must and Will,* published as *Revolution,* No. 50 (December 1981), p. 36.

percent of total weapons imports.[129] The price tag of just one nuclear aircraft carrier is more than the GNP of 53 countries; meanwhile, 40 million people in the Third World (half of whom are children) die each year from hunger and malnutrition.[130] The division of the world between oppressor nations and oppressed nations is thus materially embedded in an international division of labor and concentration of productive forces and wealth. And this lopsidedness is reflected in the structure of the economies of the oppressed nations themselves.

The concept of articulation refers to the internal coherence of a national economy, that is, to the linkages among different sectors producing specific use values and between investment and consumption, which mesh in such a way as to make for an organically integrated economic formation. This involves mutually reinforcing relations among these sectors. On the one hand, there are production/consumption functions: a derived demand for capital goods and the capacity to produce them, the final demand for wage and consumption goods and the capacity to produce them, and the overall expansion of a home market through the multiplication of forward and backward linkages.[131] On the other hand, articulation engenders the self-cheapening (through increases in productivity) of the elements of constant and variable capital, which sustains the profitable and more balanced reproduction of the aggregate capital. In the era of imperialism, with the world far more interrelated and the division between oppressed and oppressor nations assuming a particular systemic character, this process of national economic integration becomes distorted in both the imperialist and oppressed nations. As a result of imperialist penetration and domination, however, the degree and character of distortion in the dependent economies is such that they may be considered *disarticulated* in comparison with the imperialist economies.

By briefly examining the historical role of the railways in the two types of countries, we can begin to glean some fundamental differences. In the United States, the rail system, in conjunction

---

[129] *New York Times,* 25 October 1981, Sec. 4, Midwestern ed.

[130] "FAO Director-General Presents Report on World Food Security; Calls For New Action on the Issue," United Nations Press Release, FAO/3248 (13 April 1983).

[131] For a discussion of these production/consumption functions and a survey of key insights of the "Third Worldist" school, see Alain de Janvry, *The Agrarian Question and Reformism in Latin America* (Baltimore: Johns Hopkins Univ. Press, 1981), Chapter 1.

with organized terror directed against Native American peoples in particular, played a pivotal part in opening up and unifying the continental market. Where the imperialists constructed rail networks in the Third World, however, the emphasis was placed on serving external trade outlets and existing population centers. In Africa, for instance, most rail lines were grouped in localized networks along the coast or diverged inland from the chief ports to mining regions and assembly points and centers of agricultural production. (Only South Africa has a railway system of nationwide proportions.) A survey of the most general features of the oppressed countries makes it clear why the distinction between articulated and disarticulated formations is a necessary one.

The most strategic firms and sectors of the dependent economies are dominated, directly or indirectly, by imperialist capital. Where their production is export-oriented, such enterprises (or industrial enclaves) do not gird nationally-centered development. In the case of enterprises catering to the local market for consumer durables, much of this production is determined by the need of the ruling classes to create and prop up a social base of more privileged strata. Much of this commodity output (industrial luxuries) does not, therefore, enter into the necessary reproduction costs of labor power. Both types of production call forth supporting infrastructure and intermediary links (roads and steel mills, for instance) which are often quite massive in scope. It is these sectors, along with a substantial military/police apparatus, that typically lay vast claim to expenditure outlays and to the most modern and high quality investments. Consequently, much of the industrial and technical effort of these countries is not augmenting the profitability of local, national capital through the cheapening of wage goods, as well as through the more efficient production of the requisite raw materials and capital goods.

The capital goods requirements of the advanced sectors must be met in large measure through imports, thus exacerbating external dependency and balance of payments difficulties (even if some of this final output may be aimed at substituting for imports). Highly capital-intensive investments do not generate employment opportunities for the mass of laborers. And much of the imported technology has limited productive application outside these spheres. The development of an autonomous and integrated technical and industrial base is thus impaired.

Lagging behind the modern sector, and yet developing in functional relation to it, are more traditional and backward segments, particularly within agriculture. These, too, evince certain characteristics linked with the subordination of the colonial and neo-colonial countries. The traditional sectors have been utilized as a reserve of cheap labor (peasant migration to the cities) and as a source of cheap wage goods (foodstuffs produced under precapitalist or generally labor-intensive conditions, as well as under conditions of the "informal" economies of shantytowns, etc.). The inherent limitations of these backward modes have necessitated massive food imports as well as selective modernization to yield agricultural exportables or certain wage goods — and the direction and financing of these investments create new contradictions.

Finance capital permeates and dominates all of this. It siphons value from a highly differentiated circuit of local capital in the form of repatriated profits, loans and interest payments, and through various conduits of unequal trade and exchange associated with its political and economic dominance. Development depends heavily on foreign capital and world trade. Of necessity, linkages exist between the modern and backward sectors, crucial to which is the role played by cheap labor in the generation of imperialist superprofits in all economic sectors. However, the linkages are not guided by the "auto-centered" needs and motion of these economies but by their external orientation and subordination. Disjointedness characterizes them, both during fits of rapid growth and periods of deep decline.

These peculiar intersectoral relations, sharp social polarization and skewed income distribution, and pervasive value extractions impinge upon and distort the processes which might otherwise lead to an articulated national capital and market. The individual productive elements of the oppressed economies operate at very different levels of efficiency (the most modern of these sectors attaining productivity levels that compare favorably with those of the imperialist countries) and profitability; they lack a certain overall synchrony.[132] As particular branches and segments of these countries or even whole national economies are squeezed further by imperialist capital, they grow ever less capable of meeting the needs

---

[132] This in fact is the basis for the mistaken perception that these are "dual" economies composed of wholly separate or completely dysfunctional (relative to each other) modern and backward structures of production. The Third World countries are not mere shards of national economies; they are unified, but in a highly distorted manner. The various segments of these economies mesh in a different kind of way than happens in the advanced countries.

of expanded reproduction (through modernization, for example, which would cheapen the cost of particular inputs). This distorts these economies even more and is an integral element of imperialist crisis.

Relative to the Third World countries, the imperialist countries are internally articulated. The qualifying "relative" is important. Irrational allocation of capital and discordant linkages exist in the advanced countries, too. The contradictions and ruptures to which this gives rise are key features which emerge from anarchy and characterize accumulation and crisis in both the competitive and monopoly epochs of capitalism. Disarticulation, in fact, is an expression of anarchy. In the oppressed nations, however, it is qualitatively different, not merely quantitatively greater, and it stems from the place of these economies as subordinate formations in the production relations of imperialism. Further, while both groups of countries are part of the international division of labor, arising out of the specific division of the world — with a country like the United States critically dependent on inputs from abroad — here, too, the relationship of the two groups to this division is qualitatively different. It is, in short, an *imperialist* division of labor.

The centers of accumulation are situated in the imperialist countries; from here originates the essential "heartbeat" of accumulation. How capital is allocated within the imperialist countries, though inseparable from international relations, is mainly determined internally, notably by the material reality and needs of an imperialist base of accumulation. In contrast, the economic structure of the oppressed nations is shaped mainly by forces external to them: what is produced, exported and imported, financed, etc., reflects first and foremost their subordination, and not principally the internal requirements and interrelations of different sectors. They answer to another's "heartbeat." The momentum of these economies is predicated on capital infusions from and demand in the imperialist countries (what is called the center in relation to the oppressed periphery), the scope and magnitude of which depends on the overall profitability of imperialist capital. Moreover, and this will be analyzed in depth in a separate chapter, because of disarticulation they require and can only operate through steadily increasing financial injections; viewed in relation to external finance, they become what may be described as "junkie economies." Thus the staggering dependency of so-called "miracles of growth" in the Third World on imperialist loan capital. But the imperialists can only inject capital into these countries at levels required to sustain and stabilize reproduction so long as they can make continual extractions from them as well.

The lopsidedness associated with the rise and development of imperialism is also manifested in particular distortions and dislocations in social structure. In the advanced countries there is widespread stratification within the working class and considerable ossification among some of its privileged layers. The petty bourgeoisie also persists as a large and increasingly differentiated stratum. Especially since World War 2, this process of bourgeoisification, predicated on imperialist superprofits, has cut a much wider swath in the metropolitan working classes and has taken hold for more extended periods of time. In the colonial and dependent countries, a young, and in some cases rapidly burgeoning, working class exists alongside a peasantry, which generally remains an important element of the social structure, and marginalized layers. (These layers occupy a position somewhere between landless peasants and proletarians, and are forged when traditional modes of production are uprooted under conditions of disarticulation.)[133]

In this context, a comment on the modification of the law of population referred to earlier is in order. Mechanization, Marx showed, rendered a portion of the population superfluous. This industrial reserve army exerted downward pressure on wages and supplied wage-labor during periods of expansion. Mechanization does indeed lead to the formation of a reserve army, but today this must be understood internationally and with respect to lopsidedness. In the advanced countries, some sections of the unemployed become a permanent reserve which cannot be absorbed into the work force, even during booms, while, on the other hand, there is not necessarily the same crushing of large sections of the employed working class during cyclical downturns. In the oppressed nations there is, *at all times*, a huge under- or permanently un-employed urban "fringe" population and enormous wasted (unutilizable) labor in the countryside.

[133] Many of these marginalized workers are driven onto the bottom rungs of the metropolitan working classes as immigrant or so-called "illegal" workers. The United States is the world's largest de facto employer of foreign labor. In 1975, the share of foreign workers within the total labor force of Austria, France, West Germany, the Netherlands, Switzerland, and Sweden was slightly more than 10 percent. See Philip L. Martin and Alan Richards, "International migration of labor: boon or bane," and Ayse Kudat and Mine Sabuncuoglu, "The changing composition of Europe's guestworker population," *Monthly Labor Review*, Vol. 103, No. 10 (October 1980), pp. 5, 10.

With respect to this basic division in the world, three essential observations can be made. First, while accumulation proceeds on a world scale, as part of a single unfolding of the fundamental contradiction and within one highly integrated framework, this unity is structurally differentiated. Second, though surplus value is accumulated in the oppressed countries (with capital export actually promoting fairly rapid development in some of them, given certain international conditions), and though these countries are not without their internal contradictions and motion, their structural evolution is warped by and serves the needs of the dominant metropolitan centers. Breakneck and tumultuous urbanization in many neocolonial countries, the coexistence of advanced productive enclaves with backwater modes, and the differentiation of the Third World itself are necessary complements to and outcomes of imperialist accumulation. Finally, the reciprocal relations between the colonial and dependent countries on one side and the imperialist metropoles on the other constitute an active dialectic: this process of imperialist expansion and concentration produces barriers in both the oppressor and the oppressed nations that ultimately impede and undermine accumulation on a world scale.

Certain misconceptions cloud this understanding. Imperialism is not quintessentially defined by the theft of riches from the Third World; it is not merely the seizure of wealth per se. It is, rather, an internationalized mode of production subsuming others, a mode of production governed by real and dynamic value relations, whose expansion demands specific allocations of capital and concrete transformations of production relations which turn into their opposite, widening disparities and imbalances. This active dialectic is complex, but it operates so that at a certain point the center ends up lacking the stimulus from and the ability to continue pushing forward disarticulated development in the periphery. These distortions, then, do not arise out of malevolence or short-sightedness on the part of the imperialists, but flow from their objective need to overcome, or try to overcome at any given moment in time, barriers to profitable expansion. And, within a certain international framework, these relations and mechanisms are functional to imperialist capital.

The export of capital is the necessary catalyst of imperialist accumulation. But in conjunction with the financial network, it also intertwines the economies of different countries, transmitting and amplifying the tendencies of capital to crisis, which are aggravated by disarticulation in the oppressed nations and the parasitic struc-

ture and "costs of empire" of the economies of the advanced countries. The interknittedness and flexibility of finance capital enables
it to spread risks and withstand pressures, but only by raising
overall tension and explosive potential. The uneven development
of countries and regions, arising from the laws of accumulation,
creates flash points and weak links, not unlike the difficulties
associated with different units of capital within a nation dropping
out of the circuit and thereby endangering others. In the imperialist
era and in the world arena, however, these units are far more
massive and interconnected. It is, moreover, now a question of
more precariously perched national circuits jolting highly integrated imperialist empires and blocs.

What this suggests, then, is that while the tendential laws of
capital force their way through the process of accumulation, including, for instance, the tendential decline in profitability of internationalized capitals, it is the anarchy of a single global reproductive process which drives imperialism into crisis, exactly because
accumulation depends in a qualitatively new and greater way on
the functioning of interdependent and international links which
are drawn more tightly by finance capital. However, and this point
will be systematically addressed shortly, this occurs in the framework of the ever-changing balance of economic, political, and
military forces in the world. The interaction between individual
imperialists and their colonies and neocolonies or, more generally,
between imperialism and the oppressed nations, is not self-
contained, but is interpenetrated and linked with the other major
aspects and contradictions of this epoch in their specific motion and
development.

In this international system of domination and exploitation, the
separation of the forces controlling production from the actual process of production takes extreme form. Lenin wrote:

> Further, imperialism is an immense accumulation of money
> capital in a few countries. . . . The export of capital, one of the most
> essential economic bases of imperialism, still more completely
> isolates the rentiers from production and sets the seal of parasitism
> on the whole country that lives by exploiting the labor of several
> overseas countries and colonies. . . . [134]

---

[134] *Imperialism*, pp. 120-21 (*LCW*, 22, p. 277).

The export of capital, especially to the Third World, enables some countries to live off others. One might, in this connection, ponder the following statistics. By the 1960s, U.S. enterprises abroad constituted in the aggregate, on the basis of the gross value of their output, the third largest "economy" in the world — behind the United States and the Soviet Union.[135] Or, more than 10 percent of both Chase Manhattan's and Citibank's total income in 1979 came from Brazil alone.[136] Parasitism fundamentally rests on a process of accumulation that takes place in a world divided into oppressor nations and oppressed nations. All the imperialist countries thrive on superexploitation in the colonial and dependent regions of the world, whether it be through direct or more convoluted means. If particular imperialist countries have been hemmed in or cut out from a sufficient share of this booty, they must find the ways to get it.

That the advanced countries export capital to other parts of the world and in particular draw tribute from the oppressed nations has peculiar domestic effects: notably the relative displacement of both agricultural and manufacturing production (with much of this shifted to overseas enterprise), the growth of unproductive layers of the labor force, and the increasing weight of speculative activity. More generally, finance capital's mode of operation is reflected in the enormous commitment of resources to financial, circulatory, political, and military superstructures which serve the maintenance and extension of its international activities. Not only do tributaries and canals feed into the structure and process of imperialist capital, but massive sums are deducted and drained from it which make for further particularities and distortions of accumulation and crisis.

Let us pause for a moment to review some of the main points we have made thus far about the international framework of accumulation and the objective existence of a single world process. The growth of the productive forces on a world scale, specifically the development of means of transport, means of communication and other infrastructure, and the relative saturation of capital in the advanced countries have facilitated and, what is more fundamental, have compelled the international flow of capital. A new global

---

[135] Leo Model, "The Politics of Private Foreign Investment," *Foreign Affairs*, Vol. 45, No. 4 (July 1967), pp. 640-41.

[136] "Brazil Reins In Its Economy," *New York Times*, 8 December 1980, Sec. 2, Midwestern ed. This figure is for total income before securities transactions.

matrix of reproduction has emerged, accelerating the process of accumulation in countries of different types and at varying levels of development, while exacerbating uneven development within and between them. The internationalization of capital and the struggle among different national imperialist capitals has drawn the colonial and dependent countries into the swirl of international relations and integrated them into the world capitalist order in a way that trade and premonopoly colonialism did not. The pace and scope of economic development and of the transformation of social relations now reflects and is conditioned by their structured relationship to imperialism and by the important fact that it is in these colonial and dependent regions that superprofits can be massively generated.

VIII

Capital implies many capitals; this is a basic truth of Marxist political economy. But what of monopoly, does it alter things such that the driving force of anarchy can no longer be considered central? And what of the imperialist state, in what relation does it stand to the many capitals and their antagonisms? It is necessary to return to the analysis begun earlier concerning competition and rivalry under imperialism.

Large vertically and horizontally integrated units of capital significantly affect market structures. Collusion between them does indeed exist; its material basis lies in the dominance of a few giant monopolies and their mutual self-interest in preserving a certain equilibrium, which may take form in "orderly marketing agreements," for instance. At the same time — and this is related to the nature and necessity of finance capital — the mammoth scale of key investment ventures and infrastructure development (the Alaska pipeline, for instance) elicits the pooling of risks and agreed upon distribution of spoils. The intertwining of different financial groups is manifested in the practice of joint ventures, syndicated loans, etc.

Such systems of alliances and cartel-like agreements extend into the global arena. Here, too, market shares are apportioned and a framework of control established. "The capitalists," Lenin wrote, "divide the world, not out of any particular malice, but because the degree of concentration which has been reached forces them to adopt this method in order to obtain profits."[137] At a deeper level, however, these agreements must be understood as only *truces* — sometimes extended ones, but truces nevertheless — in the basic antagonism among capitals. Lenin, who treated monopoly in a rigorously Marxist framework, underscored that it grows out of and *intensifies* the inner dynamic of capital, but with features particular to the epoch.

Within various national markets, different financial groups confront each other, angling for advantage and position. The struggle is played out both in terms of overall strategy and in particular constellations of activity. A Chrysler Corporation, for instance, becomes a battleground for different strategic orientations of contending financial groups. And even the organization of a unified and integrated monopoly in "ordinary" times reflects the centrifugal tendencies of capital. For instance, ITT or a similarly large conglomerate will draw up a budget and plan to ensure that the company, with all its many subsidiaries and divisions, earns the maximum profit possible. The respective management groups to whom money is budgeted are then expected to obtain the maximum return (although sometimes they will be forced to operate suboptimally or at a loss in the "general interests" of the conglomerate) and will even enter into competition with other divisions.[138]

Under imperialism, the compulsion to transform capital values is modified; in fact, technical innovation may be *deliberately* retarded or its diffusion blocked in particular branches for a time. Thus Lenin spoke of a tendency towards stagnation and decay coexisting with the growth and further development of the productive forces:

> Certainly, the possibility of reducing cost of production and increasing profits by introducing technical improvements operates in the direction of change. But the *tendency* to stagnation and decay, which is characteristic of monopoly, continues to operate, and in certain branches of industry, in certain countries, for certain periods of time, it gains the upper hand.[139]

In other words, under imperialism the capitalists, as mentioned earlier, have recourse to means other than technical innovation and

[137] *Imperialism*, p. 88 (*LCW*, 22, p. 253).

[138] A similar process takes place in the Soviet production associations.

[139] *Imperialism*, p. 119 (*LCW*, 22, p. 276).

cost reduction to maintain and extend advantage. The waste and extravagance of styling changes and advertising in the U.S. auto industry, against a backdrop of sluggish process innovation, have been lavishly documented by muckrakers. The competitive edge and international privileges of U.S. capital rendered cost-efficient energy investments temporarily unnecessary in the domestic U.S. economy. From control of distribution networks and credit to the purchase of patents, finance capital possesses a vast array of weaponry with which to garner and distribute spoils, and this finds expression in the phenomenon of price-fixing or, as is more customary in the U.S., in the practice of price "leadership." The point is that under conditions of relative stability, the compulsion to invest in new production technique diminishes.

Nevertheless, as Lenin emphasized, this is only a tendency. Cost considerations are by no means irrelevant within cartels; there is a certain minimal efficiency which, along with other factors, girds the monopolistic position of their component firms. Alliances give rise to rifts and realignments, and this often involves competitive investments. Monopoly can only restrict competition, it cannot overcome it, and this restriction is only partial and more than offset overall by heightened rivalry. Monopolistic advantages erode and finance capital cannot, as spoken to earlier, allow its productive foundation to so deteriorate as to undermine its overall position. The motion, then, is for cartels to form and, as crisis develops, to break down. That is, centrifugal forces arising out of the anarchy of social production tear away at the stability of cartels: the battle for the cheapening of commodities asserts itself, although, as we shall see, these processes are conditioned by overall international relations.

The pace and scope of technical change (excluding the more continuously "innovative" military and allied sectors) is determined by the balance of strength among the monopolies and, most important, the relative strengths of different national capitals. For example, during long stretches of the postwar period, the so-called high growth or "high-tech" industries, like computer manufacture, have been more technologically vigorous and price competitive than basic industry. The outcome of World War 2 for a country like Japan (both in terms of the more widespread destruction to its productive base and its less privileged international position) forced its steel industry into a more technically innovative stance than its U.S. counterpart. Under favorable — or compelling — conditions, finance capital can, by mobilizing the resources at its disposal, accelerate technical progress. New investment possibilities may require technological breakthroughs, while "outsiders" may overcome barriers to entry on the basis of massive technological assaults. Given the already advanced level of development of the productive forces, innovation will, therefore, have potentially far-ranging impact, even if its introduction is artificially delayed.

It is obvious that technical change has been enormous in the imperialist era; it has been slow only in relation to its possibilities (for instance, the large-scale development of solar power is feasible in the world today), but surely not in relation to the pace of the premonopoly era. Monopoly can restrict technical progress, but the expand-or-die urging of capital makes it impossible for the bourgeoisie to carry this too far and certainly to embrace an ideology that liquidates science as such. The further development of the productive forces calls forth more socialized forms of scientific research and development (state-subsidized research, etc.). Capital presses science and technology into its service as weapons in the competitive struggle and, quite literally, as weapons to insure its domination. The systematic application of science is part of the increasing socialization of the productive forces, which comes into increasing conflict with capitalist production relations; it is a moving, intensifying contradiction.[140] The distinguishing feature of capital (and technical) transformation in this era is its *uneven and spasmodic* character — over time and among different capitals, within different spheres of the national economy, as well as among different national economies.

Monopolistic agreements and arrangements are inherently unstable. The barriers impeding the mobility of capital are neither permanent nor absolute: new entrants appear, certain zones of expansion may be more "up for grabs" than others, merger and diversification activity may leave things unchanged in one sector but strengthen the hand of one financial group overall. Different units of national capital enter into competition with foreign capitals: auto firms, steel companies, banks, etc. Not only, then, is the kind of collusion described earlier temporary, but, in the final analysis, it serves the cause of contention.

As emphasized, imperialism cannot free itself from its foundation in commodity production and competition. Every level of the world economy enveloped by the capitalist mode of production is,

---

[140] This anticipates a line of argument against the theory of "general crisis," which will be taken up in the third chapter.

so to speak, awash in the contradictoriness of capitalist expansion. Thus, discrete and separable capitals anarchically interact within and between both the groupings and alliances established by the agreement of particular capitals and the political boundaries and configurations established by the force and *diktat* of imperialism. In whatever way and to whatever degree domestic and international arrangements facilitate growth over a given period, the very process of expansion brings the "many capitals" into conflict with each other and ultimately dictates that they do battle to create a viable basis for continued expansion. In other words, what imperialism cannot eliminate — what it, in fact, heightens — is the compulsion of particular units (or coalitions) of capital to outstrip, outflank, and defeat their opponents: the long-term survival of some depends on the demise or obliteration of others. But this is not the end of the matter.

In *Anti-Dühring*, Engels made the point that the anarchy/organization contradiction, which leads to conflicts among local producers, also leads to conflicts among national capitals. In a footnote in Volume III of *Capital*, he further explained:

> [C]ompetition in the domestic market recedes before the cartels and trusts, while in the foreign market it is restricted by protective tariffs. . . . But these protective tariffs are nothing but preparations for the ultimate general industrial war, which shall decide who has supremacy on the world market.[141]

It was Lenin, however, who systematized an understanding that went beyond such observations which, insightful and suggestive as they were, could not anticipate a new stage of capitalist development. There is indeed, Lenin pointed out, a struggle among monopoly capitalists over the economic division of the world; this is a struggle which involves the interaction of cartels and other economic groupings whose agreements break down. But the main rivalry is not between this or that firm and its foreign counterpart — it is that rivalry which is fought out in the realm of the superstructure among national capitals as represented by their respective states. This rivalry, Lenin stressed, ultimately develops into the struggle for a new political division of the world, which subsumes the struggle over economic division.

There is a world imperialist system, but this is not tantamount to

---

[141] *Capital,* III, p. 489, note by Engels.

the existence of a single capital formation coterminous with it. The imperialist system is not, therefore, the same as an individual capitalist country in the premonopoly period. A specific feature of this world system that differentiates it from the capitalist mode of production in particular countries before the rise of imperialism is that it is composed of discrete national capital formations. These national formations are not merely larger-scale versions of individual capitals; they are geopolitical complexes with distinct superstructures, and their existence and character play an extremely important role in the process of internationalized accumulation. That finance capital's moorings happen to be national ones is a result of the historical evolution of capitalism.

A particular capitalist can perhaps insinuate himself into another national market, but as a class the bourgeoisie cannot. It cannot easily dislodge another national imperialist capital from its home base. And, in dialectical relation, finance capital cannot, for politico-strategic and economic reasons, afford to lose power where it is. American capital in a country like Indonesia is concerned about stability in that country, but not to the same degree as it is about the stability of its home front (without which it loses, among other things, its capacity to be in Indonesia, as well as other places). There must, in short, be a state to back up economic interests. The process of internationalization might appear to undermine nationality. In fact, by intensifying and concentrating the contradictions of accumulation in the international arena and spurring inter-imperialist conflict, internationalization actually compels the violent assertion of nationality, the defense and extension of specifiable and common national interests. Capital must have the means as well to short-circuit and suppress the resistance it provokes from the oppressed of the world.

The military functions of the imperialist state impact enormously on the physiognomy of advanced capitalism. War and the production of weapons have, of course, played a major role in human history. The use of organized violence to extend markets and the interaction between arms production and industrialization have also been major factors in the development of capitalism. But with the rise of imperialism, arms production and military expenditure in general take mind-boggling leaps, both as ongoing shares of economic activity and in the extraordinary dimensions they reach during periods of international conflict. The major capitalist states doubled their annual military expenditures between the mid-1870s and 1908.[142] The management of war-induced and military-associated debt has been a decisive object of fiscal and monetary policy in the twentieth century. The military sector has also preempted a large fraction of human and technical resources in the advanced countries. In the United States about one-third of all scientists and engineers (and this is a conservative estimate) are engaged in defense-related work, while two-thirds of total federal budget obligations for research and development were channeled into military and space programs during the 1970s.[143] In the Soviet Union during the mid-'70s military uses absorbed, according to U.S. government estimates, about one-third of the output of the machine-building and metalworking industries, while a critic of the U.S. "military-industrial complex" estimates that Soviet military industry uses a work force numbering 4.8 million.[144]

There is a material and political unity of interest, a unitariness (as well as contradictoriness) of a national capital, stemming from the imperatives and objective coordinates of imperialist accumulation, interpenetrated by the class contradiction in its various manifestations. A Japanese multinational corporation, for example, can economically jeopardize and subvert an American multinational, but in today's world they rarely enter into combat alone. There is political and military power, concentrated in the national state, which both galvanizes and defends national capital. This is one reason that the forces binding cartels made up of different national capitals are less durable than those binding national capitals. In the world, then, there are objective social formations, each of which boasts an army and political apparatus, culture, etc., which constitute the superstructure. But if political power grows out of the barrel of a gun, guns must be produced — there must be a base, and a relatively secure one, underlying and supporting the superstructure.

Economically, finance capital is still grouped around national

[142] Richard Krooth, *Arms and Empire* (Santa Barbara: Harvest Publishers, 1980), p. 40.

[143] Lloyd J. Dumas, "Military Spending and Economic Decay," in Lloyd J. Dumas, ed., *The Political Economy of Arms Reduction* (Boulder: Westview Press, 1982), pp. 7, 11.

[144] U.S. government data cited in Abraham S. Becker, *The Burden of Soviet Defense* (Santa Monica: Rand, 1981), p. 18; Seymour Melman, "The Conversion of Military Economy: The USSR," in Dumas, ed., *The Political Economy of Arms Reduction,* p. 90, note 1.

markets.[145] There are national circuits with articulated relations (though not without contradiction) between department 1 (the sector producing the means of production) and department 2 (the sector producing means of consumption), furnishing and cheapening the necessary elements of constant and variable capital. There are strategic concerns which must be propped up — not only the military industry, but other pivotal segments of the economy. There is an extraordinary build-up of fixed capital that cannot, in its great mass, be profitably liquidated or just physically dismantled and shipped abroad. Finally, the biggest hunk of surplus value produced by these capitals still issues from this domestic base. In short, finance capital cannot profitably and safely extricate itself from its national base. Of course, national boundaries are not inviolate — they have been and will continue to be changed by force of arms. Nevertheless, there are objective interrelations and levels of integration of capital to which correspond a national market and class formation. And there is a real, powerful tendency for these particular interrelationships, for these national social formations, to assert themselves.[146]

We have stressed that the nationality of capital acquires cohesiveness precisely in antagonistic relation to other imperialist capitals. *The inexorable logic of capital mandates that individual capitals unite with others. . . but only for the purpose of struggling with yet others.* This results in combines, trusts, and trading blocs. But in a world dominated by the capitalist mode of production, the only way that national capitals can decisively confront and overcome their adversaries — a concrete imperative posed at certain turning points of world history — is through military means. This movement and logic of capitalist accumulation culminates in imperialist

---

[145] The term national market as applied to a multinational state denotes a certain level of coherence of production and exchange relations. It should not be taken to mean that there are not separate nations within the confines of these states.

[146] This is one reason that the victorious powers of the last two world wars did not simply absorb those they vanquished. To be sure, there were both important political factors associated with securing internal stability and strategic international considerations influencing the treatment of the defeated bourgeoisies. But to swallow these national markets would require an exceptionally high degree of integration and centralization — far beyond, for instance, what is embodied in the International Monetary Fund (which in no way obliterates national capitals) — and a kind of international division of labor presupposing a sharp break with the historically evolved interrelationships within the structure of national capitals. A United States of Europe is not inconceivable in a future period, but it would require enormous changes, not only in the economic base but also in the superstructure.

wars. And the antagonisms of capital, in all their different dimensions, will tend eventually toward the bipolarization of imperialist relations, toward the formation of two war blocs comprising different national capitals — each bloc defined in relation to its opposite and arrayed against its opposite.[147] The highest expression of the organization/anarchy contradiction is that the political and military representatives of imperialist capitals, that is, national states, must fight the political and military representatives of others.

Hence, it is the policies of the imperialist state and not those of particular enterprises or monopoly groups which are most decisive. Yet the latter are hardly irrelevant. These are links and component parts of accumulation on a world scale; their motion and interaction cannot but build up tension and conflict in the international arena. Contradictions are neither eradicated at these lower levels nor are they somehow displaced or simply "dumped" into the world market. The international arena is at once a concentration point of the contradictions of capital as capital and the consummate battleground where these contradictions are fought out to their provisional resolution through the medium of national states and by repartitioning the world. The idea that cartels can abolish crisis was properly scorned by Lenin as a "fable."[148]

Exactly because of the centrality of international connections, the imperialist state functions, on the basis of its all-around maintenance of internal class rule, as the key instrument deployed by imperialist capital to secure its environment. In general, the increasing socialization of the productive forces and the inherent difficulties of imperialist accumulation (and the necessity of offsetting the disturbances arising out of it) implicate the state far more widely in the reproductive process than was the case in the premonopoly period. This also has its peculiar expression in the Third World where the state, especially in its financial provision for and share of investment in gross fixed capital formation, has been central to accumulation in countries as diverse as Brazil and

---

[147] The exact character of such bipolar configurations is a function of specific political and economic factors. Further, imperialism may face the necessity to bloc as a whole against a socialist state or system of states. An important particularity of the present period — in contrast to the pre-World War 1 and pre-World War 2 situations — is that political-military blocs are coextensive with the existing economic blocs. The United States forged a highly integrated economic and political alliance in opposition to the socialist camp at the end of World War 2, an alliance which faces a rival bloc headed by a now imperialist Soviet Union.

[148] *Imperialism*, p. 28 (*LCW*, 22, p. 208).

Iraq. In the social-imperialist countries, the state is the main lever of accumulation (the bourgeoisie controls the principal means of production through it and appropriates surplus value preponderantly at this level); in the countries of the U.S.-led bloc it is, to varying degrees, a major vehicle for restructuring capital, both directly (nationalization) and indirectly (monetary and fiscal policy). Still, in both blocs the principal function of the imperialist state is not explicitly economic, but political — to maintain the rule of the bourgeoisie and to preserve the social and production relations of capital. At the same time and directly related, the state must organize the national capital and fight for its interests in the international arena.[149]

The state is the institutional embodiment and expression of the total national capital. However, the national capital is not literally a single capital. The imperialist state collectively represents the many capitals composing the national capital; they do not fuse into one (not even in the Soviet Union) and this representation is itself fraught with contradiction and conflict. But the state has the ability to forcibly mitigate conflicts between fractions of the national capital. And since there is that unitariness of interests of a national capital with an objective mooring, anarchy within the national capital is restricted. It is restricted, however, only in relation to the joint rivalry of all its components with other national capitals (which itself has been conditioned historically by and subordinated to the rivalry between different coalitions or blocs of national capitals), and as a function of the crisis and conflict which grow out of the anarchy of "many capitals" in the international arena.

In this connection, an historical aside becomes quite relevant. Nikolai Bukharin, who by 1929 had emerged as leader of the right wing of the Communist Party of the Soviet Union, had earlier suggested in several studies that in developing toward state capitalism, capital was basically transforming itself into a single national trust capable of surmounting intra-class strife and economic crisis.[150] Bukharin argued that stable, self-regulating, and statified national capitals would find their limits in the international arena, where

---

[149] This function is revealed in the elaboration of national economic policy, export promotion, the use of diplomacy, protection of vital sea routes and raw materials sources, colonial policy (from propping up particular regimes to waging colonial wars), and mobilization for and prosecution of world war.

[150] In fact, Bukharin saw in the state's regulative and integrative capabilities the basic carapace of socialist organization.

they would confront each other.[151] But Bukharin ignored, or seriously downplayed, the basic fact that as long as capital remains capital (resting on its material foundation of commodity production), it will always divide into many capitals; the organization aspect of the organization/anarchy contradiction embodied in the national imperialist state is relative. Lenin chastised Bukharin for sundering imperialism from its capitalist foundation.[152] It is important to note that Lenin also included among the chief characteristics of imperialism the economic division of the world by different monopolies, although the political division was more powerful and ultimately subsumed it. This emphasizes again how internal anarchy is not overcome, but canalized. Moreover, Lenin stressed throughout his writings on imperialism that partial organization and planning in the long run intensify the anarchy of capitalist production as a whole. Bukharin situated the key conflicts in the international arena, but he metaphysically separated these conflicts from the contradictory motion and anarchic nature of capital in general. A national capital, though cohesive, is highly striated, and composed of elements of varied efficiency and profitability; there is anarchy and competition among them.

The rivalry among different national capitals foists a new calculus on the capitalists. The world is transformed into a chessboard on which investments, loans, and aid have become elements of broader strategic consideration. Such strategic considerations range from denying adversaries access to certain raw materials to shoring up whole countries for geopolitical reasons (these countries might even be only of marginal importance in terms of productive investment). Capital exports do not simply gravitate directly to the highest rate of profit; actually, preventing rivals from securing important markets or raw materials may result in short-term losses. The search for greater profitability interacts continually with the exercise of domination and control.

Profit is the soul and commander of the imperialist formations. But the whole international framework within which capital accumulates and the intensification of its contradictions *qualitatively heighten the significance of political and military struggles,* both in or-

---

[151] See Nikolai Bukharin, *The Politics and Economics of the Transition Period,* edited with an introduction by Kenneth S. Tarbuck (London: Routledge and Kegan Paul, 1979), pp. 57-63, 73-79.

[152] See "Report on the Party Programme" (Eighth Congress of the R.C.P.[B.], 18-23 March 1919), *LCW,* 29, pp. 165-69.

dinary and extraordinary times. Indeed, in the imperialist era the very process of accumulation is highly intertwined with politics.[153] The political role of the state must be seen in this light.

That the imperialist state collectively represents a multiplicity of capitals produces a certain imperialist "largeness of mind." The warfare and welfare functions of the imperialist state are pre-eminently political. The war in Vietnam was not, for instance, carried out by the U.S. principally to gain profits in Vietnam. The military costs far outweighed any such potential.[154] Likewise, the poverty program in the United States was not undertaken to turn profits for individual firms, nor did it reflect some hybrid capitalism which had grown socially constructive. Both of these policies served the needs of empire more broadly, through force on the one hand, and concessionary pacification on the other. The state must also undertake investment projects (like the seeding of strategic new industries and infrastructure development) and bail-out operations which are not necessarily profitable in themselves but which, nonetheless, are essential to the reproduction and over-all profitability and stability of the national capital. In all the imperialist countries, the technical-educational and military sectors are highly subsidized through various mechanisms.

All this flows from the objective need of imperialism to secure the general political and economic conditions within which capital can successfully accumulate. Price regulation and the mobilization and transfer of surplus value to enterprises or activities which may be unprofitable or unproductive of surplus value represent, therefore, a modification by the state of the operation of the law of value.[155] But the ability of the imperialist state, by means of direct investment and fiscal and monetary authority, to centralize and re-distribute surplus value in accordance with political priority (as against simple profitability) is anchored in the real production of values internationally — and state expenditure reacts back upon ac-

[153] The economic structure of society ultimately determines political, military, and ideological lines and policies — this is basic to Marxism — but these policies in turn react back upon the economic structure — and this, too, is basic to Marxism.

[154] Similarly, Israel and Cuba are kept afloat by the U.S. and Soviet imperialists, respectively, for political, strategic, and ideological reasons. Evaluated simply as economic investments, they are very much losing propositions.

[155] These state activities and functions are analytically distinct from, though they overlap with, productive state-run enterprises and industries (as exist in the Western imperialist bloc), and the generalized extraction of surplus value through a system of state enterprises (as exists in the social-imperialist bloc).

cumulation, generating new contradictions. Moreover, even if in the imperialist era the law of value is mediated through complex mechanisms, and if politics continually and powerfully interact with economics, these imperialist politics are still ultimately grounded in the expand-or-die nature of capital, and in the regulating role of the law of value.

IX

The capitalist mode of production has become dominant throughout the world. Within the oppressed countries, precapitalist relations and modes are increasingly shaped by and subordinated to the needs of the expanding capitalist sector. Further, and more important, these countries taken as a whole — including their capitalist sector — are dominated by imperialism, whatever the level of their internal transformation. This represents one crucial aspect of the change in world relations that has occurred. On the other hand, each grouping of imperialists and colonies must take account of and can only expand in relation to and ultimately at the expense of others. The further unification of the world market — in particular the higher forms of global integration associated with and generated by capital export — and the territorial division of the world fix capital in a world dynamic that is both economic and political. Accumulation now proceeds in this context. What distinguishes imperialism is the qualitative dominance on a world scale of the fundamental contradiction of the bourgeois epoch between socialized production and private appropriation.

The fundamental contradiction develops through two forms of motion. The antagonism between different (national) imperialist capitals chiefly grows out of, extends, and, further, is a qualitative development of the contradiction between organization at the enterprise level and the anarchy of social production. But this fundamental contradiction is also manifested in class terms. The contradiction between the proletariat and the bourgeoisie in the imperialist countries, the contradiction between the oppressed nations and imperialism, and the contradiction between the socialist camp and the imperialist camp (when socialist countries exist) are chiefly products and expressions of this second form of motion, the class contradiction of capitalism. These three contradictions plus the interimperialist contradiction form the main content of the development of the fundamental contradiction in the contemporary era; they arise from and are integrated into the overall process of transition from the bourgeois epoch to the communist epoch.

These contradictions do not develop as metaphysical isolates. They continually interact with each other and react back upon the totality of this process (along with other contradictions which play exceedingly important roles at times). Moreover, one or another of these major contradictions may, in any period, be principal, that is, influence the overall development of the others more than it in turn is influenced by them, and thus most determine how the fundamental contradiction will develop at a given stage. Their interrelationships, however, are fluid; even as they reach certain relative limits in their own development, these contradictions transform one another. At particular turning points a formerly principal contradiction achieves a certain degree of resolution (or mitigation) and is superseded by a new principal contradiction. But, to stress the point again, movement compelled by anarchy is the principal form of motion of the contradiction between socialized production and private appropriation. This form of motion – the qualitative impact of the contradictions of world accumulation and the consequent role of wars of redivision – is more determining of the overall process by which these other contradictions unfold, at least so long as the bourgeois mode of production is dominant in the world.

The internationalization of capital has profound repercussions on revolutionary class struggles. Imperialism violently draws the masses of the colonial regions into the maelstrom of world history. At the same time, the export of capital creates new legions of gravediggers of imperialism. The resistance of the masses in those regions now takes place on the stage of a single international process and assumes a tremendously important role in this process. The contradiction between the proletariat and the bourgeoisie within the imperialist countries and that between the oppressed nations and imperialism become intertwined, and their character and relation with each other change. Imperialism opens new prospects for the subjective factor, for the dynamic political role played by the masses. Indeed, it was only in this era that the proletariat ever seized and successfully consolidated political power.

If such prospects are enhanced and if the various manifestations of class contradiction may principally shape the course of world events over any given period of time, might it not be argued, then, that the press and propulsion of mass struggles is actually more determining of the overall process by which imperialism is headed towards its extinction? Certainly, as Marxism affirms, the fundamental contradiction can only be resolved through protracted and all-around revolutionary struggle. However, it is the underlying expand-or-die compulsion of capital, not the various expressions of the class antagonism, that chiefly confronts the imperialists with the repeated need to redivide the world, and it is movement compelled by anarchy that sets the overall terms for these other contradictions and ultimately determines the parameters and possibilities of the class struggle. This does not contradict the fact that the fundamental contradiction can only be resolved in the political sphere. The terrain on which the class struggle is fought is not merely a given — just "there," as some static platform consisting of the capitalist mode of production. The concrete development of the anarchy/organization contradiction lends necessity and freedom to both the bourgeoisie and proletariat and, at certain times, qualitatively increases the objective freedom of the international proletariat to act decisively in its world-historic interests.

To approach the question from another angle: the Great Depression of the 1930s was not the outcome of mass political upsurges in the world nor was it overcome, in a country like Germany, for instance, through economic assaults on or the political dismemberment of the German working class. World War 2 was not the cumulative response to blows inflicted against imperialism in the Third World, nor was its main and immediate purpose to suppress and contain the masses in these countries. (Similarly, while contradictions between individual imperialist countries and the Third World are factors that increase the antagonism between the two imperialist blocs in the world today, these are not the main cause of the conflict between the two blocs, nor have struggles in the Third World had the effect of overriding or mitigating that antagonism; they have not, for example, foisted on the imperialist blocs the necessity to overcome their divisions and unite against these struggles.) On the other hand, the historical factors conditioning imperialist crisis and war are interwoven with and inseparable from the class contradiction. And precisely during such critical moments of global dislocation, the scope for revolutionary initiative and struggle increases vastly, and with this, qualitatively greater possibilities emerge for accelerating the worldwide destruction of imperialism. The intensification and internationalization of the contradictions of capitalist accumulation have everything to do with why imperialism is the era of proletarian revolution.

X

We have treated the concept of the fundamental contradiction mainly in terms of its dominance on a world scale and the resulting integration of particular development processes into a single world process through which this fundamental contradiction intensifies and is ultimately resolved in the passage to world communism. It is now possible to introduce and elaborate on a second major thesis of this work, concerning the particular motion and development of the fundamental contradiction in the imperialist era. Again, what must be grasped is the relationship between the specificity of imperialism, on the one hand, and its roots in the economic laws and contradictory character of capital, on the other. Capital cannot exist without constantly developing the productive forces. As a condition for this, it must, within the framework of private appropriation, reorganize its relations of production. Yet owing to the anarchy of this mode of production, such a process leads, by way of its internal contradictions, to sharp and radical interruptions of accumulation — to crises which, by destroying inefficient capitals and altering the relations among capitals, actually lay the basis for renewed and profitable accumulation. What emerges is a distinctive cyclical movement; the process of accumulation develops through expansion and crisis. Exactly because capital grows more concentrated, each forward thrust creates the conditions for more devastating crisis.

The basic laws of accumulation are modified when capitalism develops into imperialist-capitalism. But capitalism can neither overcome its inner compulsion to expand nor prevent its inner contradictions from exploding: it is still a dynamic mode of production. In fact, in important ways, under imperialism these basic laws assert themselves more intensely, but within the context of international relations and of the changes within them. The laws of accumulation interact with the division of the world and international political struggles. Although there has never been, nor could there ever be, an economic process (or cycle) dissociated from political phenomena, in the imperialist era a far more complex dialectic linking politics with economics now operates, with politics itself assuming greater importance than ever before.

We have reached a critical point in our analysis. The argument is this: with the rise of imperialism a new structural dynamic begins to govern the development of world history, and as long as the bourgeois mode of production remains dominant it will continue to govern that development. If we consider the course and the major turning points of the twentieth century, it is possible to discern certain striking features which suggest the existence of just such a dynamic. First, interimperialist wars have played the principal role in temporarily resolving the political conflicts and antagonisms among imperialist capitals which became concentrated in open military confrontation between rival imperialist blocs. Second, the two world wars have also been accompanied by major revolutionary upheavals, the Bolshevik and Chinese Revolutions standing as the most significant examples. Third, as a general tendency, interimperialist wars, in their preparation, prosecution, and outcome have played the principal role in restructuring capital, the result of which has been the temporary economic revitalization of imperialism. Fourth, the specific outcome of each of the two world wars and accompanying revolutionary outbursts has lent a distinct political and economic character to each of the extended periods of peace (that is, absence of world war) which have followed. Finally, these intervening periods have been just that — periods of movement toward yet another explosion. For the imperialists, these interim years have always seen the various alignments, transformations, advances, etc., produced by the preceding war period, turned into their opposite. That so much of the social, political, and economic history of the twentieth century is chronologized and categorized in terms of "prewar" or "postwar" periods is not without objective significance.

We have spoken already of spiral motion as a general characteristic of historical development. But we have also chosen to employ this term *spiral* in a specific historical sense. By spiral we mean a definite stage or period in the development of the contradiction between socialized production and private appropriation during the imperialist epoch. Historically, the stages in the development of the imperialist system have been punctuated by imperialist world wars for redivision. These wars have been at once products of distinct and historically determined political and economic contradictions and also more general expressions of the fundamental laws governing the accumulation process in the imperialist era. Hence, world wars in the imperialist era are not simply individual events but must be understood as demarcating one spiral from another, resolving the particular set of contradictions of one period while, at the same time, beginning to set the stage for the next period. This does not mean that only such wars could have been or must in the future be the turning points in a spiral — major revolutionary initiatives or upheavals could play that role.

Thus far in the history of imperialism, each new stage of development — or spiral — has been set in motion by the new division of the world and changes in alignments among the imperialists achieved as a result of war's outcome, on the one hand, and by the degree of revolutionary advance, consolidation, and the potential for further advance achieved in periods of international crisis and war, on the other. A spiral is colored by particular contradictions arising from these changes while incorporating new contradictions that will play a greater or lesser role in its unfolding. The contemporary era has seen two complete spirals. The first began with the rise of imperialism and ended with World War 1. That war and its outcome initiated a new spiral, the contradictions of which were resolved through World War 2. We are presently entering into a resolution phase of the spiral set in motion by World War 2. How this third spiral ultimately ends will of course be determined by the actual events of history.

There is tremendous complexity, particularity, and contingency here. We live in an epoch of transition. Capitalism is in its highest and final stage, but its decline and overthrow will be a drawn-out process and the proletarian revolution is itself in its infancy. It is possible, however, to uncover certain basic features of these spirals, traceable to the laws of accumulation in the imperialist era, and to generalize from their historical development. A spiral is a structured process: a structure of international relations which, precisely because it is internally contradictory and conditioned by the laws of capital, is a process whose motion is towards its violent transformation. *Imperialism is heading towards its extinction through spirals, which operate on an international level, and whose turning points are world-historic conjunctures.* This spiral/conjuncture motion is the structural dynamic of the imperialist era.

Major turns in the political economy of imperialism do not develop out of the periodic overproduction of capital (arising from the contradictions in the accumulation process) within different countries taken by themselves, as was the case with the cyclical crises of competitive capitalism. Under imperialism, cyclical motion becomes part of and subordinate to the motion of a larger, international process involving the balance of power among the imperialists and the forces ranged against imperialism. (For example, whether competitive pressures dissolve cartels depends on a global framework including not simply economic rivalry but political configurations and ultimately war blocs.[156] The centrality of the world arena to the process of accumulation thus does not hinge on international relations or a world market in the abstract, but on concrete economic processes, on the concrete alignments and struggles of rival imperialists, and on class and national struggles in their concrete development. Politics, world events, major changes in the balance of world forces decisively influence how particular spirals unfold. A spiral, in the sense that we are now speaking, is not static; it expresses from start to finish the transformation of the world through the struggle of opposites and the interpenetration of contradictions.

The basic laws of capitalist accumulation continue to assert themselves, then, in the framework of the relation of forces in the world in which interimperialist wars have been nodal points. The division of the world through such wars creates a certain context for and has a profound impact on each new spiral. For instance, the concrete relations between victors and vanquished at the end of World War 2, in particular the dominant and orchestrating role won by U.S. imperialism through that war, and the more thorough redistribution of colonies (as compared with that of World War 1) were major factors setting the stage for the development of the fundamental contradiction in the present spiral.

This is a fundamental reason for the very different scope and duration of expansion following World War 2 relative to that following World War 1. Why certain sectors of the U.S. economy were modernized while others atrophied in the postwar period can only be understood in terms of the prerogatives and necessities of empire flowing from the outcome of World War 2. The international position of U.S. imperialism dictated that it maintain and expand an immense and highly advanced military sector; at the same time, the establishment of specific political and financial arrangements strengthened its ability to garner surplus value internationally and enabled it to profitably delay the retooling of some basic industry.

The path these spirals take is also influenced by the long-term development of imperialism. For example, the various "land reform" programs sponsored by U.S. imperialism in the Third World

---

[156] Hence, there is renewed and predatory price competition within the U.S. bloc at the same time as efforts are made to maintain more stability and cooperation in order to confront the adversary bloc. However, such competition would be far more destructive were there not this common political necessity to strengthen a war bloc.

during the present spiral could not have been carried out in the pre-World War 2 period, even had there been the resources to carry them out. These "reforms" presupposed a certain degree of infrastructure development and capitalist penetration of the countryside that had been achieved during the two preceding spirals.

Yet there is no predetermined course to which these spirals will hew; they are complex and variegated, involving the continual interaction of political and economic factors. The U.S. imperialists had to consolidate, defend, and extend the spoils of World War 2, and this inevitably gave rise to and intensified contradictions and resistance. It was no accident that U.S. imperialism was the main target of the national liberation struggles in the postwar period. But it was not "written on a rock" that U.S. imperialism would face its most severe trial of strength in Vietnam, that it would meet defeat there, or that this defeat would mark a major turning point in the development of imperialist crisis. By the same token, the restoration of capitalism in the Soviet Union was not inherent in the outcome of World War 2. This certainly had its historical roots in and was conditioned by the international situation, but such a reversal for the international proletariat constituted a major new factor in the spiral. Why the downturn of 1958 was experienced in depth in the major imperialist countries and yet overcome without a major explosion can only be understood in connection with a certain international constellation of forces, central to which was this very reversal in the Soviet Union.

The sharpening of contradictions on a world scale gives rise to struggles and upheavals which profoundly influence the course and structure of accumulation, as well as the international class struggle. This has been touched on already, but requires further discussion. Lenin wrote that "the awakening of Asia and the beginning of the struggle for power by the advanced proletariat of Europe are a symbol of the new phase in world history that began early this century."[157] Indeed, Lenin conceptualized this era as one of revolutionary storms. This was not mere exhortation or wishful thinking. The revolution that Lenin led radically altered the course of world history, both in its direct challenge to imperialism and in the inspiration, example, and support it gave to the oppressed throughout the world. Mao Tsetung, through the course of the Chinese Revolution after World War 2, led the struggle of the inter-

---

[157] "The Awakening of Asia," *LCW*, 19, p. 86.

national proletariat to its highest pinnacle thus far. That struggle for the future — as exemplified by the slogan "it is right to rebel against reaction" which rang out during the Cultural Revolution — sent shockwaves throughout the imperialist-controlled world, and it raised the sights of hundreds of millions of oppressed across the planet. During this century the imperialists have had to continually contend with major revolutionary struggles and with the prospect of losing control in various regions of the world. [158]

The division of the world between, on one side, a handful of advanced capitalist countries and, on the other, a great number of oppressed nations embracing the largest part of the world's territory and population and figuring integrally and indispensably into the process of imperialist accumulation, underlies the existence of two great forces of the revolutionary struggle against imperialism in the world: the proletarian-socialist revolution in the capitalist-imperialist countries and the anti-imperialist democratic revolution in the colonial (or neocolonial) and dependent countries, which holds the potential for socialism if led by the proletariat. Of great historical moment — and very much related to the lopsidedness analyzed earlier — is the fact that the focal point of revolution since the Bolshevik Revolution has shifted from the advanced countries to the colonial and neocolonial regions of the world. These have indeed become storm centers of revolution, particularly since World War 2, while the same period has seen a certain retarding of the revolutionary movement among the working class in the advanced countries. Although the stabilization in the advanced countries has complicated the world-historic process of proletarian revolution, whatever degree of stability has been or might be established in any particular country (or even region) is always relative to and deeply affected by the existence of revolutionary class and national liberation struggles in the rest of the world.

The multifarious effects of the Vietnamese national liberation struggle underscore the important role played by revolution in the working out of spirals. Here was a struggle that pounded the great military colossus of the imperialist world. What began as a surgical "police" action on the part of the U.S. imperialists grew into a ma-

---

[158] Had there been a significant revolutionary advance in the earlier part of the present spiral or a world war involving the then socialist Soviet Union and China together against imperialism, a major shift, perhaps one of qualitative proportions, in the relations of strength between the international proletariat and imperialism might have resulted.

jor war of aggression requiring massive commitment of financial and military resources and incurring a high political cost. The world was far from quiet during a period of robust expansion in the West. The Vietnamese resistance sparked other struggles, particularly in Asia; and, in the imperialist countries themselves, this war ignited and fueled powerful mass movements. At the same time, the war jarred the dollar/gold standard and opened certain opportunities for the other imperialists in the U.S.-led bloc to angle for momentary advantage. The weakening of the U.S. and the concomitant necessity to cut its losses also allowed the Soviet social-imperialists to make new inroads in various parts of the world.

The present spiral is replete with examples of how such conflicts, struggles, and revolutions influence the freedom and necessity of the imperialists: the specific route to reconstruction taken by West Germany was closely linked with U.S.-bloc encirclement of the Soviet Union; the structure and internal contradictions of the South Korean economy in the postwar period cannot be understood apart from the existence of the Chinese Revolution; the Alliance for Progress, with all its imperialist "social reform" and infrastructure development, is inexplicable without reference to the Cuban Revolution. The Cultural Revolution in China had far-reaching influence on both the international class struggle and the constraints acting on imperialism and social-imperialism; its long-term ideological impact will bear directly on the outcome of this spiral.[159]

Politics and class struggle are not exceptional or ancillary events; they affect — at certain times, decisively so — the course and resolution of imperialist spirals. Mass revolutionary stirrings and upheavals challenge the imperialist order, rend its political, social, and ideological fabric, and contribute to the destruction of that order. These struggles are truly of world-historic significance.[160]

[159] To emphasize the centrality of the international context, that the Cultural Revolution had to be launched and could be conducted in the fashion it was had everything to do with the struggles and alignment of forces in the world at that particular time. It, too, was part of a single world process. See Bob Avakian, *The Loss in China and The Revolutionary Legacy of Mao Tsetung* (Chicago: RCP Publications, 1978), especially pp. 53-55.

[160] Such an understanding clashes with various economist notions of class and national struggle. These typically focus narrowly on a certain sphere of production relations and their reform. This may assume its classic trade-unionist form in the struggle for improved terms of the sale and conditions of employment of labor power or turn on the quest of neocolonial and dependent regimes for improved terms of trade. Whether such strategies are presented as means to make imperialism "work" or to bring it to its knees, they will do neither, but only help prolong its existence and in the long run reinforce the misery it produces.

Yet for all these diverse, interweaving, and contingent factors, there is a very definite, though dynamic, international framework within which capital accumulates. And, again, at least so long as the bourgeois mode of production is qualitatively dominant in the world, the assertion of the capitalist laws of accumulation, particularly the motive force of anarchy, will overall set the terms and parameters of these spirals.

To return to the example of the Soviet Union: the restoration of capitalism in the Soviet Union expanded the maneuvering room of the Western imperialist bloc — in the 1960s in particular when, for instance, the Soviet Union was encouraging restraint and accommodation on the part of national liberation forces. But this reversal could not create a wholly new set of circumstances such that imperialism could surmount its basic contradictions. The developments towards crisis and world war growing out of the fundamental contradiction, a process into which the exigencies of the now social-imperialist Soviet Union were integrated, continued to exert themselves. Similarly, the loss of proletarian power in China in 1976 is a major new factor in the relation of forces internationally. This loss, while not preordained, was completely bound up with the developments toward world crisis and war and by itself is not enough to outweigh the crisis of the world economy or to increase the leverage and opportunities open to imperialism in a way comparable to the effect of the earlier Soviet reversal. The primacy of the laws of capitalist accumulation has everything to do with why, thus far in the history of imperialism, interimperialist wars have been concentration, or nodal, points of these spirals.

The international development of what we have called spirals, involving the dynamic interplay between economics and politics and the relationship between the two forms of motion of the fundamental contradiction, provides a basis for analyzing world events. This framework also enables us to more fully understand an important feature of imperialist accumulation which arises from and influences the laws of motion of capital, specifically, the modifications in the role and character of the cycle.

It is of more than passing interest that Lenin did not dwell on cyclical movements within the accumulation process, though this was by no means extraneous or unimportant to what he described and analyzed in his study of imperialism. To a certain extent, his work did not focus on this question and, in another sense, the experience he summed up centered on both the formative stages of imperialism and its first cataclysmic eruption; it was not possible to answer every question posed by the emergence of this new framework of capitalist accumulation. But Lenin's point of emphasis, even if all its implications were not fully drawn out (as only further experience would permit), was a profound one. He argued powerfully that the underlying contradictions of the first fifteen years of the twentieth century could only be mitigated for any particular imperialist power through a favorable redivision of the world — not by a more "efficient" cycle or series of cycles. But what is the status of the cycle under imperialism, what is its relation to the international spirals referred to, and to what extent are these spirals really analogues to the cycle?

The cyclical character of accumulation persists and cannot be eliminated under imperialism. Accumulation proceeds unevenly, by way of expansion and contraction, because of the anarchy of social production. At the same time, as emphasized earlier, particular national capitals do not lose their identity or meld into a single cycle of a single world capital formation; accumulation on a world scale proceeds through national and bloc configurations in interaction with each other. However, the cycle is greatly distorted as a result of both the internationalization of capital and the intervention of the imperialist state, that is, the cushioning yet ultimately exacerbating effect of international capital flows and countercyclical measures. Insofar as cartelization permits maintenance of excess capacity (to limit output) and seeks to minimize predatory price conflicts among monopolies, thus keeping prices higher, the existence of monopoly distorts the cycle still further. The duration and frequency of these cycles grow more irregular and they are stamped with peculiar features (such as perverse price movements).[161] More important, the regular motion of the accumulation cycle no longer fundamentally determines the essential structural and performance characteristics of the imperialist economies. Cyclical motion is subordinated to and conditioned by the international framework and the changes within it; in fact, more protracted and gripping international crises envelop cyclical oscillations. International relations and connections are more determinant of the phases and trend-lines of accumulation, of investment patterns, waves of technological innovation, the constitution

---

[161] Lenin, it should be noted, observed that contemporary crises of overproduction occurred "at more lengthy and less definite intervals" than they had during the earlier stages of capitalism ("Karl Marx," *LCW*, 21, p. 64).

and reconstitution of cartels, and even the weight and significance of cyclical turns, than are cyclical movements themselves.

With respect to economic trends of the postwar period, a distinct pattern of development can be traced throughout the U.S.-led bloc. In simplified terms, there was a period of stabilization and growth in the 1950s, the most vigorous and sustained expansion in the 1960s, and heightened instability and precipitous decline in the 1970s setting the stage for the present decade. Prior to the world downturn of 1973-75, recessions in most of the Western imperialist countries (including Japan) were milder and shorter than in the pre-World War 2 period. In West Germany, there was no classical cyclical downturn to speak of until 1966-67.[162] Clearly, cyclical movements — muted or otherwise — can explain neither the growth of the 1950s and 1960s, nor the generalized crisis of the present period.

As for the Third World, by stimulating the growth of a capitalist sector, the export of capital also imparts a cyclical motion to these economies. Given their external dependency and internal disarticulation, however, the cycles which they experience are even less autonomous and determinant. Which parts of these economies grow, which do not, and which get pinched in crisis, or why some of these economies can only be "bled" with caution by the imperialists during crisis (since critical weak links could destabilize the entire edifice), is completely bound up with international relations. External conditions actually become internal to individual countries.

To be sure, the pattern of cyclical motion in the premonopoly period was also hardly invariant, and this cyclical movement was itself part of the historical development of capitalism to a higher level. But the spirals of the twentieth century pivot on a more multi-dimensional dialectic of economics (with all the complexity of imperialism as a world system) and politics (in which revolution plays a central role). In general, these spirals possess certain common features associated with the convulsive redivision of the world, and particular spirals are marked by more dominant and determining elements, lending a distinct contour to their development. But this is not an extended cycle. There is no characteristic shape or time-frame, i.e., so many years of upward and downward phases of ac-

---

[162] Philip A. Klein, *Business Cycles in the Postwar World* (Washington, D.C.: American Enterprise Institute for Public Policy Research, 1976), pp. 21-27.

cumulation to each spiral.[163] We are dealing with the violent recasting of international relations and the transformation of inter-related factors into their opposites on a global plane. Such is the fundamental process through which capital expands, lunges into crisis, and undergoes stark reorganization in the imperialist era.

XI

Uneven development is a general law of capitalism — in fact, of society (and nature) generally — but it assumes particularly acute form under imperialism. "Finance capital and the trusts," Lenin wrote, "do not diminish but increase the differences in the rate of growth of the various parts of the world economy."[164] The global effect of the mobility and centralizing capacities of finance capital is to heighten and create new imbalances, even if in particular countries and for particular periods capital is marshaled to over-come such imbalances. With respect to the colonies and the im-perialist-sponsored international division of labor, this has already been addressed: the characteristic disarticulation in the oppressed nations and lopsidedness internationally. Further, the level of de-velopment and growth rates within different sectors of the colonial economies and among the colonies show marked differentiation.

Within the imperialist countries, investment trends and rates of growth vary among individual firms and branches of industry. The sluggish modernization of the U.S. steel industry relative to that of the information industry, for instance, offers an obvious case in

---

[163] Our conception of the spiral differs radically from the highly deterministic "long-wave" theory which does indeed incorporate and project elements of an ex-tended cycle, though by no means a cycle in the sense that Marx analyzed. Its point of departure is usually some variant of technological determinism whereby massive technical changes or innovations first induce a protracted period of growth but then gradually exhaust themselves. Ostensibly accounting for long-term historical devel-opment and purporting to examine economic trends in an international context, "long-wave" theory blurs the distinction between the competitive and monopoly epochs of capitalism (and between social systems in some cases) and tries to fit diverse phenomena into a procrustean bed of regular and predictable 50- or 100-year waves. Basically, it suggests that as long as capitalism can eke out a new technology it enjoys indefinite staying power. Despite its sometimes Marxist trappings, this theory is rooted neither in the imperatives of capitalist accumulation nor in a real dynamic of international relations. The question will be more fully addressed in a subsequent volume.

[164] *Imperialism*, p. 116 (*LCW*, 22, p. 274).

point. Gaps between the conditions of reproduction in the monopoly and nonmonopoly sectors will ultimately widen. These are obviously phenomena of capitalism per se, but the imperialist internationalization of capital and the whole mechanism of capital centralization and reallocation accentuate differences, particularly as these processes cease to stimulate production in the same way. Among the imperialist economies, some are more dynamic than others, and different powers are more or less successful in politically and strategically advancing their international interests vis-à-vis others, that is, in maintaining or challenging the existing framework of international power relations.

On this last point, there looms an important dialectic between the victors and vanquished in interimperialist wars. It will tend to be to the advantage of the victors to massively export capital, and a significant portion of this exported capital may flow to the economies of the defeated imperialist powers. Compared with the victors, the vanquished are more compelled to invest domestically since, precisely because of their defeat, their ability to invest abroad is more restricted. Finance capital may reap greater profits through monopolistic control and concentrated investments outside its national basin — and it is exactly a favorable division of the world which permits this volume and direction of capital export.[165] As a result, those imperialist economies which are the recipients of capital export, including especially the previously vanquished — although they, too, carry on international investments — may actually grow faster than the principal capital exporters. On the other hand, the economies of the major capital-exporting countries expand more than they would without the stimulus coming from the new situation. This stimulus may operate in a different way, however, in these countries, spurring overall growth but more in the shape of the rapid expansion of the financial, luxury, and military sectors than in modernization of more bedrock and basic industries.

Thus, there are exigencies and prerogatives stemming from the monopoly of political power, and such a division of the world also

---

[165] To take one example: it redounded to the advantage of U.S. finance capital for a period to have its fingers in the reconstruction of the productive bases of the European and Japanese economies (if through highly complex financial interrelations) rather than to simply retool U.S. industry. Although this involved important particularities of the postwar period, especially in relation to the previously mentioned political concerns, there also exist certain general features associated with the privileges of the victors.

impacts on the defeated imperialists. Again, there are no inviolate patterns of growth: among the winners there are those who win more than others, there are long-term historical factors which play their part, as well as contingent political factors. Most important, the dialectics of the situation, with initial advantages and stimuli turning into their opposites, will be asserted. The impetus given accumulation in those economies which are largely recipients of capital export tends to immediately forestall yet ultimately compound crisis, within these countries as well as internationally. The drawbacks of particular disfigurations, warpings, and inefficiencies of the domestic base of those powers enjoying certain international privileges tend to grow more manifest and serious as, by way of its contradictions, expansion leads to crisis. The point is that these individual national economies form elements of an international dynamic; collectively, in interaction with one another, they contribute to overproduction in a larger international setting, and it is the international framework which is the limiting factor against which they collectively strain.

Capitalism is characterized by highly developed productive forces which undergo rapid change. In its later, imperialist stage, the changes capitalism stimulates are far more convulsive. Growth in particular sectors and countries is more spasmodic, while decay and ruination in others is more pervasive, all of which fundamentally weakens the imperialist system. In sum, uneven development under capitalism is a specific manifestation of the anarchy of social production and a factor which, especially in the imperialist era, compounds its destructive expression.

Before turning to the question of interimperialist war in its own right, a few additional points about uneven development (and the tendentious interpretations of this phenomenon) must be raised which relate directly to that discussion. If the specific treatment of this law by Lenin has a sharp polemical edge, it is because he was challenging and refuting a sophisticated theory of *organized* capitalism (as applied to the international arena) promulgated by the man who was perhaps the most influential "Marxist" of his day, Karl Kautsky of the German Social-Democratic Party. Kautsky argued that imperialism represented a certain policy of a certain fraction of the bourgeoisie and was not a structural, economic necessity. In fact, Kautsky posited that the resort to force, which he alleged to be the essence of imperialist expansion, was counterproductive to capital. He further suggested that the same processes which produced monopoly could theoretically induce capitalism to evolve in a more rational and less bellicose direction:

> From the purely economic point of view it is not impossible that capitalism will yet go through a new phase, that of the extension of the policy of the cartels to foreign policy, the phase of ultra-imperialism....
>
> Cannot the present imperialist policy be supplanted by a new, ultraimperialist policy, which will introduce the joint exploitation of the world by internationally united finance capital in place of the mutual rivalries of national finance capitals? Such a new phase of capitalism is at any rate conceivable.[166]

Lenin's critique, spelled out in *Imperialism, The Highest Stage of Capitalism* and other writings of the war period, showed, on the one hand, that Kautsky detached the politics of imperialism from its economics and, on the other, that his was an attempt to substitute abstract economic trends and possibilities (the evolution toward a single world trust) for the real concrete development of society and the world, development fraught not only with economic antagonisms but political contradictions and conflicts as well, all of which grow more intense in this era.[167] Kautsky papered over the explosive qualities intrinsic to imperialism and denied the qualitative leaps (revolutions) necessary to transform it. "Ultra-imperialism" was nothing less than an opportunistic pipe dream.

Imperialism is a dynamic system, and the correlations of strength within it change continually. Were it actually the case that patterns and rates of growth of the various imperialist powers were always and everywhere in lockstep and the distribution of colonies among them such that minor reshuffling and trade-offs were all that was required to satisfy their needs of expansion and reorganization, then Kautsky's conceit of an imperial order capable of peacefully resolving differences among contending international interests would only be half wrong. The imperialists could then, as they now only do at certain stages of their rivalry, negotiate orderly marketing agreements and political treaties and either accept the existing division of the world as a permanent framework within which to iron out differences or peaceably adjust that framework.

---

[166] Quoted in *Imperialism*, pp. 112, 142 (*LCW*, 22, pp. 271, 293); an English translation of Kautsky's most infamous article on "ultra-imperialism" can be found in *New Left Review*, No. 59 (January-February 1970), pp. 41-46.

[167] See, for instance, "Preface to N. Bukharin's Pamphlet, *Imperialism and the World Economy*," *LCW*, 22, p. 107.

But capital develops unevenly, the more so under imperialism. This is true at any level of its existence: financial group, cartel, national capital, bloc, etc. And even if particular national capitals uniformly encountered the same obstacles to accumulation internationally, they would still face the necessity to expand or die at each other's expense. Like monopolistic agreements, the established partition of the world is inherently unstable, and the imperialists are inevitably compelled to go over from a relatively peaceful reshuffling (of gains here and losses there) to armed struggle for the repartitioning of colonies and spheres of influence in toto. In short, the necessary redivision can be effected neither piecemeal nor peacefully.

Lenin's emphasis on uneven development flows from his emphasis on the anarchy of capitalist production. It was in the heightening of this anarchy – and the intensified rivalry among different imperialist powers, which is a concentrated expression of it – that Lenin sought an explanation for the volatility of the modern era. (He did not narrowly focus on cyclical developments in individual countries, nor did he look principally to the aggregate global profit rate, to discover the cause and form of world crisis.) Because of the driving force of anarchy, imperialism cannot be permanently stabilized. And the law of uneven development helps explain why this is not possible, whether through intensified exploitation, mutual respect for spheres of influence, trade protocols, or any other measure.

Nevertheless, a great deal of confusion surrounds the concept of uneven development, especially its political implications. Lenin did not reduce the compulsion to redivide the world to this law as such; for him it was but one very important manifestation of the more fundamental and underlying anarchy of social production. At the same time, Lenin stressed, political and superstructural factors play a very crucial role in the actual constellation and collision of international forces. The law of uneven development neither adduces an archetypal scenario of how imperialist powers array themselves in the drive towards war, nor does it lead to the proposition that some powers face greater necessity – or justification – to seek out a redivision than do others.

There is a tradition that actually runs counter to Leninism, and that twists the law of uneven development into a mechanistic and economist rendering of world events. In the aftermath of World War 1, for instance, the international communist movement predicted military conflict between the United States and Great Britain, based on the differences and divergence in their growth rates and economic development. This distortion has also been linked historically with attempts to extract from the law of uneven development a rationale for politically expedient and self-serving policies. During the 1930s and 1940s — at those times when the Soviet Union was working for and entering into alliance with the Allies — it was argued that the fascist powers posed more of a danger to the people of the world than did their democratic counterparts and stood more to blame for the outbreak of World War 2. This notion that some imperialist powers have more aggressive designs on the world, based on some confection of political-military strength and economic weakness (or vice versa), has been a philosopher's stone for outright social-chauvinism. In the name of a "greater fascist danger," the Communist Parties in the Allied imperialist countries pursued policies that objectively aided the conquests by their own bourgeoisies. In the name of a "greater" Soviet danger, the "three worlds theory" propagated by the Chinese revisionists, headed by Deng Xiaoping, sanctifies capitulation to the Western bloc (a position which could easily flip to capitulation to the Soviet Union since it is predicated on a "main danger"). With the accumulation of further experience and understanding, it becomes necessary and possible to build on Lenin's scientific and internationalist explanation of the underlying cause and class character of interimperialist war.

Let us begin with the role of superstructural influences and the relation between political and economic factors. The principal and decisive rivalries in a particular spiral are not merely extensions of economic competition, and war does not invariably break out when a major change occurs in the balance of economic strength between vying imperialist powers. Many other developments in the political and economic realm occur which shape particular alignments and which may precipitate the actual escalation to military conflict.[168] We mentioned the erroneous conclusions drawn by the Comintern from the real economic combat between the two strongest industrial powers in the 1920s. Similarly, there is today intense economic competition between Japan and other imperialists in the U.S.-led bloc, including the U.S. but even more so the various West European powers — indeed, this may well be the sharpest economic competition raging in the world — and yet these

[168] The political division of the world also includes as a major element the strength and actual disposition of forces of the international proletariat. This was one very important factor that helped weld together the imperialist bloc headed by the U.S. at the end of World War 2.

powers are not preparing to assault each other militarily. They are, in fact, lining up in the same war bloc, for the time being at least, and even should they end up in opposing blocs as a result of some "switching of sides," that would not be a direct outcome of the economic competition between them, but a product of overall world relations and the overall intensification of contradictions, in particular among the imperialists. Rivalry expresses the underlying economic contradictions of capital, but not as a direct or immediate correlate.

This phenomenon of "lining up" is of necessity mainly a matter of political and military strength; in the context of the present spiral, the United States and the Soviet Union are the two major imperialist powers capable of mobilizing the military resources and marshaling the political strength in the international arena to forge and lead war blocs. In fact, the United States and the Soviet Union have not been mainly engaged in an economic contest that has suddenly become military. Their interaction has not principally taken the form of outproducing and out-trading each other in the same markets, nor have they been busily invading and muscling into each other's markets. Essentially, their contention on a *strategic* level has subsumed and conditioned economic conflicts.

The ability of each imperialist country to contend internationally depends on its *aggregate* power, which is not reducible to the size of its GNP or the volume of industrial output. In this connection Lenin noted:

> [S]trength varies with the degree of economic and political development. In order to understand what is taking place, it is necessary to know what questions are settled by the changes in strength. The question as to whether these changes are "purely" economic or *non*economic (e.g., military) is a secondary one, which cannot in the least affect the fundamental views on the latest epoch of capitalism.[169]

Quite obviously, for instance, the political strength of the Soviet Union is far greater than what its economic base, pure and simple, would suggest. Although its clout is hardly unrelated to that economic strength — which is indeed important — by itself, this is secondary.

Now Lenin's application of the concept of uneven development

---

[169] *Imperialism*, p. 89 (*LCW*, 22, p. 253).

to the relations between nation-states — i.e., that different imperialist powers at any given time experience unequal rates of growth and occupy different positions in the structure of international relations — has been invoked by various opportunists to support national defensism. This is the notion that the cause of interimperialist war resides in a certain disequilibrium between, on the one side, those advanced powers which enjoy political hegemony in the world (over colonies, well-developed trade and currency zones, etc.) and yet whose economic strength is no longer commensurate with such spoils and, on the other side, the parvenus whose economic dynamism is constrained by the political muscle of the "privileged" powers. Depending on the imperialist loyalties of the particular theorists, one side or the other is the culprit. The "underdogs" who had been "pushed around" and denied their "rightful" place in world affairs by the more established powers have no choice but to regain or assert their national rights and even to "liberate" the oppressed in countries dominated by their rivals; or, alternately, these upstarts, who are more aggressive, bellicose, and the real instigators of war, force the dominant powers to "defend" a "legitimate" status quo and to "protect" those under their jackboot from the onset of worse horrors. Such arguments were flung about and canonized during the last two world wars; they were pernicious and self-serving then and are every bit as wrong and chauvinist today.

Is it true that some imperialist powers are "hungrier" than others? Is the root cause of interimperialist war the disparity originating in the outcome of previous wars between the victors and vanquished or between imperialist "haves" and "have-nots"? Scientific analysis proves otherwise. We are dealing with the complex modalities of internationalized capitals. These nodal points in the development of a spiral, which world wars have to date signified, arise when the structure of capital on a world scale and the structure of international power relations compel the imperialist powers to seek a new, more favorable division of the world. With respect to the current spiral, the Soviet Union has not surpassed the U.S. in overall economic strength or grown faster than Japan; yet it requires a larger sphere of influence than it now has to resolve the crisis within its bloc. The United States, on the other hand, has not completely lost its economic preeminence, yet it no less desperately needs a redivision of the world. All imperialisms must restructure on the basis of expansion. Not only this, but each must prevent the other from obtaining a more favorable division of the world.[170]

That the "lesser" imperialists of this spiral must "line up" with either the U.S. or the Soviet imperialists scarcely lets them "off the hook." They are no less subject to these objective laws and, actually, uneven development among the U.S. and its European and Japanese allies is one factor inducing these "lesser" imperialists themselves to seek a more favorable division of the world, although, paradoxically, they can only do this by allying with the United States (or switching to a comparable "junior slot" in the opposing Soviet-led bloc). And, so, while superstructural factors interpenetrate with economic laws — in this case, strategic necessity mutes the anarchy and uneven development among the imperialists within one bloc — anarchy and rivalry in the world as a whole cannot be overcome. The contradictions arising from the accumulation process within one bloc cannot be permanently contained. Rather, they are desperately channeled into antagonistic confrontation with another bloc (although contention will continue within these blocs). Thus, there is necessity on both sides and within both blocs.

The only way that the requisite recasting can be effected is through war. At a certain point, particular national capitals (or blocs of such capitals) emerge as direct and immediate barriers to each other. What transforms a particular international framework into an obstacle to the continued expansion and reorganization of capital is the dialectical interaction of economic crisis, developing out of a specific dynamic of internationalized accumulation, with the political challenge of rival imperialist powers — all of which is affected as well by revolutionary struggles in various countries (and the class struggle, on one level or another, within all countries).

In this context we must examine how relatively separate imperialist capitals codetermine the barriers each confronts. We have spoken of internationalized capital flows, yet these are deformed and broken up by monopoly, national states, blocs, and colonial systems. In the previous spiral, there was a specifiable sterling zone, a franc zone, etc., and in this spiral there are two relatively independent blocs. As a result, varied but definite patterns of ac-

---

[170] Here it might also be pointed out that in World War 1 and World War 2, imperialist powers lacking a favorable division of the world and beset with major weaknesses could be found on both sides.

cumulation can be discerned in individual countries and blocs and a rather clear bloc-wide dynamic of crisis can be mapped in the U.S. and Soviet blocs, respectively; in the U.S.-led bloc, this dynamic found concentrated expression in the synchronized downturn of 1973-75 which was linked with an ensemble of historical factors, including capital flow patterns among the imperialists, the Vietnam War, and other phenomena. However, particular national and bloc formations are indissolubly part of a single, world imperialist economy. They are mutually determined and integrated into a single process of world accumulation.

In essence, division into countries and blocs is relative and conditional. Capital tends to flow, albeit unevenly, to the maximum extent permitted by the bounds of a specific political division. Within the whole of the imperialist-dominated world, imperialist capitals act reciprocally on each other, exactly because capital accumulates internationally and exactly because capital remains profoundly national. That is, they interact as rivals in a world that can only be redivided among them. In short, these discrete elements taken together constitute and are integrated into a single process, a process which reacts back through these boundaries and divisions. Whatever particular configuration political alliances and boundaries, currency and trade zones may take, there is but one world to be divided. Hence, the thrust of accumulation in particular countries and blocs must bear on others.

On the most obvious level, capital flows tend to penetrate barriers erected by other imperialist states (or blocs), if initially as a trickle. In this spiral, for instance, the two blocs have been more isolated from each other than were the opposing groups of imperialist capital in the pre-World War 2 period (although the world as a whole is far more integrated). Nevertheless, an increasing degree of interpenetration could be observed through the 1970s and early 1980s. This is especially true in the neocolonies, like India, but is also of some moment in Western and Eastern Europe, with Poland, perhaps, the most striking example. Clearly, such flows are connected with the economic crisis in the Western alliance (and earlier attempts to expand investment opportunities) and with certain long-term structural weaknesses and deformations in the Eastern bloc. But these capital movements have also had distinctive political and strategic overtones. This emphasizes the role of rivalry in establishing contact points and transmission belts of crisis between such blocs (although these flows have not eroded the structure or obliterated the dynamics of bloc-wide development).

Indeed, as emphasized, rivalry is inseparably linked with the internationalization of capital. Yet the impact of rivalry is not reducible to the sheer magnitude of inter-bloc capital flows nor is reciprocal influence tantamount to the possible "echo" effects of crisis in one bloc on conditions in another. Some further illustrations from the current spiral will help clarify the fact that imperialist capitals, by dint of their internationalized mode of existence in a world completely divided up, mutually condition each other.

In the early and mid-1960s, particularly after the Cuban missile crisis, there was no military confrontation between the United States and the Soviet Union; in many parts of the world they actually colluded with each other. Nevertheless, the United States did not at this time simply export capital on the basis of where it could obtain the highest rate of return. The U.S. imperialists took into account the position of the Soviet Union as a potential global adversary. Even though the Alliance For Progress was carried out mainly to restructure capital and to derail mass struggles in Latin America, it was also formulated with an eye towards countering Soviet influence, or, more precisely, preserving the upper hand for U.S. imperialism in the context of U.S.-Soviet collusion. The Soviets, needless to say, also made similar calculations. Yet more striking, perhaps, is how such rivalry, even when it is not filtered through such capital flows, still has important economic repercussions.

One of the major expressions of uneven development between the two blocs is the extremely unbalanced structure of the Soviet economy, specifically a bloated, resource-draining military and an associated heavy industrial sector, which lends a peculiar complexion to crisis in that country and its bloc. But this can hardly be separated from the necessity faced by the Soviets to respond to the United States on the international plane. When the Soviet Union emerged as an imperialist power in the 1950s, it confronted a previously determined division of the world, largely reflecting the dominance of U.S. imperialism, which influenced how and to what degree the Soviet social-imperialists mobilized and allocated capital. The prevailing division of the world, coupled with a complex of international economic relations and political struggles, reacted upon the internal necessity of the Soviet Union to expand and ultimately to recast this very division of the world.[171]

---

[171] If the Soviet Union faces in the United States a stronger imperialism, with a more developed international network, it is also the case that the Soviet Union has not "come out of nowhere." It was able to pull an entire part of the world, notably large sections of Eastern Europe which had been in various stages of political transi-

This international framework and rivalry, interacting with the historical foundation upon which capitalism was restored in the Soviet Union (a highly centralized, planned economy) and with revisionist ideology itself, has resulted in a massively bureaucratized and militarized economy that is at once an Achilles' heel and a source of strength. In one context, then, the Soviet bloc's economic problems are external to those of the West; in another, broader context they mutually and reciprocally interpenetrate with Western problems — and only by dealing with its global antagonist can the Soviet bloc overcome its crisis.

XII

Thus far in the history of imperialism, world war has constituted a nodal point in the transition from one spiral to the next; objectively, these have been war-to-war spirals. Indeed, one of the most crucial features of the imperialist epoch is the purgative function world war plays in the accumulation process. World war is mainly a product of the anarchy/organization contradiction. Polarization into and the confrontation between two political-military blocs is a concentrated expression of the struggle among "many capitals" and the underlying necessity of capital to reorganize its conditions of existence. Not until imperialism is overthrown can such wars be eliminated; their basis lies in the very requirements of this mode of production.

In the imperialist era, the appearance of crisis signifies that certain economic contradictions and political conflicts have arisen in the context of the existing division of the world and, yet, cannot be overcome within it, thrusting the world imperialist system into convulsions. This is distinct from premonopoly crisis which arose mainly from within a national framework. To be sure, classical crises were never "purely economic" affairs. But the preconditions for

---

tion, into its imperialist orbit, based on the leadership it previously exercised over them in the socialist camp, on a critical mass of military strength, and on the forms of economic integration previously established. This, along with its ability to also transform its relations with some Third World countries relatively quickly, provided it with certain reserves useful to its interests. Though not so significant a factor as the division of the world it faced, the fact that it could begin to forge its own international division of labor also influenced the internal structure of its economy and imposed new requirements on it.

the resolution of imperialist crisis are more emphatically and decisively situated in the realm of the superstructure. The destruction and reorganization of capital is now bound up with and ultimately hinges on the political-military defeat of some imperialisms by others. War and its outcome create a new structure for the world economy and establish an environment within which it becomes possible to do certain things. A new division of the world is the main determinant, apart from the limiting factor of revolution, of capital's ability to reorganize its international coordinates. So, if one were to ask what catapulted the United States to the top of the imperialist hierarchy, the answer is World War 2, not the gradual economic or technological overtaking of others. To account for the twenty-five year period of relative stability and expansion in the U.S. bloc after World War 2, one must start with the economic and political changes wrought by that war, the total reorganization of capital, and the redistribution of colonies and spheres of influence its outcome entailed. These were what enabled the U.S. imperialists to restructure the world capitalist order, in a manner favorable not only to their own interests but to the accumulation process in general.[172]

We have stressed that imperialist capital is anchored to national markets and states at the same time that it must function as internationalized capital. With the accumulation and sharpening of contradictions in the international arena, a threshold is reached when only the establishment of new power relations, by and to the advantage of particular imperialists, will permit the institution of new economic relations adequate to the global needs of imperialist capital. Things are not simply put back to where they were before the outbreak of war; the same capitals are not born again out of the ashes. The violent recasting of the international framework through war represents a leap in the organization of internationalized capital: the structure and allocation of capital, within national formations and on a world scale, is transformed. Crisis is the real concentration and forcible adjustment of the contradictions of bourgeois economy. In the imperialist epoch *interimperialist war is the only substantial "adjustment" of these contradictions that can occur, that is, outside their worldwide revolutionary resolution.*

---

[172] That the other imperialists were "dealt in" to the postwar arrangements was connected to the confrontation with the socialist camp, and that such an order was established was connected to the overwhelmingly dominant position of U.S. imperialism.

War, however, is not an economic phenomenon, like merger, although war mobilization has important economic effects which will be discussed shortly. The imperialists do not consciously go to war to restructure capital; they wage war because they must defeat global rivals and redivide the world. Interimperialist rivalry culminating in the violent collision of imperialist national capitals is not, therefore, the same as economic competition or simply a response to economic pressures; interimperialist rivalry and war have their own internal logic. More specifically, the intensification of contradictions in a particular spiral reaches a point past which a major strategic gain by either side can no longer occur without rupturing the whole framework. Any change of such magnitude in the international equation might embolden the immediate beneficiary to launch a bid for decisive advantage and supremacy or precipitate a massive, preemptive response from the other. Given these conditions, a major revolutionary upsurge or economic jolt in one or several countries or within a bloc would seriously affect the balance of strength and perhaps decisively influence the whole matrix and the imperialists' whole calculus. In any case, an inherently unstable and mutually threatening situation must be overcome — one side must prevail over the other.

War, then, has its own dialectic. The imperialists do not go to war to escape depression or only after economic crisis has deteriorated to a predetermined breaking point. World War 1, for example, did not occur amidst a worldwide depression, yet World War 2 did. And the Depression of the 1930s was not the key moment of that spiral; the war itself was. The destruction and carnage of that war was not somehow a direct function of the preceding level of unemployment or decline in industrial output. It was linked with the intensity and scope of interimperialist rivalry (which was entwined with but not reducible to economic crisis), further developments in military technology (weapons, transport, and delivery systems), and the whole motion of imperialism towards further integration of the world and the intensification of its major contradictions. In the present spiral, there may be a depression like that of the 1930s prior to the outbreak of world war, but the imperialists may well have to go to war (unless this war is prevented by revolution) before the world economy reaches such a pass. Nevertheless, imperialism is today confronted with its most serious crisis.

Still, if war has its own logic, that logic and the resultant destruction are a continuation of a certain class politics, serve specific class ends, and grow out of the environment of commodity production. And the transformations and outcome of interimperialist war make it possible and necessary for the victorious capitals to put things back together on the most favorable footing, in accordance with the laws of capitalist accumulation as expressed in the imperialist epoch. Again, the imperialists cannot escape their environment and capital cannot simply maintain itself and its international inter-relations as they have been. The contradictory process of the destruction and restructuring of capital — which is at the heart of capitalist accumulation — is heightened in this era.

The immediate object of interimperialist war is to knock down rivals, to qualitatively enhance and bolster the global leverage and freedom of expansion of some imperialist capitals at the expense of others. Whether or not the imperialists subjectively recognize this, the economic factor objectively compelling world war is the inabili-ty of capital to adequately reorganize its overall relations of produc-tion, its general international framework. Yet war is more than a singular concentration of the contradictions of accumulation and the struggle between imperialist rivals. The intensification of rivalry and the murmurings of upheaval in the colonies and ad-vanced countries, or the potential for and the actual eruption of really cataclysmic revolutionary struggles, are all dialectically related. As contradictions gather force and become more explo-sively concentrated in the international arena, the imperialists recognize that their entire order — and their own place in it — is at stake; which is to say, they must deal with economic dislocations, global adversaries, and the oppressed people in a more conclusive fashion. Put differently, world war becomes, for the imperialists, the only way out of this kind of all-consuming and multidimen-sional crisis.

If they are to temporarily resolve any of the major contradic-tions they face, the imperialists must go to war and carve out a new division of spoils. Again, not to risk war is to guarantee losing con-trol over everything, since the contradictions can only grow more intense and the contagion of political and economic crisis will spread. These pressures and constraints are transmuted into the drive for global power and supremacy. Consider the situation of Nazi Germany. Suppression of the masses and war mobilization were quite obviously related to economic crisis and rivalry, in par-ticular, to satisfying the international requirements of German capital. But the temporary stabilization associated with mobiliza-tion and, more important and fundamental, the struggle for redivision and its fruits were also essential towards combating the reemergence and exacerbation of the very conditions that bred insurrection and threatened the very rule of German capital in the post-World War 1 period. This is not to say that the imperialists specifically launch war to forestall revolution, or that it is only under revolutionary pressure that they will pursue this form of conflict. Rather, it is to underscore both the omnibus crisis conditions which engulf them and the limited number of actual options at hand.

In a certain sense, the metaphor "window of vulnerability" (or "opportunity") that has been bandied about by the U.S. imperialists captures the reality of their situation. If the Soviets do not act against the U.S. within a certain time frame — and the U.S. imperialists also apply this logic from their perspective — then, given the overall situation, they may suffer a catastrophic defeat. For both blocs, there exists the danger of unraveling and crumbling on many different fronts, economic and political, including revolutions in the Brazils or Indias and the possibility of social-political crises in the imperialist citadels themselves leading to revolutionary initiatives, perhaps even successful revolutions. Indeed, countering this pervasive vulnerability — even at the cost of wiping out much of human civilization — is part of the underlying, if obscene, logic of imperialist war.

The redistribution and concentration of political power among the imperialists is the fundamental condition for recomposing the international interrelations of capital in a manner favorable to renewed accumulation. One or the other antagonist must be knocked down and subordinated.[173] Capitalism's ability to overcome global crisis hinges on the wholesale reorganization of the imperialist-dominated world, within which the reallocation of colonial territories plays a pivotal role. That many of the most crucial battles during the last two world wars were fought in Europe is not at odds

---

[173] Consequently, while the imperialists might factor the preservation of some productive forces into their military calculations — in the choice, for instance, of military or population versus industrial targets — this is secondary to and overridden by the need to cripple the war-making capacity of an adversary. The basic law of warfare holds: to preserve oneself it is necessary to destroy one's enemy. On the other hand, it is not always possible — or necessarily desirable — for some imperialists to fully vanquish their rivals. Rather, they seek the most favorable terms of victory given the actual military course of war and the various political factors that come to bear on its resolution, including domestic morale and revolutionary advances in various parts of the world.

with the fact that the most decisive areas into which imperialist capital must expand are the colonies.

The object of the struggle for world supremacy is not the plunder of the domestic imperialist economies; the previous two world wars have not resulted in the wholesale colonization of some imperialisms by others. Of course, the exigencies of war dictate invasions and occupations; moreover, the victorious imperialists will (or can, for that matter) hardly reorganize things on the basis of equality among imperialisms. But previous interimperialist occupations have, despite the practice of annexation and the redrawing of boundaries, been largely temporary and selective (the partition of Germany and the deployment of NATO troops in West Germany is inseparable from the "containment" of the Soviet Union), and the bourgeoisies of these countries have generally neither lost their independence nor ceased being imperialists, although imperialism can certainly create new states (as it did out of the Austro-Hungarian empire, for example).

It is, above all, the redistribution and more thoroughgoing penetration and subordination of already oppressed nations for which the imperialists fight, and, in the aftermath of war, the social structures and political economies of the oppressed nations reflect this.[174] To the victors goes the fundamental right and privilege of

---

[174] The very cohesiveness of the imperialist social formations presents obstacles to long-term external control of these countries and the deracination of a national imperialist bourgeoisie. Their social and historical development militates against wholesale domination by other imperialisms. Germany, for instance, was divided at the end of World War 2, but it was not annexed or turned into a French department like Algeria. The imperialists require a modicum of allegiance, or at least passivity, from the metropolitan working classes; they also face the task of forging new interimperialist alliances. Hence, there are political imperatives which impede the "colonization" of the advanced countries and which preserve the distinction between the oppressor and oppressed nations (even where some of the former have been defeated in war). The working class can be put on rations in the imperialist countries, but this itself bespeaks an objective necessity to attend to the maintenance of a work force. In the oppressed nations, where traditional, subsistence modes of production persist to varying degrees and where there is a huge surplus layer of the work force, the imperialists need not concern themselves to the same extent with the reproduction and sustenance of a local proletariat. With respect to the colonies, the territorial division of the world need not assume the form of open colonization or formal agreements and condominiums. It is bound up with the overall exercise of political, economic, and military control — thus the widespread practice of neocolonialism, especially since the end of World War 2. Rarely are colonial preserves or national markets in general wholly protected from other capitals, although the preponderant influence of one or allied powers over particular markets and regions establishes the objective basis for spheres of influence and blocs.

becoming the dominant exploiters of the colonies: this is the foundation of a new imperial order. Still, the determining element overall is the *international framework as a whole, not the colonies taken by themselves.* With the establishment of new imperialist power relations and a new structure of capital it becomes possible to exploit the colonies on terms and in a context which pushes accumulation qualitatively forward. [175]

But even the restructuring of the entire imperialist order can only be partial and temporary; the convergence and intensification of world contradictions also propel major revolutionary advances, and the outcome of these wars ultimately intensifies the fundamental contradiction of the bourgeois epoch. In this light, let us turn to the question of restructuring.

Classical overproduction crises resolved themselves, it will be recalled, through the destruction of a portion of the total capital; out of the struggle for survival emerged not only larger, but more efficient units of capital. The restructuring of a critical segment of the total capital altered the overall value composition and structure of capital, thereby restoring conditions of profitability. In the imperialist stage, world war objectively performs a similar purgative function. The purgative thrust of world war interacts with other political factors and the crisis tendencies of capital. In the dynamic of events and transformations leading up to war, and still more in its prosecution and aftermath, a complex process of destructive renewal and reorganization takes place. This results in more efficient capitals within the imperialist countries, that is, a more efficient mass of national capital, predicated on modernization and capital's distribution in new proportions. And it can effect the establishment of a more efficient international division of labor.

---

[175] This means that even the opening of a vast new market in the colonies may not, at a given point in a spiral, substantially push forward accumulation. That China, for instance, has thrown itself open to Western capital — its capitulation at least now taking the form of moving into the orbit of the Western bloc — has had no significant leavening effect on crisis, nor has it obviated the need for total redivision, visions of a one-billion person consumer market notwithstanding. The depth of the world economic crisis, from which China is now hardly immune, sets limits to the tapping of these possibilities and the intensity of interimperialist rivalry imposes additional constraints on the viability of piecemeal restructuring. The primacy of the international framework does not mean, then, that with some switches by particular countries from one bloc to another the international conditions will thereby ripen for accumulation — it is precisely this entire framework as such that must be altered as the necessary condition for thoroughly exploiting such areas of investment and markets.

Crisis continues to play a purgative role in the imperialist era. There is still a process of "weeding out" and "eating up" going on, and it is raised to a higher level, with the very big absorbing the very big. In the monopoly stage of capitalism, however, the maneuvering room of the bourgeoisie, as concentrated in the countercrisis measures of the imperialist state (the scope of which depends on international reserves and political necessity), increases for a time, only to turn into its opposite and impose far greater necessity. These attempts to broadly counteract disruptive trends and to forestall the collapse of large monopolized capitals, with its potentially devastating consequences, are particular to the development and unfolding of imperialist crisis. But at a deeper level, countercrisis initiatives are a manifestation of the heightening of the contradiction between organization and anarchy — because they only make for a more explosive situation. [176]

Hence, if the destructive force of crisis is temporarily attenuated, eventually it will assert itself more powerfully. Yet exactly because capital functions in an international framework, central to which is imperialist (nation-state) rivalry, this dynamic is linked with and becomes part of an even more violent struggle for the "survival of the fittest" — interimperialist war. The economic processes associated with crisis do not in themselves, either in individual countries or aggregately, generate the requisite conditions for the successful renewal of accumulation, for the qualitative recasting that is objectively demanded.

The centralized mobilization of human, technical, and financial resources is the sine qua non of total war. The organization of war production is founded on unprecedented rationalization, the concrete forms of which vary according to historical circumstances. The state must intervene more forcefully, mandating and presiding over merger and financial restructuring, and the selective disbursement of war contracts promotes further centralization.

War production in general elicits expansion and facilitates economies of scale, while raw materials must be husbanded and waste reduced, and labor discipline must be exacted more ruthlessly. At

---

[176] Indeed, the unprecedented seriousness of the current crisis stems in part from the "pressure-cooker" atmosphere as the imperialists have tried to keep so many different components of internationalized accumulation intact. Another sign of the increased anarchy of capitalism is that more powerfully situated monopolies may weed out more efficient nonmonopolies and more efficient, but "lesser," monopolies; in this sense, the purgative function is also distorted.

the level of productive technique, new or previously unprofitable technologies are tapped and pressed into service, even spawning new industries. For example, the fundamental impetus for large-scale airplane manufacture came from World War 1, and various synthetic materials and the modern electronics industry were basically products of the Second World War. The "eating up" of less efficient capital by more efficient capital and the rechanneling of resources as part of war-related investment spur higher levels of productivity. Although such measures are temporary, their effects are long-term.[177] And on the heels of war, an initial stimulus to production comes from the reconversion needs associated with pent-up demand and reconstruction.

If the imperialists can embark on such rationalization, then why do they not continue with such domestic restructuring instead of going to war? Simply because they can do this only for so long. The allocation and absorption of resources required by an enlarged military sector create massive imbalances, result in the severe restriction of consumer goods production (with all the political fallout that entails), and lead to the erosion of the very base on which the military rests. Without a redivision of the world, militarization only aggravates the dynamic of crisis and actually accelerates the drive toward war precisely because it throws the economy even more off-balance and cannot be profitably sustained. A war economy, then, is itself not the fundamental solution to crisis, but only a means to obtain and protect the spoils of conquest. Lacking this, it loses not only its raison d'être, but the means to continue.[178]

---

[177] For a considerable period during World Wars 1 and 2, capital was operating more efficiently in all the adversary economies. In the immediate aftermath of these wars the surviving mass of imperialist capital was still on the whole newer, relative to prewar productive capacity.

[178] One hackneyed social-reformist argument holds that war is in essence a plot by the munitions makers (or, less crudely put, that war production simply makes for profitable business). The imperialists go to war, it is argued, to rev up their flagging economies. This denies both the reality of interimperialist rivalry, stemming from real material conflicts, and the very character of armaments production. In the final analysis, without an international base of surplus value to support it, military expenditure is a drag on the reproductive process, as essential as it is to the demands of empire. (The political economy of military expenditure will be analyzed in a subsequent volume.) The corollary proposition, i.e., that the imperialists should be building schools and hospitals instead of tanks and missiles, masks the fact that profit rules production and that the imperialists must at certain points redivide the world through war, which means they must prepare for it, and that they must have massive military strength for "lesser wars" and for the purpose of intimidating actual or potential rivals as well as oppressed masses.

Nor does physical destruction in itself render capital more profitable. If this were all that was required, the capitalists could just as well blow up their own factories and burn down their cities — a veritable orgy of self-destruction as a basis for reconstruction. Certainly, a considerable portion of the productive forces is physically wiped out by war, but what facilitates recovery and expansion is not the simple act of rebuilding. The point is that this rebuilding can now be accomplished in a more concentrated and centralized way and on a new political basis, that is, in the context of new international alignments and division of colonies.

All these economic changes — through crisis, war production, and reconstruction — are secondary to and only become operative as more or less stimulative factors in connection with the concrete shift in international political relations achieved through war and the reorganization of production relations made possible on the basis of its outcome. This process of reorganization goes on all the time, but it now takes a qualitative leap. What is the relationship between the politics of redivision and the economics of a massive and global restructuring of capital? The key link in this process is the triumph of some imperialist powers over others and the degree to which they can stave off revolutionary advances in various parts of the world.

Crisis grows out of the interaction of many capitals in the international arena. This driving force of accumulation is conditioned by the general features of the epoch — the modus operandi of finance capital, the structural differences between the oppressor and oppressed nations, etc. — and by the particularities of each spiral, such as the political alignments defining a specific "operating fraternity" of imperialist capitals and the various political and revolutionary struggles in the world. The accentuated anarchy to which this gives rise can only be overcome by the victory of some over others. This is principal. Secondarily, within all these countries, the weaker (and often less efficient) capitals, as we have seen, are absorbed or eliminated in the centralizing tendencies which gather momentum through crisis and war preparations. The defeat and subordination of certain imperialist powers diminishes for a while the intensity of global antagonism among the imperialists. The economic base from which and the international network through which the defeated powers formerly pursued their imperial ambitions at cross-purposes with the ambitions of others, are shattered or greatly weakened. As a consequence, the victorious powers obtain a new degree of flexibility and maneuverability in the world. But pounding a rival into submission and restructuring capital are, of course, not one and the same thing. While dependent on the former, the latter is a distinct process and its substance requires closer examination.

One aspect of reorganization is its impact on the international division of labor, the specific range of which is established by the concrete relations between victors and vanquished among the imperialists and by the scope of revolutionary advance (the imperialists must maintain their rule over the masses in their citadels and maintain their hold over as many of the colonies as possible). The international division of labor involves the allocation of social labor towards the production of specific material elements entering the reproductive process. The enlargement or contraction of international spheres of influence and their overall level of integration condition the nature and forms of international specialization of production of particular use values. And this bears directly on the degree to which the comparative productivity advantages of particular national units of capital can be brought into play.

Where capital is exported, which industries are expanded overseas relative to their previous domestic concentration, and, in general, what is developed and where, are all principally determined through the international restructuring of capital. Within a new imperialist hierarchy the possibilities for a new and more rational distribution of productive efficiencies are enhanced. Through World War 2 the victorious imperialists lifted various trade and investment barriers in order to facilitate more extensive capital flows, access to raw materials, etc. Some illustrations may be useful. Post-World War 2 West Germany did not rebuild its economy or trade patterns along the model of Germany's prewar structure. As it had now become part of a more integrated bloc, this national capital could, for instance, rely on other imperialists for certain inputs which previously it produced domestically, though less efficiently. Consequently, investment resources were directed into other areas. Moreover, since much of the rebuilding was from the ground up, the new capital formed was more technically advanced than its counterpart in some other imperialist countries, and this in turn contributed to the overall productivity of the bloc.[179] And since West Germany and Japan were dealt in to the

---

[179] The victors reorganize on the basis of spoils; they do not face the same necessity (as the vanquished have) to largely build from scratch to catch up and eventually overtake. Here the question of which use values are produced in which proportions dovetails with the question of the internal expansion of parasitic sectors in the economies of the victors as a function of their international position.

new intra-bloc arrangements (indeed, Germany's historical pattern of trade with the primary producers of Eastern Europe was radically altered as a result of the new political situation), they could, for example, receive cheap oil from the Middle East, which also influenced both the allocation and profitability of the mass of West German and of Japanese capitals.

Yet another example of the transformation of the international structure and efficiency of capital can be seen in the colonies. In the oppressed nations, the utilization of land and allocation of capital are, in the aftermath of war, fixed by a whole new international arrangement. Where previously, perhaps, the expansion of certain industries, raw materials exploitation, or the amount of land in cultivation was limited by the particular configuration of existing imperialist relations to which the oppressed nations were subordinated, their integration into a new imperial order recasts all of this.

Capitalism cannot exist without continually modifying its production relations, and the redistribution and concentration of political power enable the imperialists, especially the victorious ones, to carry this out in a more thoroughgoing way. This is completely bound up with new opportunities for expansion, and embraces both quantitative and qualitative transformations. In the advanced countries, capital grows more concentrated and centralized through the press of events; these are mainly quantitative changes that continue as new production possibilities open up. However, qualitative changes occur as well — during the postwar period in Italy and Japan, for instance, the continued transformation of handicrafts production and peasant agriculture had as its counterpart a huge influx of rural inhabitants into modern industry. Concentration also has a direct international thrust. The financial order set up under the baton of the U.S. imperialists, for instance, served, on the one hand, to facilitate retooling and reorganization throughout the bloc and, on the other, as a means through which, especially in the face of recessionary pressures, the U.S. imperialists gained control of productive resources and further concentrated capital on an international scale. Concomitant with this concentration are the deeper penetration of imperialist capital into the oppressed nations and the transformation of some precapitalist relations of production.

In the current spiral, this phenomenon has found significant expression in certain parts of the Third World, and the expansion of the postwar period is inseparable from it. It is not merely a matter of which crops, for instance, can be grown on previously un- or under-utilized land, but of the installation of new production relations. Such changes, particularly in the countryside, have been of great moment in the process of imperialist accumulation during this spiral, and they have interacted with tremendous quantitative changes as well: the further concentration of capital and the striking and unprecedented expansion of the already existing industrial urban centers in the oppressed nations under the domination of imperialist capital. These changes react back upon a new international structure of capital as a source of superprofits.

The most fundamental product of the new totality of international connections and internal interrelations established through war is the radical transformation of value relations and the constitution of conditions which permit profitable expansion in its international dimensions. The new political alignment sets the general framework within which occur the interrelated processes that have been described. The expansion of production in the colonies as part of their integration into a new order and the breaking up of some (and generally not all) precapitalist relations; the establishment of a new international division of labor and new intra-imperialist investment and trade patterns; the further concentration of capital — these will result in a general cheapening of the elements entering into the reproduction process, both as constant and variable capital. Centralization and access to more open and integrated markets facilitate economies of scale and the profitable and extensive application of new technologies. West European and Japanese expansion and modernization, for example, involved huge and costly fixed-capital investments. The existence of vast and interrelated export markets and the continuity and scale of production they afforded made it possible, along with other factors, to recoup and make good on these investments. Similarly, U.S. capital could spread its huge research and development outlays over a large total output (much of which is produced overseas), thereby reducing such outlays per sales dollar.

However, overcoming barriers to accumulation is not simply a matter of altering the aggregate composition of capital. We have stressed that the aggregate capital, on the national or the bloc level, is composed of discrete and competing capitals which develop unevenly. The other side to this question of value relations is the recomposition of relations within this total capital, that is, the transformation of the interrelations among particular units of capital nationally and internationally such that they stand in a more proportional and articulated relation to each other. Objectively, these units form part of the international division of labor and distribution of capital, of a highly socialized and interdependent mass of capital. But, again, this mass of capital is individuated into discrete capitals of different composition which reproduce at differing rates and levels of efficiency. Towards the end of a spiral, the specific global distribution of the "many capitals" comes into conflict with the general requirements of accumulation. Capital is tied up where it is not needed while sectors or industries crucial to counteracting declining profitability are undercapitalized and therefore frequently fail to keep pace with the needs of others. All these are major elements of anarchy and crisis.

War clears the ground, so to speak, to start anew. Through liquidation, new international investment, state subsidies, joint ventures in infrastructure development, etc., this situation is temporarily overcome. The imperialists effect a new proportional allocation of capital so that the forward motion of the individual units, elements, and circuits of capital corresponds more to the overall needs and contributes more to the overall profitability of internationalized imperialist capital. But what this represents is a higher degree of order within disorder. Exactly because capital cannot consciously organize itself as a totality, such a redistribution of capital must inevitably lead again to crisis and explosive antagonism.

To sum up: the establishment of a new global complex of accumulation, the various links of which stand in a definite relation to and are conditioned by this complex, gives impetus to accumulation on a world scale. It is effectuated by a process of destruction — the defeat of rivals, the dismantling of old empires, and the annihilation of weaker capitals. But just as there is no predetermined pattern to the spirals of imperialism, there is no archetypal redivision of the world. The struggle for world supremacy and the class contradiction mutually condition each other. Each redivision reflects contingent political factors and will be invested with specific properties. There is no law which says that a single dominant power must emerge out of world war and there is no determined line of development, for instance, toward larger blocs or a more comprehensive international division of labor.[180] A more in-

---

[180] Had the division of the world following World War 2 been more like that following World War 1, it is very unlikely that agriculture would have been modernized to the degree and in the way it was in the United States or that industrialization would have gone so far in Brazil, to take two significant developments in this spiral. This emphasizes again how international conditions are the basis for change in particular countries.

tegrated pre-World War 1 global financial network, organized around the pound, gave way after that war to fragmented (and ultimately fractious) currency and trade blocs, given the specific outcome of that war. The highly integrated dollar-based international monetary order, established as a result of the massive U.S. victory after World War 2, and the related extension of international credit facilitated the more rapid international turnover of capital and its expansion. Further, since interimperialist world wars are, after all, military contests fought through to lesser or greater victory, their immediate outcome may not, in some important aspects, correspond to the economic requirements of durable expansion (even though such wars objectively recompose the conditions for renewed accumulation). But whatever the specific terms of redivision and reorganization, leaps are made in organization at the level of individual and national capital — and in the dissolution of precapitalist relations throughout the world. There are factors inherent in the accumulation process which make larger and more integrated international forms of organization a desideratum of growth and expansion. Yet capital is locked into modes of private appropriation and grounded in national markets. In the imperialist epoch, *both aspects of the contradiction between organization and anarchy intensify.* Capitalism is in violent transition to something higher.

XIII

The outcome of interimperialist war engenders a new spiral of development, marked by new contradictions and the emergence of new forces. For the imperialists, war is a specific kind of resolution of contradictions, but the reorganization this dictates and makes possible will, over the actual course of a spiral, lead to an increase in international disorder. The transformations and thrusts forward actuated by redivision turn into their opposite. And this is interpenetrated by and interconnected with diverse political and revolutionary struggles which themselves sharpen as crisis and interimperialist rivalry intensify. In other words, the same process bringing the imperialists into violent collision with each other accentuates the major contradictions of this era, including the various forms of expression of the class contradiction. In the modern epoch, the spiral motion on an international plane reaches a point of conjuncture at which the major contradictions of the spiral, mutually determining and interpenetrating each other, are, as Stalin aptly put it, gathered into a "single knot" and thrown "on to the scales."[181] In such periods of conjuncture, developments towards war and revolution are heightened.

The concept of conjuncture figures centrally in Lenin's political writings. It lay at the very core of his strategic perspective of preparing for an eventual revolutionary situation when, as Lenin powerfully and graphically expressed it, days count for more than do years or scores of years in "normal" times.[182] History in a sense becomes telescoped during these relatively brief historical "moments," when sudden and dramatic leaps and changes in the objective situation take place, when quiescent masses are jarred and jolted awake, when fissures and cracks in the world imperialist order widen into cleavages which threaten its very existence. It is this Leninist stress on preparation, on preparing especially for the heightened opportunities to storm the heavens in such historic conjunctures, that has been both revived and deepened in the writings of Bob Avakian:

> Actually it has always been a basic tenet of Marxism that, while the exploitation, oppression and all-around suffering of the masses, especially the masses of workers, is a consistent, inevitable and fundamental condition of capitalist society, and while there will be in one form and on one level or another resistance to this on an ongoing basis, it is not all the time that it is possible to overthrow capitalism. Rather, it is only under certain conditions, particularly with the eruption of a profound crisis, that the objective possibilities for the revolutionary overthrow of capitalism emerge. The analysis of and emphasis given to the role of capitalist crisis in the *Communist Manifesto* is an expression of this. Further, Marxism has always stressed the relation between capitalism and the world market, the international character of capitalist production and exchange and the increase of this with the development of capitalism, and the relation between international events and crises in specific countries. . . . But with the development of capitalism into imperialism all this has assumed even more pronounced and profound importance. And Lenin, as a key part of his overall analysis of imperialism and its relation to and effects upon prospects for proletarian revolu-

---

[181] J. V. Stalin, *The Foundations of Leninism* (Peking: Foreign Languages Press, 1970), p. 6.

[182] *The Collapse of the Second International, LCW,* 21, p. 254.

tion, recognized, emphasized and systematized the understanding of the qualitatively new and greater role of international relations and the development of world-historic conjunctures whose outcomes determine the direction of things. . . for decades to come.[183]

Avakian has situated the concept of conjuncture in the political economy of imperialism and the spiral development of the world proletarian revolution. Conjunctural episodes represent the extreme concentration of the contradictions of imperialism and, in particular, those contradictions characteristic of a specific spiral. War, then, is not the end of crisis (or even of a particular spiral); rather, it signifies the boiling over of contradictions on a world scale. Some imperialists must win the war, redivide the world favorably, and at the same time prevent or significantly limit revolution leading to socialism in various parts of the world. Indeed, while the imperialists may appear to be the strongest at these times, as they spare no effort to launch their juggernauts, it is precisely in such periods of turmoil and desperation that they become most vulnerable to revolutionary assaults. Crises and wars are filled with devastation and horror, the daily horrors of capitalist exploitation and oppression raised exponentially. But they are also replete with unprecedented opportunities to rip away chunks of the world from the imperialist system and to hasten its doom. Such is the objective significance of world-historic conjunctures.

Imperialism is a web of international relationships. Many different weak links emerge throughout the world imperialist network and there is a back-and-forth motion between tenuous individual elements and the system as a whole. As the system grows more exposed and fragile on many different fronts and flanks, the situation is least in hand and under control for the imperialists. Indeed, for both the imperialists and the masses, the stakes are raised as never before. The imperialists must put everything on the line to preserve their system, while the international proletariat, amidst all this madness, is challenged to enter into and wage battles which can prove truly decisive and historic. To be sure, these are highly complex situations whose exact features and outcome, especially their outcome, cannot be divined or assured in advance. However, if there is, as has been repeatedly stressed, a dialectic between the

---

[183] Avakian, "For Decades to Come — On a World Scale," *Revolutionary Worker*, No. 98 (27 March 1981), p. 10.

operation of capitalism's underlying laws of motion and the fact that these laws operate in historical contingency and through the crucible of class struggle, it is still true that these laws do indeed exist and make certain developments inevitable...notably such conjunctures with all their acute and unpredictable features.

The point is that particular spirals cannot go on forever. They have a definite trajectory and are rooted in the basic anarchy of capital; they unfold, in the final analysis, according to the basic laws of capital, as expressed in ways particular to this epoch. The contradictory development of internationalized accumulation, global rivalry, and class struggle is a process of the worldwide intensification and transmission of contradictions. It is exactly when contradictions reach a conjunctural point, a point of wild interaction, convergence, and explosion — reflecting the objective character and international dominance of the bourgeois mode of production — that politics itself assumes even more profound importance. It is hardly happenstance that the Bolshevik and Chinese Revolutions, which were themselves crests of revolutionary waves, triumphed amidst the storm and stress of world wars and their aftermath. Further, and this takes us back to lopsidedness and the division of the world into oppressor and oppressed nations, the extended periods of relative political and economic stability that often characterize life in many of the imperialist countries are, with the emergence of such conjunctures, shattered by the dislocations of crisis and war. Rare opportunities, including the likely emergence of revolutionary situations in at least some of these countries, present themselves in such unique historical circumstances. (Of course, this is not to say that these are the only times that insurrectionary situations can possibly arise in these countries.) In the colonial countries, where the more desperate conditions of the masses lend themselves to more frequent outbursts, at conjunctural moments the prospects for revolution are vastly increased. And so, in a world that is quite literally "up for grabs," the conscious dynamic role of the masses can affect world history (as Avakian puts it, echoing Lenin) "for decades to come."

In *Capital*, Marx wrote: "Capitalist production seeks continually to overcome these immanent barriers, but overcomes them only by means which again place these barriers in its way and on a more formidable scale."[184] We have had occasion to return to this

---

[184] *Capital*, III, p. 250.

theme throughout the course of this exposition. It is only fitting that it frame the concluding summation.

Capitalism is a dynamic mode of production which undergoes breakneck leaps through which it temporarily overcomes barriers. Accumulation is necessarily punctuated by destructive crises and periods of more open and critical class conflict. All this is heightened as well as distorted in the imperialist epoch. Imperialism is throbbing and staggering capitalism which lurches forward into ever more severe crises and convulsions. Even during phases of expansion and relative calm it faces conflicts, armed struggles, and crises in different parts of the world. During those historic "moments" of which we just spoke, the imperialist system is shaken on a world scale by cataclysmic eruptions and revolutionary onslaughts of unparalleled ferocity. These conjunctures are not fortuitous; their material basis lies in the specific nature of imperialism. As we have argued, imperialism does not operate in the same way as competitive capitalism and it actually supersedes many of the particular features of the earlier stage. Yet it rests on the same foundation. What makes imperialism so explosive is precisely that it is a mode of production which is highly parasitic, highly socialized, and marked by a high degree of internationalization, yet it is one that cannot transcend the limits of nationality of capitalism and commodity production in general — anarchy continues, and ever more forcefully, to assert itself. This is capitalism violently straining against its limits, which advances and develops only through massive fits and starts.

Now the basic truth that Marx approached from many different angles and that is encapsulated in Engels' description of the "circle that is gradually narrowing" is this: the forward motion of capital itself prepares the conditions for its own undoing. The advance of the capitalist mode of production resides in the perfection and extension of the division of labor, in the intensive and extensive development of markets, in the continual commodification of social life and the proletarianization of the masses throughout the world, and in the further concentration and centralization of capital — in short, in the development of the productive forces in an overall sense. But in so doing capitalism only intensifies its major contradictions and strengthens the basis for its overthrow and destruction.

In the imperialist era, capital is constantly confronted by the necessity to take ever more extraordinary measures to profitably reproduce and extend itself — and such measures, along with the mobility and flexibility of finance capital in general, rebound ever more wrenchingly back on themselves. The imperialists do not simply start all over in restructuring capital, they start each time from a world which is more capitalized. The struggle for redivision, as the necessity asserts itself, becomes more destructive and reorganization more complex. Tendencies towards greater concentration and socialization, towards deeper crisis, weaken the imperialist system and drive it closer towards its extinction.

But all this cannot be divorced from consciousness and the material force of revolutionary struggle. On the one hand, these form part of the necessity faced by imperialism. On the other hand, the destruction of imperialism does not await the approach of some abstract limit or state of crisis. Imperialism will never reach a point past which it will fall of its own and give way to a higher social order as a consequence of the operation of its economic laws pure and simple. These only provide the basis and offer opportunities — especially at moments of conjuncture — for conscious struggle and action. The struggle for socialism and communism can only be the product of the fiercest and most conscious leaps to transform the world. The historical advance of proletarian revolution is itself a spiral-like development of victories and temporary setbacks, of massive surges forward and periods of retreat. Yet, through these twists and turns the international proletariat has accumulated experience and understanding which increase its capacity to make such leaps. The objective motion of imperialism creates more favorable material conditions to do just that and, especially as conjunctural moments approach and unfold, to accelerate its final destruction as contradictions come to a head in the international arena. This, too, is part of the "narrowing circle."

There is a definite dynamic of crisis, war, and revolution under imperialism, a general process which will continue for some time. In the era of imperialism, the contradiction between socialized production and private appropriation becomes the underlying contradiction in a single, overall world process of the advance from the bourgeois epoch to its replacement by the epoch of world communism. Capitalism in its highest and final stage is headed towards its extinction through a spiral/conjuncture motion. It is a protracted process and struggle which is at once punctuated and accelerated by major leaps and massive upheavals.

Marx once described the condition of wage-labor as "the last form of servitude assumed by human activity."[185] The enslavement of one human being to another and the subordination of productive and creative activity to the imperatives of profit no longer correspond to the needs of advancing society. Humanity has reached an historic threshold: it can move beyond the horizon of scarcity, which is the taproot of social antagonism, and can begin to overcome the divisions and inequalities of class society. For the first time it can collectively and consciously transform nature. This is the profound outcome of successive modes of production based on an exploitative division of labor and, in particular, the unprecedented technical and scientific achievements of capitalism, "achievements" resting on exploitation, plunder, and murder, the horror and scope of which far surpass that of any other epoch of human history.

Capitalism has created the basis for a whole new and qualitatively higher mode of social existence, and yet its social relations constitute the very obstacle to realizing it. This is the significance of the conflict between socialized production and private appropriation. In the imperialist era this conflict grows more intense and violent. The internationalization of the capitalist mode of production and the aggravation of its contradictions heighten revolutionary possibility. Lenin wrote the following passage during a period of acute crisis and world war out of which came a revolution that indeed shook the world. It remains quite relevant as we approach another such world-historic conjuncture, one that may open the possibility for even more extraordinary breakthroughs:

There had been an epoch of a comparatively "peaceful capitalism," when it had overcome feudalism in the advanced countries of Europe and was in a position to develop comparatively tranquilly and harmoniously, "peacefully" spreading over tremendous areas of still unoccupied lands, and of countries not yet finally drawn into the capitalist vortex. Of course, even in that epoch, marked approximately by the years 1871 and 1914, "peaceful" capitalism created conditions of life that were very far from being really peaceful both in the military and in a general class sense. For nine-tenths of the population of the advanced countries, for hundreds of millions of peoples in the colonies and in the backward countries this epoch

---

[185] *Grundrisse*, p. 749.

was not one of "peace" but of oppression, tortures, horrors that seemed the more terrifying since they appeared to be without end. This epoch has gone forever. It has been followed by a new epoch, comparatively more impetuous, full of abrupt changes, catastrophes, conflicts, an epoch that no longer appears to the toiling masses as horror without end but is an end full of horrors.[186]

[186] Lenin, "Introduction" to Nikolai Bukharin, *Imperialism and World Economy*, this translation taken from Monthly Review Press edition (New York: 1973), p. 10.

2

Towards the American Century: The Rise of U.S. Imperialism

God has . . . made us the master organizers of the world to establish system where chaos reigns. He has given us the spirit of progress to overwhelm the forces of reaction throughout the earth. He has made us adepts in government that we may administer government among savage and senile peoples. Were it not for such a force as this the world would relapse into barbarism and night. And of all our race He has marked the American people as His chosen nation to finally lead in the regeneration of the world. This is the divine mission of America, and it holds for us all the profit, all the glory, all the happiness possible to man. . . .

That flag has never paused in its onward march. Who dares halt it now — now, when history's largest events are carrying it forward. . . .

— from Senator Albert J. Beveridge's speech
in the U.S. Senate, January 9, 1900[1]

We have a record of conquest, colonization and expansion unequalled by any people in the Nineteenth Century. We are not about to be curbed now.

— Henry Cabot Lodge, 1895[2]

---

[1] *Congressional Record,* 56th Congress, 1st Session (Washington, D.C.: Government Printing Office [GPO], 1900), Volume XXXIII, Part I, p. 711.

[2] Quoted in William Appleman Williams, *The Contours of American History* (Chicago: Quadrangle, 1966), p. 345.

Empires are forged through decades of economic expansion, geographic extension, and foreign plunder. Yet the antagonistic aims and requirements of rival imperialist empire-builders find their highest moment in world war. The idea of an American Century had obviously been gestating in the minds of America's rulers since at least the turn of the century. But the possibility of shaping and dominating a new global order was not within their reach until World War 2. This chapter surveys the ascension of U.S. imperialism through these first two world wars.

The central argument can be summarized briefly: the key gains and advances of U.S. imperialism were the product of the two major interimperialist conflicts. In each instance, the U.S. imperialists' peculiar relationship to these world wars allowed them to make far greater gains than did any other imperialist power. Not so directly embroiled in the intra-European contest during World War 1, the U.S. imperialists could utilize vast internal reserves, especially oppressed nationalities, and they could take advantage of their proximity to Latin America to bolster capitalist expansion. During the opening years of the war they were able to avoid direct military involvement, exploit the combatants' difficulties to advance U.S. interests, and then finally enter the war on the winning side at the propitious moment to maximize their share of the spoils while minimizing political and economic losses. A similar pattern was repeated in the second interimperialist war. But if in each of these wars the U.S. imperialists were "sitting on top of the mountain to watch the tigers fight," while benefiting from the mutual weakening of the belligerents, they hardly remained passive. They formulated clear war aims and pursued them vigorously. And they seized on opportunities during and between the wars to angle for influence and control in the Third World, especially (though not exclusively) in Latin America and the Pacific. The relative hemispheric insularity of the U.S. was an important source of strength in U.S. imperialism's bid for world supremacy.

The principal goal of *America in Decline* is to trace and interpret the course of the post-World War 2 imperialist spiral, which has been characterized by the worldwide dominance of U.S. imperialism, the eventual decline of U.S. power, and the growing challenge to that power as the spiral has entered its conjunctural phase. In subsequent volumes we shall simultaneously test and apply the general theoretical propositions expounded in the preceding chapter so as to both explain the roots of the current world crisis and examine its implications for revolutionary resolution. However, at this point, in order to grapple with the theoretical issues raised by the expansion of the U.S. in the post-World War 2 period, some historical background is necessary. This chapter offers a panorama of the forces and events leading up to and underlying the achievement of a Pax Americana following World War 2, emphasizing the emergence of those factors that would eventually play a critical role in the unfolding of the current spiral.

The U.S. Quest for Empire: The Early Decades and the First World War

Capitalism became capitalist-imperialism around the turn of the century, and capitalism in the United States was certainly no exception. Having attained a high degree of concentration and monopoly, U.S. imperialism announced its arrival at the imperialist banquet table by displacing Spain, the last of the old feudal-based colonizers, as overlord of colonial subjects from Puerto Rico to the Philippines. By the century's turn, the world was completely dominated by and divided among a handful of capitalist powers. As the British imperialist ideologue Joseph Chamberlain declared in

1902: "The day of small nations has long passed away; the day of Empires has come."[3]

During the final quarter of the nineteenth century, rapid economic expansion hastened the concentration and centralization of capital. The process was perhaps most advanced in the U.S., where an extraordinary merger wave took place, involving at least 15 percent of all plants and employees in manufacturing by the turn of the century.[4] This merger wave, along with the internal expansion of those firms which had prevailed in the competitive struggle, cemented the foundations of a highly concentrated economy. A study conducted at the time found that of 92 large consolidations, 78 gained a market share of 50 percent or more and 26 gained control of at least 80 percent.[5] By 1909, 43.8 percent of the total industrial output was produced by a mere 1.1 percent of all industrial enterprises.[6]

Closely linked to monopolization of production was the increased importance of capital export. U.S. overseas investments soared from $500 million in 1900 to $2.5 billion in 1914 — a fivefold increase, as indicated in Table 2.1. According to the same set of figures, U.S. foreign investment rose from a negligible share of the total of the major capitalist countries in 1885 to 2 percent in 1900, to over 6 percent of the total by 1914. The rapid emergence of the U.S. as a foreign investor, however, did not mean that its internal sources of expansion were exhausted. On the contrary, the U.S. was able to exploit crucial internal reserves: the semifeudal Black Belt South, in particular the Black nation centered there; the far from completely tapped lands of the West, forcibly seized from the Native American and Mexican peoples, as well as the oppressed nationalities concentrated there, particularly the Mexicans and later

---

[3] Quoted in Dan Nabudere, *The Political Economy of Imperialism: Its Theoretical and Polemical Treatment from Mercantilist to Multilateral Imperialism*, 2nd ed. (London: Zed Press, 1978), p. 101.

[4] Historical data summarized by F. M. Scherer, *Industrial Market Structure and Economic Performance*, 2nd ed. (Chicago: Rand McNally, 1980), p. 119.

[5] See Scherer, *Industrial Market Structure*, p. 121.

[6] V.I. Lenin, *Imperialism, The Highest Stage of Capitalism* (Peking: Foreign Languages Press, 1965), p. 14; also in *Collected Works (LCW)* (Moscow: Progress Publishers), 22, p. 197 (based on official U.S. government statistics). On the emergence of finance capital and the formation of the first financial groups, see Matthew Josephson, *The Robber Barons* (New York: Harcourt Brace Jovanovich, 1962) which, despite its petty-bourgeois moralism, contains much useful information. See also Glenn Porter, *The Rise of Big Business, 1860-1910* (Arlington Heights, Ill.: Harland Davidson, 1973).

TABLE 2.1

Growth of Foreign Investment of Selected Leading Capital–Exporting Countries: 1870, 1885, 1900, 1914, and 1930

(in millions of U.S. dollars to the nearest $100 million)*

Country	1870	1885	1900	1914	1930
United Kingdom	$4,900	$7,800	$12,100	$19,500	$18,200
France	2,500	3,500	5,200	8,600	3,500
Germany	–	1,900	4,800	6,700	1,100
Netherlands	500	1,000	1,100	1,200	2,300
United States	–	–	500	2,500	14,700
Canada	–	–	100	200	1,300

*Not directly comparable with other figures in this chapter or with other figures in Woodruff, who bases this series on the comparability of Eugene Staley's figures for this time frame (see Staley, *War and the Private Investor, A Study in the Relations of International Politics and International Private Investment* [Garden City, New York: Doubleday, Doran, and Co., 1935]).

Source: William Woodruff, *Impact of Western Man*, 2nd ed. (Washington, D.C.: University Press of America, 1982), Table IV/1, pp. 150-51.

the Chinese; a large pool of immigrant labor; and uncommonly plentiful natural resources (compared with the old nations of Europe). At the same time, new acreage, unfettered by the constraints of precapitalist landholding patterns, was brought into cultivation, a factor which contributed to the thriving U.S. agricultural export trade. But, as the substantial increase in foreign investment during the early years of the century revealed, the U.S. imperialists just as avidly pursued global interests and sought to export capital with as much vigor as did their European counterparts.

During the late nineteenth century, the major European powers were scrambling for control of colonies, as dramatically exemplified by the Berlin Conference in 1884-85 which divided Africa among the great powers. The United States, however, was not yet in a position to partake of the African depredations nor to enter many of the other contests among the European imperialists. Rather, it aimed at vying with these powers in Latin America, the Pacific rim, and China, as well as scooping up colonies from the crumbling Spanish empire.

Despite its self-serving anticolonial fables, the U.S. opposed Spanish colonialism only to replace it with its own brand of imperialist domination. In the Philippines, after the U.S. defeat of the Spanish in a brief naval encounter in Manila Bay, the entire thrust of U.S. operations in that country was directed toward the bloody suppression of the Filipino people (the U.S. imperialists even turned on the moderate leader Aguinaldo who had previously been brought back from China in a U.S. warship to oppose the Spanish). The historians Morison and Commager described the situation: "...the United States now found that it had purchased, for $20 million [in payment to Spain for an armistice], a first-class Filipino insurrection....[When] Aguinaldo's troops disregarded the command of an American sentry to halt, the United States army undertook to 'civilize them with a Krag' [a standard-issue U.S. Army rifle]." [7]

The Philippine insurgency was quelled with the aid of concentration camps and water torture. Before it was over, hundreds of thousands of people, the overwhelming number of them Filipino, had been killed. As a result of the Spanish-American War, the U.S. also acquired Guam and Puerto Rico, along with the other territories "freed" from Spanish colonialism, while Cuba was also effectively brought under U.S. domination with the same duplicity and violence. During this period, the U.S. imperialists also annexed the Hawaiian Islands, occupied Wake Island, divided the Samoan Islands with Germany and Britain, continued to struggle with the other imperialist powers over the partition of China, and expanded their influence in Latin America and the Caribbean. [8]

The main focus of the U.S. imperialists' efforts was in Latin America, where they sought to wrest as much as possible from long-established British economic and political control and to counter rising German imperialist influence. Their methods were none too subtle. When Colombia, for example, refused a U.S. "proposal" to surrender control of land where the U.S. wanted to build a canal, Teddy Roosevelt simply "took the Canal Zone," to use his own words. The U.S. backed a motley group in declaring Panama's

---

[7] Samuel Eliot Morison and Henry Steele Commager, *The Growth of the American Republic*, 5th ed., Volume 2 (New York: Oxford Univ. Press, 1962), pp. 429-30.

[8] Howard Zinn, *A People's History of the United States* (New York: Harper and Row, 1980), pp. 303-13. The Philippines remained a U.S. colony until 1946 (at which time it gained its "independence" and became a neocolony of the U.S.); Puerto Rico, Guam, and the Virgin Islands remain under formal U.S. control to this day.

independence (according to one history, "the Panamanian 'revolution' was announced in Washington practically before it broke out"), sent a warship to "show the flag," and immediately recognized the "new, independent Republic of Panama," which promptly accepted Roosevelt's terms for a canal zone.[9]

In order to justify their rivalry with the other imperialists and their suppression of the Latin American masses, the U.S. rulers formulated the "Roosevelt Corollary" to the Monroe Doctrine; this completed the transformation of a policy aimed originally *against* European meddling into one *justifying* U.S. meddling — and, ultimately, U.S. domination. In the words of one Latin American scholar: "just as President Polk had amended the Monroe Doctrine half a century earlier in order to 'legitimize' annexations like that of Texas, Theodore Roosevelt attempted to justify aggressions under his own administration and those which were to follow in country after country by adding what became known as the Roosevelt Corollary. According to this new amendment proclaimed by Roosevelt in 1904, lack of order in any country called for the intervention of civilized states, 'and in the Western Hemisphere the adherence of the United States to the Monroe Doctrine may force the United States, however reluctantly . . . to the exercise of an international police power.' "[10] Some examples of the "reluctant" hemispheric policing activities that followed this edict include: the withdrawal of Germany from Venezuela in 1903 under the threat of force from the U.S.; the takeover, by executive action of President Roosevelt, of the customs houses in Santo Domingo in 1905; the arrival of a U.S. warship in Nicaraguan waters in 1908; and a treaty negotiated with Honduras in 1911, at the suggestion of New York bankers, which extended U.S. authority over that republic.[11]

All of the advanced capitalist countries were involved in a breakneck chase to carve up portions of the globe previously un-

[9] Alonso Aguilar, *Pan-Americanism from Monroe to the Present* (New York: Monthly Review Press, 1968), pp. 47-49; John M. Blum et al., *The National Experience: A History of the United States* (New York: Harcourt, Brace and World, 1963), p. 533. The construction of the Panama Canal was mainly guided by strategic considerations, in particular the need of the U.S. fleet to pass quickly between the Atlantic and Pacific Oceans, thereby undercutting British naval dominance in the hemisphere. Today the Canal Zone remains a critical outpost for the U.S. and is seat of the combined Army, Navy, and Air Force Southern Command.

[10] Aguilar, *Pan-Americanism*, pp. 50-51.

[11] Charles A. and Mary R. Beard, *The Rise of American Civilization*, Volume 2 (New York: Macmillan, 1931), pp. 502-3.

TABLE 2.2

Colonial Possessions of the Great Powers
(in millions of square kilometers and in millions of inhabitants)

	Colonies				Metropolitan countries		Total	
	1876		1914		1914		1914	
	Area	Pop.	Area	Pop.	Area	Pop.	Area	Pop.
Great Britain	22.5	251.9	33.5	393.5	0.3	46.5	33.8	440.0
Russia	17.0	15.9	17.4	33.2	5.4	136.2	22.8	169.4
France	0.9	6.0	10.6	55.5	0.5	39.6	11.1	95.1
Germany	–	–	2.9	12.3	0.5	64.9	3.4	77.2
United States	–	–	0.3	9.7	9.4	97.0	9.7	106.7
Japan	–	–	0.3	19.2	0.4	53.0	0.7	72.2
Total for 6 Great Powers	40.4	273.8	65.0	523.4	16.5	437.2	81.5	960.6

Colonies of other powers (Belgium, Holland, etc.)	9.9	45.3
Semicolonial countries (Persia, China, Turkey)	14.5	361.2
Other countries	28.0	289.9
Total for the world	133.9	1,657.0

Source: V.I. Lenin, *Imperialism, The Highest Stage of Capitalism, Collected Works* (Moscow: Progress Publishers), 22, p. 258.

claimed by capital. As can be seen in Table 2.2, between 1876 and 1914 this small club of capitalist powers annexed almost 25 million square kilometers of territory in formal colonies (half a billion people now in thrall to formal empire), not to mention the very considerable extension and consolidation in the way of neocolonies and semicolonies. Even Germany, which arrived late at the banquet, still managed to amass a not inconsiderable empire.

This division of the world reflected the relative economic and political strength of the various powers. Clearly, Britain had by far the most foreign investment and the largest empire. Because of British preeminence in industrial development and the immense advantages of the British empire, British commodities dominated world trade and the pound sterling functioned as the linchpin of the international monetary system. As one observer has described the situation:

> It was not simply that Britain provided the long-term and short-term capital necessary to keep the system going, but that the specific evolution of the world economy in the nineteenth century was integrally related to Britain's own economic development. As the world's strongest industrial and mercantile power, Britain used its diplomacy and military strength to create a world economy that gave maximum freedom to trade and investment. The gold-standard mechanism assured freedom of trade and the security of foreign investments. The use of sterling as the main international currency and the pivotal role of British bankers were, in turn, indications of the success of Britain in making the entire world its trading area.[12]

But once the other capitalist countries had developed to a point where they were both able to and compelled to challenge British supremacy, "free" trade — which reflected British economic and political predominance — gave way to protectionism and intensified economic and political rivalry. Tensions were mounting within a world order and during a period which saw the rise of the major imperialist powers. The configuration of rivalry which gradually emerged was complex, shaped by geopolitical and historical factors, as well as the conflict of economic interests. On both the economic and political levels, the greatest potential challenges to British power came from the United States and Germany. As for the U.S., its more dynamic economy was on a collision course with British world preeminence. Between 1870 and the outbreak of World War 1, U.S. GNP grew at a rate more than twice that of Great Britain.[13] Yet in Latin America, for instance, the Monroe Doctrine notwithstanding, the U.S. could only secure a $1.65 billion investment while the British could claim $3.7 billion in 1914.[14] Nevertheless, the specificity of the situation was such that Germany stood in a more desperate position vis-à-vis the existing international order.

---

[12] Fred L. Block, *The Origins of International Economic Disorder: A Study of United States International Monetary Policy from World War II to the Present* (Berkeley: Univ. of California Press, 1977), pp. 12-13.

[13] U.S. Bureau of Economic Analysis, *Long-Term Economic Growth, 1860-1970* (GPO, 1973), Table 7, p. 99.

[14] See Table 2.3, p. 191.

The U.S., therefore, was not compelled to challenge the British in a direct, all-around way. On the one hand, the U.S. (and also Japan) stood outside that framework of European power politics which imperialism inherited from late feudalism and competitive capitalism. It was this framework which was shattered in the two world wars, creating a more appropriate global political framework for imperialist accumulation. On the other hand, unlike its European counterparts, U.S. imperialism could still concentrate on developing the vast territories it had recently annexed. Like all the imperialist powers, the U.S. was increasingly driven to expand outward. But even though they were quick to grab at the remnants of Spain's decrepit empire, the U.S. rulers could for the time being mainly rest content with a somewhat secondary role in the overall imperialist scramble for power. (Where it did exert influence, as in China, the U.S. pushed for the maintenance of an "open door" to all national capitals. The assumption, of course, was that in such "free competition" for influence the U.S. would ultimately come out on top given its prodigious internal rate of growth and modernization.)

To a considerable extent, imperialism emerged within an institutional framework dominated by the European market and political state system. The great powers were predominantly European nation-states and world politics largely reflected the legacy of nineteenth-century European power politics. Partly for this reason, the principal challenge to British leadership came from Germany. As a leading chronicler of the economic history of Europe has emphasized: "The rapid industrial expansion of a unified Germany was the most important development of the half-century that preceded the First World War — more important even than the comparable growth of the United States, simply because Germany was enmeshed in the European network of power and in this period the fate of the world was in Europe's hands."[15] Indeed, in the first decade of the twentieth century, Germany was relatively more dynamic, could boast of greater increases in productivity, and had a much higher rate of domestic capital formation than did Britain, whose parasitism stood in striking contrast to German growth. Nevertheless, while German exports hammered at British control of foreign markets, German foreign investment was restricted by

---

[15] David S. Landes, *The Unbound Prometheus: Technological change and industrial development in Western Europe from 1750 to the present* (London: Cambridge Univ. Press, 1970), p. 326.

the unfavorable balance of political and military power.

Thus, Germany needed a new division of the world and (unlike the U.S.) had to play a frontline role in attempting to achieve a favorable redivision, while for their part, the British imperialists needed both to defend the old division, which was favorable to them, and to expand further. The U.S. could continue to pursue the conquest of "its" newly acquired West, consolidate its holdings in the Pacific and the Caribbean, and nibble at British commercial and financial control in Latin America — while the European powers were more immediately forced to gear up for a life-and-death struggle for empire. The hemispheric insularity of the U.S. afforded its leaders considerable maneuvering room in comparison with the other imperialists (who were also choked by the British-dominated world order).

The not inconsequential domestic reserves of U.S. imperialism, along with its "extra-European" situation, help explain why U.S. interests were not as hemmed in by British dominance as were German interests. The U.S., as a result, could deal with both Germany and Great Britain in ways that they could not deal with each other. True, in the prewar decades the United States was a rising dynamo. But, as emphasized in Chapter 1, there is no strict correlation between indices of economic vitality and specific political alignments (and conflicts). The overall politics and economics of the international situation dictated that Germany lead a direct challenge to the existing interimperialist relations.[16]

Lenin characterized the war that broke out:

> The first imperialist war of 1914-18 was the inevitable outcome of this partition of the whole world, of this domination by the capitalist

---

[16] A German historian, Fritz Fischer, has discovered that several years before the start of the war the German government and high command had developed extensive plans for a far-reaching German empire, rivaling and similar to those later formulated by Hitler, including colonization of the Ukraine (see Fritz Fischer, *Germany's War Aims in the First World War* [New York: W.W. Norton, 1967]). This is understood by some as a refutation of the correct argument that the first imperialist war was the responsibility of both groups of imperialist combatants, and as confirmation that "German expansionism" was the sole cause of it. In point of fact, however, besides reflecting that Nazi expansionism was not something different from "ordinary" imperialism, this merely shows that Germany was conscious of its role as imperialist challenger in the First (and Second) World War and, it would seem, confident of its ultimate success. The far-flung and already existing empires of Britain, France, and Tsarist Russia were no less founded on pillage, plunder, and exploitation than the fledgling empire of the Germans.

monopolies, of this great power wielded by an insignificant number of very big banks — two, three, four or five in each country. This war was waged for the repartitioning of the whole world. It was waged in order to decide which of the small groups of the biggest states — the British or the German — was to obtain the opportunity and the right to rob, strangle, and exploit the whole world. You know that the war settled this question in favor of the British group. And as a result of this war, all capitalist contradictions have become immeasurably more acute.[17]

World War 1 was the first imperialist war for world redivision, the first mass slaughter of modern history. On the first day of the Battle of Somme in 1916, 60,000 people lost their lives. This monstrous conflict not only drove millions to an early grave, but also left most of Europe physically and economically devastated. In France alone, 2.7 million people were left homeless; 285,000 houses were destroyed and 411,000 damaged; 22,000 factories, 4,800 kilometers of railroads, 1,600 kilometers of canals, 59,000 kilometers of roads, and 3.3 million hectares of arable land lay useless.[18] Currency inflation was astounding. In victorious Britain, prices in 1920 stood at three times their prewar levels. But the worst inflation by far was in the defeated countries of Central Europe. In Austria, prices rose to 14,000 times prewar levels; in Hungary, the multiple was 23,000; in Poland, 2,500,000. In Germany, by November 1923, the mark was worth one-trillionth of its prewar value.[19]

But, as a result of previously unimaginable death and destruction, empires were recarved and capital restructured on an international scale. The German challenge to Britain was defeated — temporarily as it turned out — and German military, political, and economic might was significantly restricted. Germany lost its entire colonial empire and some minor portions of territory. The old semi-feudal Russian, Austro-Hungarian, and Turkish empires vanished from the stage of history. The spoils of war went to the victorious powers, but not all the winners emerged with greatly expanded strength. Italy, a lesser partner in the wartime alliance against Germany, gained virtually nothing for its efforts, as the British and

---

[17] "Report on the International Situation and the Fundamental Tasks of the Communist International" (19 July 1920), *LCW*, 31, pp. 216-17.

[18] Nabudere, *Political Economy of Imperialism*, p. 131.

[19] Landes, *Unbound Prometheus*, pp. 361-62.

French were far from willing to cut Italy in on the spoils of war which hardly made up their own losses. France lost an estimated 23 billion out of 45 billion francs in foreign investment, in part on account of war expenditure needs, but mainly because several of her debtors defaulted. The French imperialists lost 12 billion francs (or one-quarter of their overseas holdings) in Russia alone, debts that the proletariat now in power was not about to pay back.[20]

Although Britain was generally successful in defending her share of the world, the war's aftermath saw the near total stagnation of her economy and the collapse of the sterling-based gold standard. To finance the war, the British were forced to sell off £207 million of £800-900 million in dollar-denominated investments, plus another £54 million of sterling-denominated investments.[21] Britain's total foreign investment in 1929 was at no higher level than it was in 1913-14.[22] With France and Germany mainly tied down in Europe, Japan seized the opportunity to grab German colonial holdings in the Far East and to consolidate a powerful position in China.

Among the imperialist powers, the principal victor was the U.S., which emerged from the war in the most economically powerful position and whose gains will be documented below. Taking advantage of their geographic position, the U.S. rulers managed to remain largely aloof from the entanglements of prewar alliances, enabling them to implement the strategy (to again use Mao Tsetung's colorful description) of "sitting on top of the mountain to watch the tigers fight." U.S. troops accounted for only 2.4 percent of all Allied troop deaths in battle.[23] In the early stages of the war, the U.S. maintained a formal neutrality while supplying the combatants, mainly the British and French, with war materiel and financial backing. Once the tide had begun to turn, the *Lusitania* sinking became a convenient excuse for the cry to go up, "the Yanks are coming" — to claim, of course, a full "fair share" of the spoils.

While the U.S. imperialists sat out the early stages of the military conflict in Europe, they waged their own war against Latin

---

[20] Landes, *Unbound Prometheus,* p. 362.

[21] Landes, *Unbound Prometheus,* p. 362.

[22] United Nations, Department of Economic Affairs, *International Capital Movements During the Inter-War Period* (Lake Success, N.Y.: 1949), pp. 2, 29.

[23] *Encyclopedia Americana* (1983), s.v. "World War I: War Casualties."

America and the Caribbean. In 1914, U.S. Marines invaded Vera Cruz to protect considerable U.S. interests in Mexico. After some eight rebellions against U.S. domination rocked Haiti in less than four years, President Woodrow Wilson sent the Marines to occupy that country a second time, installing a puppet regime and then annexing the island outright as a U.S. protectorate in 1915. Troops were to stay there for nineteen years. In 1916, U.S. Marines similarly invaded and occupied the Dominican Republic for the fourth time (and kept troops there for eight years), and the U.S. Army went on a "punitive expedition" to Mexico to go after revolutionary forces led by Pancho Villa. As Wilson explained, "I am going to teach the South American Republics to elect good men."[24] Smedley Butler, commandant of the U.S. Marines, later exposed the role of U.S. armed force during this time. After bluntly characterizing his function as that of "a racketeer for capitalism," he went on:

> . . . I helped make Mexico and especially Tampico safe for American oil interests in 1914. I helped make Haiti and Cuba a decent place for the National City Bank boys to collect revenues in. . . . I helped purify Nicaragua for the international banking house of Brown Brothers in 1909-12. I brought light to the Dominican Republic for American sugar interests in 1916. I helped make Honduras "right" for American fruit companies in 1903. . . . Looking back on it, I feel I might have given Al Capone a few hints. The best he could do was to operate his racket in three city districts. We Marines operated on three continents.[25]

From the standpoint of world history, the new interimperialist alignments were not the most important product of World War 1. With the First World War, the legitimacy of bourgeois rule was called into question as never before. In the immediate aftermath of the conflict, a tremendous leap forward in revolutionary consciousness and struggle swept through Europe and spread rapidly to the colonies and, to some extent, to the U.S. as well. The masses would not supinely return to the "peaceful" oppression of the

---

[24] Quoted in Ernest Gruening, *Mexico and Its Heritage* (New York: Century, 1928), p. 578. On the diplomacy of Woodrow Wilson, see also "The Sanctimonious Piffle of Woodrow Wilson," *Revolutionary Worker,* No. 158 (24 June 1982), p. 8; and V.G. Kiernan, *America: The New Imperialism* (London: Zed Press, 1978), pp. 134-35.

[25] Quoted in Leo Huberman, *We, the People,* 2nd ed. (New York: Monthly Review Press, 1964), p. 253.

prewar period. The British Prime Minister Lloyd George cringed: "The whole of Europe is filled with the spirit of revolution. There is everywhere a deep sense not only of discontent, but of anger and revolt amongst the workmen against prewar conditions. The whole existing order in its political, social, and economic aspects is questioned by the masses of the population from one end of Europe to the other.... Much of this unrest is unhealthy."[26] For the imperialists, unhealthy it surely was. And the "disease" was worst in Russia where, in October 1917, the Bolshevik Revolution removed most of the empire of the tsars not only from the war but from the imperialist system itself.

The Russian Revolution was truly an earthshaking event. This establishment of the world's first proletarian state (excepting the Paris Commune of 1871 which lasted but a few months) ushered in the epoch of proletarian revolution. The new Soviet state inspired the working class and oppressed peoples both in the imperialist countries and in the colonies.[27] The existence of a socialist country even introduced radical new elements into world diplomacy — in all their actions, imperialist diplomats now had to reckon with the

---

[26] Quoted in Nabudere, *Political Economy of Imperialism,* p. 132.

[27] The revolutionary insurrections that broke out in Berlin, Munich, Vienna, and Budapest in the aftermath of World War 1 have been well documented, particularly the rise of workers' and soldiers' councils. But in the first few years after the October Revolution, the organization and influence of the proletariat in the oppressed nations also grew tremendously. The Second Congress of the newly formed Communist International in 1920 included in its ranks delegates from India, Turkey, Persia, China, Korea, Java, and the Soviet Asian peoples. By 1925, communist parties had been established in several oppressed nations: Indonesia, Palestine, Burma, and Malaya. Further, several underground parties and organizations were formed in the Middle East. Parties affiliated with the Third International were also founded in Argentina, Brazil, Chile, Cuba, Mexico, Uruguay, and elsewhere in Latin America. Close political relationships developed between the new proletarian dictatorship and the leading political representatives of the nationalist movements in countries such as Turkey, India, and China, sites of upheavals against foreign rule. The revolutionary outbursts in Afghanistan, Korea, Egypt, Iraq, and Mongolia in the 1919-1922 period were all closely connected with the October Revolution. In Java and Sumatra, in the mid-1920s, communists led armed rebellion against Dutch rule (see William Z. Foster, *History of the Three Internationals* [New York: International Publishers, 1955], pp. 307-8; Foster, *Outline Political History of the Americas* [New York: International Publishers, 1951], pp. 378-79; and Harry Magdoff, *Imperialism: From the Colonial Age to the Present* [New York: Monthly Review Press, 1978], p. 65). The rise and development of the Chinese Communist Party is well known, as is Mao's classic statement of its origin: "The salvoes of the October Revolution brought us Marxism-Leninism" (Mao Tsetung, *Selected Works* [Peking: Foreign Languages Press, 1969], Volume 4, p. 413).

existence of Soviet power. Indeed, the shadow of the Bolshevik Revolution loomed large over the "peace negotiations" which brought the war to a close. Woodrow Wilson's famous "Fourteen Points" and his rhetorical promise of "self-determination" and a "just peace" were in great measure a response to this — one perceptive historian even titled the final chapter of his book on the diplomacy of these years "Wilson Versus Lenin."[28]

The U.S. Extends Its Empire in the Wake of the First World War

In 1918, the Armistice was signed. Germany, which suffered greatly in terms of casualties and war destruction, also paid a heavy price in the form of industrial dispossessions, colonial losses, and reparations as a vanquished power. Its colonial territories were apportioned among the winning powers as mandates of the League of Nations, as Wilson had urged. While the U.S. had furthered its characteristically neocolonial influence during the war years (especially in Latin America), it did not do as well with respect to the redistribution of formal colonies. At Versailles, the imperialists gave Britain control over German New Guinea, German Samoan Islands (through Australia and New Zealand, respectively), German Southwest Africa (through the Union of South Africa), and German East Africa. France divided the Cameroons and Togoland with the British. Ruanda and Urundi were "allocated" to Belgium, the Portuguese also obtained some territory in Africa, and the Japanese imperialists "acquired" the Caroline, Marshall, and Mariana Islands (they had already seized Korea and the southern half of Sakhalin) and consolidated gains in China.[29]

But the dragooning of subject peoples into the imperialist armies and the maraudings of these armies unleashed new actors on the stage of history in the colonial world. What the British historian Arnold Toynbee described about the French position in northern Africa has broader significance: "At the very moment...when France triumphed decisively over her Western rivals, the general

---

[28] Arno J. Mayer, *Political Origins of the New Deal Diplomacy, 1917-1918* (New Haven: Yale Univ. Press, 1959), p. 368.

[29] See H.W.V. Temperley, ed., *A History of the Peace Conference of Paris*, Volume 6 (London: Henry Frowde and Hodder and Stoughton, 1924), pp. 503-4.

ascendancy of the Western world over [northwest Africa]was challenged — suddenly and unexpectedly — by the native peoples.''[30]

A page from the history of the Middle East illustrates how the victorious imperialists dealt with the struggles of the oppressed in the countries they had "won" in battle. During the war, the British and French promised the Arab peoples of the Ottoman Empire that Britain would guarantee their independence if they fought the Ottoman Turks (allied with Germany). At the conclusion of the war, an agreement was hammered out at a European conference table: France would rule Syria and Lebanon while Britain would take charge of Palestine (divided a few years later into Palestine and Trans-Jordan) and Iraq. The decisions could only be enforced through massive suppression of indigenous forces demanding independence. The nationalist movement in Syria was quelled early, but the British met a serious challenge to their rule in Iraq, where aerial terror bombings of peasant villages figured prominently in the campaign to put down the resistance. In the early 1920s, Italy seized several islands in the Mediterranean and finally conquered Libya after more than a decade of struggle. It was not until 1926 that the Riff zones of Morocco were finally subjugated by France and Spain.[31]

Among the imperialist powers, the United States was most favorably situated to expand internationally. Although it did not obtain significant new colonies through the Versailles Treaty, it was able, on the basis of the leverage it gained, to open up new investment and trade opportunities, both in Latin America and in the colonies and neocolonies of the other imperialists. "We have advanced from the period of adventure," explained the American Director General of the Pan-American Union in 1928, "to the period of permanent investment in our relations with the nations of Latin America. . . ."[32] Achieving such "permanency" required nothing less than "gunboat diplomacy" and, during the decade of

---

[30] Arnold Toynbee, *Survey of International Affairs,* Volume 1: *The Islamic World Since the Peace Settlement* (London: Oxford Univ. Press, 1927), p. 94.

[31] See Joe Stork, *Middle East Oil and the Energy Crisis* (New York: Monthly Review Press, 1975), p. 15; see also Temperley, ed., *Peace Conference of Paris,* Volume 6, pp. 41-192; and Toynbee, *The Islamic World,* pp. 105-63.

[32] As stated by the Director General, Leo S. Rowe, in his foreword to Max Winkler, *Investments of United States Capital in Latin America* (Boston: World Peace Foundation, 1929).

the 1920s, naval forays into Central America continued to be commonplace. All this was carried out in the "fraternal" spirit of the Monroe Doctrine. In 1920, the U.S. "fraternally aided" the people of Guatemala with U.S. naval armed force. The U.S. launched similar attacks on Honduras in 1924. Nicaragua was invaded, for the second time, in 1926. Such gunboat diplomacy produced a situation in which, at one point, U.S. officials directed the financial policies of eleven of the twenty Latin American countries — and U.S. banking agents in six of them were backed on the spot by U.S. troops.[33] Largely on the basis of its new share of the world, the internal strength derived mainly from this, and such "gunboat diplomacy," U.S. capital export continued to grow throughout the 1920s.

The dramatic rise of the U.S. as a major capital exporter also included substantial loan operations, particularly in Europe. The U.S. emerged from World War 1 as the world's main creditor nation, which had significant political and economic repercussions. The French were indebted to the U.S. bourgeoisie for some $4 billion, lesser combatants for $3.2 billion. The British had themselves lent heavily to their allies but in turn were forced to borrow from the U.S. and, at the war's end, owed $4.7 billion.[34]

In the postwar period, the U.S. was the major international supplier of capital and New York began to supplant London as the world financial center. In 1924, the volume of U.S. foreign lending reached a new annual high of more than $900 million, and rose to a level of $1.25 billion in 1927 and 1928. Between 1924 and 1929, the U.S. exported almost twice as much loan capital as did Britain, and much of this capital went into Europe.[35] There, the influx of U.S. capital mainly took the form of short-term loans rather than long-term investment. In particular, U.S. financiers played an important role in funding German recovery, taking advantage of the favor-

---

[33] Beard, *The Rise of American Civilization*, Volume 2, pp. 503-4; J. T. Whitaker, *Americas to the South* (New York: MacMillan, 1939), p. 3; and Zinn, *People's History*, p. 399. According to Zinn: "Between 1900 and 1933, the United States intervened in Cuba four times, in Nicaragua twice, in Panama six times, in Guatemala once, in Honduras seven times." See also James Cable, *Gunboat Diplomacy* (New York: Praeger, 1971), Appendix: "Fifty Years of Gunboat Diplomacy," pp. 175-229.

[34] Charles P. Kindleberger, *The World in Depression 1929-1939* (Berkeley: Univ. of California Press, 1973), p. 40.

[35] Kindleberger, *World in Depression*, pp. 54, 56.

able climate for foreign investment in Germany during the 1920s.[36]
U.S. loan capital enabled Germany to meet its reparations obligations; both the Dawes Plan of 1924 and the Young Plan of 1929
established payments schedules linked to international, mainly
U.S., loans.

The U.S. position on reparations and repayments, along with
the mechanisms and arrangements worked out to finance them,
very much influenced the economic and political struggles of the
interwar period. Their fabled isolationism notwithstanding, the
U.S. imperialists positioned themselves to play the major investor
role in Germany and, linked with this, strengthened their hand vis-
à-vis Great Britain and France as well. All told, the U.S. acquired
considerable leverage over the other great powers, enabling it to as-
cend the imperialist hierarchy.

The expansion of the post-World War 1 period cannot be understood outside the new investment opportunities opened up in the
Third World. The magnitude of colonial acquisitions is certainly
not the only factor underlying growth potential — but it is decisive.
The dialectics of international expansion and domestic growth cannot be treated here; besides the general discusson in the preceding
chapter, the theoretical argumentation and concrete substantiation
of this thesis is contained in a subsequent volume dealing with capital accumulation in the post-World War 2 period. Yet that linkage
must be underscored in the present narrative if we are to understand the relative buoyancy and prowess of the U.S. economy in
the 1920s.

Let us consider the international expansion of U.S. capital. U.S.
foreign investment grew more than fivefold between 1914 and

---

[36] Despite the much ballyhooed "rape of Germany" via the Versailles Treaty, the
facts show that while Germany was severely beaten, it was not destroyed as an imperialist power. It suffered the loss of its colonies, restrictions were placed for a time
on German freedom to act in the Rhineland and on the country's military capacity,
and it was saddled with reparations payments (which proved largely unenforceable).
Despite the loss of some domestic territory, however, the German imperialist industrial base in the Ruhr and Silesia remained intact. As one historian perceptively
noted: "Germany had only to secure a modification of the treaty, or to shake it off
altogether; and she would emerge as strong, or almost as strong, as she had been in
1914" (A.J.P. Taylor, *The Origins of the Second World War*, 2nd ed. [Greenwich,
Conn.: Fawcett, 1966], p. 28). This situation did not stem mainly from the leniency of
the victorious imperialists, but from the practical necessities of dealing with a
defeated but still imperialist nation in the context of imperialist international relations, both economic and politico-strategic.

TABLE 2.3
Geographical Distribution of Foreign Investments of the United Kingdom, France, Germany, and the United States at the Outbreak of the First World War[1] and on the Eve of the Second World War[2]

(in millions of U.S. dollars to the nearest $50 million)

Destination		Country of Origin									
		U.K.		France		Germany		U.S.		World[3]	
		1914	1938	1914	1938	1914	1938	1914	1938	1914	1938
Latin America	1914	$3,700		$1,600		$900		$1,650		$8,900	
		41.8%		18.1%		10.2%		18.5%		100%	
	1938		$4,900		$400		$150		$4,150		$11,300
			43.4%		3.5%		1.3%		36.7%		100%
Asia and the Pacific	1914	$3,250		$1,050		$700		$200		$6,300	
		51.6%		16.7%		11.1%		3.2%		100%	
	1938		$5,000		$900		$150		$650		$10,650
			46.9%		8.5%		1.4%		6.1%		100%
Africa	1914	$2,450		$900		$500		—		$4,050	
		60.5%		22.2%		12.3%				100%	
	1938		$2,150		$1,050		—		$150		$4,050
			53.1%		25.9%				3.7%		100%
Oppressed Countries Total[4]	1914	$9,400		$3,550		$2,100		$1,850		$19,250	
		48.8%		18.4%		10.9%		9.6%		100%	
	1938		$12,050		$2,350		$300		$4,950		$26,000
			46.3%		9.0%		1.2%		23.1%		100%
Capitalist and Imperialist Countries[5]	1914	$10,600		$5,500		$3,700		$1,650		$26,200	
		40.5%		21.0%		14.1%		6.3%		100%	
	1938		$10,800		$1,500		$350		$6,700		$28,950
			37.3%		5.2%		1.2%		23.1%		100%
World Total	1914	$20,000		$9,050		$5,800		$3,500		$45,450	
		44.0%		19.9%		12.8%		7.8%		100%	
	1938		$22,900		$3,850		$700		$11,650		$54,950
			41.7%		7.0%		1.3%		21.2%		100%

[1]Generally 1914.
[2]1938.
[3]The sum of the three regions above.
[4]Total foreign investment of all capital-exporting countries.
[5]Includes all of Europe, U.S., Canada, Japan, Australia, and New Zealand.

Source: William Woodruff, *Impact of Western Man*, Tables IV/3 and IV/4, pp. 154-57.

TABLE 2.4

Stock of Foreign Investment*
of Leading Imperialist Powers:
1900, 1914, 1930
(percentage distribution)

Country	1900	1914	1930
United States...........	2.0	6.3	35.3
United Kingdom	50.8	50.5	43.8
France	21.8	22.3	8.4
Germany..............	20.2	17.8	2.6
Canada	–	0.5	3.1
Netherlands	4.0	3.1	5.5

*distribution of all foreign investment, including portfolio.

Source: Richard S. Newfarmer and Willard F. Mueller, *Multinational Corporations in Brazil and Mexico, Report to the Subcommittee on Multinational Corporations of the Committee on Foreign Relations, United States Senate, August 1975.* (Washington, D.C.: GPO, 1975), page 31.

1930. This compares dramatically with the investment positions of the other major powers — British, French, and German overseas investment declined during the same period (see Table 2.1). And, as can be seen in Table 2.3 (which shows the change in volume and geographic distribution of the foreign assets of the leading imperialist powers from the outbreak of World War 1 to the eve of World War 2), the U.S. even raised its investment profile over fourfold in Asia and Africa (taken together), regions which were more the bailiwicks of the other imperial powers. The distribution of ownership of the aggregate stock of all foreign investment shifted radically. As can be seen in Table 2.4, the U.S. share of the total stock of foreign investment of the six major Western capital-exporting powers was under 7 percent in 1914. Only twenty-five years later, in 1930, the U.S. share accounted for over 35 percent of the total!

In the realm of trade, the U.S. also scored impressive gains. In fact, during this period trade was the leading edge of U.S. economic expansion in many of the areas dominated by other imperialists. As is the case today with Japan and West Germany, the vitality of the domestic industrial base of the U.S. gave it commercial advantage. In 1913, U.S. exports to China stood at $26.1 million; by 1930, they had soared to $190 million.[37] The U.S. even made inroads into Britain's most highly prized colonies. In 1930, the total value of U.S. exports to India, Egypt, Nigeria, and Malaya reached 17 percent of Great Britain's total.[38]

Still, in the majority of colonial regions in Asia, Africa, and the Middle East, Britain retained the upper hand politically. France, too, retained large colonial holdings, as did most of the other European imperialist powers and Japan. Under monopoly capitalism, no less so than under earlier capitalist colonialism, the primary vehicle for securing economic advantage in a colony is political control of its state apparatus. Old-style colonialism, particularly as practiced by the European powers through the mid-twentieth century, centered on formal control of the oppressed nations through colonial administration and military occupation. Neocolonialism, particularly as perfected by the U.S. in the post-World War 2 period, revolves around very real control of formally independent oppressed social formations through a variety of mechanisms, including puppet regimes and military pacts, as well as foreign investment, aid, and trade.

It was principally in the Western hemisphere where the U.S., given the political control it exercised, made the greatest gains in overseas investments. U.S. investments in Latin America increased more than fourfold between 1913 and 1929.[39] By 1929, its assets in the Caribbean, Mexico, and Central America far exceeded those of Britain. In South America, the British were mainly protecting and consolidating their holdings in Argentina, Brazil, and Uruguay,

---

[37] Williams, *Contours of American History*, p. 435. Viewing the movement of this trade from the other direction, between 1913 and 1931 the U.S. share of China's exports rose from 9.3 percent to 13.2 percent of the total. By 1936, the U.S. was taking 26.4 percent of China's exports. The increase in U.S. foreign investment in China, while impressive, lagged behind increases in the domain of trade. In 1914, the U.S. owned 3.1 percent of the total foreign investment in China. By 1931, its share had increased to 6.1 percent as compared with its 13.2 percent share of China's exports and 22.2 percent share of China's imports (Albert Feuerwerker, *The Chinese Economy, 1912-1949*, Michigan Papers in Chinese Studies, No. 1 [Ann Arbor: Univ. of Michigan Press, 1968], pp. 63-75).

[38] R. Palme Dutt, *World Politics: 1918-1936* (New York: International Publishers, 1936), pp. 196-97.

[39] Winkler, *U.S. Capital in Latin America*, p. 284.

TABLE 2.5
Growth of Latin American Trade, 1913-1927
(in millions of U.S. dollars to the nearest million)

	Britain			U.S.			World		
	1913	1927	Percent increase 1913-27	1913	1927	Percent increase 1913-27	1913	1927	Percent increase 1913-27
South America	595	742	24.6%	381	991	160.0%	2,313	3,825	65.4%
Central America[1]	83	113	36.2%	436	792	81.8%	688	1,314	91.1%
Total for Latin America	678	855	26.0%	817	1,783	118.3%	3,001	5,139	71.3%

[1] Including Cuba, Mexico, and the West Indies.

Source: Max Winkler, *Investments of United States Capital in Latin America* (Boston: World Peace Foundation, 1928), Tables IV and IX, pp. 277, 282.

while U.S. investments were growing far more rapidly and displacing them everywhere else. U.S. investments in South America grew 1,226 percent from 1913 to 1929, compared with a 17 percent increase in British investments.[40] A further indication of increasing U.S. influence and economic advantage in Latin America is to be found in Table 2.5, which reveals the far greater ability of the U.S. imperialists, relative to the British, to expand trade in the region.

The sharp increase of its overseas investments and the general bolstering of its international position spurred overall growth for the U.S. An additional stimulus came from rationalization and restructuring induced by the exigencies of war: new production techniques found widespread application; scientific research expanded greatly; and the automobile complex emerged as a major component of the industrial structure. The liquidity of large firms increased as a result of war contracts, and new government-built facilities passed into the hands of large corporations after the war. With its productive base undamaged by the conflict, the U.S. greatly increased an already substantial technological edge over the other imperialist powers and put it to competitive use.

These advantages were reflected in the trajectory of the U.S. economy during the interwar period. After a brief inflationary boom in 1919-20 and a severe but brief downturn in 1920-21 (attributable largely to short-term causes), the years 1922-29 saw relatively impressive growth. Between 1919 and 1929, capital per worker, which had shown practically no increase between 1909 and 1919, grew at an impressive 3.2 percent annual rate.[41] The volume of manufacturing output in 1928-29 was 70 percent greater than prewar levels.[42] In the 1920s, a stupendous merger boom accompanied and fed this expansion. Between 1913 and 1929, U.S. GNP grew at an average annual rate of 3.1 percent. Of the major capitalist powers, only Japan had a higher rate of growth (Japan, like the U.S., had been able to sit out, yet benefit from, the war).[43]

The 1920s were years of expansion throughout the imperialist countries, although its pace and scope was uneven. We have already chronicled the robust expansion of the big gainer in the

---

[40] Winkler, *U.S. Capital in Latin America,* pp. 284-85.

[41] David M. Gordon, et al., *Segmented Work, Divided Workers* (New York: Cambridge Univ. Press, 1982), p. 104.

[42] Landes, *Unbound Prometheus,* p. 368.

[43] U.S. Bureau of Economic Analysis, *Long-Term Economic Growth 1860-1970* (GPO, 1973), Part IV, Table 7, p. 99.

war, the U.S. Because Great Britain still held on to a considerable portion of its empire and because of the overall expansion in the imperialist world, it was capable of sustaining a modicum of growth. New industries took root in the advanced countries: electrical power generation, synthetic chemicals, and motor transport were among the most prominent. Deprived of expanded international opportunities for accumulation, Germany, the big loser in the war, was forced to more radically restructure its domestic base (thus the extensive modernization of the steel sector), and this had a certain stimulating effect on its economy. France undertook a massive program of reconstruction and during the years 1921-29 could boast an average annual rate of increase of total real output of 7.8 percent. By the same measure, Japan showed a rate of increase of 4.8 percent (the same as that of the U.S.); on the other hand, Great Britain grew at a rate of only 2.5 percent.[44]

This economic performance can only be understood in light of the respective international positions of the great powers. Great Britain and France had successfully defended their colonial empires — but they were not to substantially enlarge them, notwithstanding gains in the Middle East. Japan expanded its colonial holdings and export markets through the war, while the war mobilization itself spurred industrialization (particularly in the iron and steel sectors) and led to big increases in concentration. Germany, of course, found itself hemmed in by the postwar arrangements; for example, the dissolution of the Austro-Hungarian empire seriously compromised its historical patterns of trade. The collapse of the tsarist empire represented a different kind of loss for all the imperialist powers. The removal of a large part of the world from the imperialist orbit, especially in view of the historical role of the European market, compounded the difficulties of international restructuring. This was of some moment for France: many of Russia's metal works were French-owned, and half of Russia's oil output was controlled by French and British capital.[45]

Thus, while a new context was established for world accumulation, the contradictory outcome of and constraints imposed by this first redivision of the world also asserted themselves: in the decade

---

[44] U.S. Bureau of Economic Analysis, *Long-Term Economic Growth*, pp. 274-75.

[45] *History of the Communist Party of the Soviet Union (Bolsheviks): Short Course* (New York: International Publishers, 1939), p. 162.

of the 1920s Europe experienced persistently high rates of un-employment; investment as a share of GNP in Great Britain was half that of the investment share in the U.S.;[46] and expansion proved especially turbulent and short-lived in Germany.

Let us sum up, then, what World War 1 accomplished. The war was a turning point in world history. Much of the institutional and economic framework of European power politics, out of which imperialism had emerged, was destroyed. Indeed, the war years were accompanied by a widespread cultural malaise in Europe and, on the other hand, a sense of anticipation as the "old world" seemed to shatter and decay on the battlefield. The growing importance of the United States, inside and outside Europe, was testimony to the collapse of that framework. Objectively, imperialist capital needed to make a leap and, by virtue of the war, it did so. In terms of inter-imperialist relations, the war temporarily diminished the intensity of world rivalry enough to permit the international reorganization of capital. New spheres of influence were chiseled out and growth ensued. On the other hand, unlike the overall redivision effected by the Second World War, this one was not as great, both in the re-distribution and concentration of colonies and in the recasting of interimperialist alignments. While the U.S. exploited the burdens and dislocations of the war to strengthen its hand against victors and vanquished alike, it did not "clean up" against its allies as it did during World War 2. At the same time, in the war's aftermath the imperialist states as a whole did not face the same overriding polit-ical necessity to bloc against a socialist camp, a necessity that miti-gated imperialist antagonisms following World War 2. And in this overall context, the absence of a leading imperialist power — in contrast both to pre-World War 1 British preeminence and post-World War 2 U.S. dominance — had an impact on the course of development of the interwar period.

For these reasons, the contradictory thrusts of imperialist accu-mulation led to a decade of expansion (in which some powers parti-cipated only minimally) followed abruptly by an unprecedented global crisis of which the crash of the U.S. stock market in 1929 was the bellwether. The Great Depression was the most acute eco-nomic collapse in the history of the capitalist system. Especially

[46] See W.W. Rostow, *The World Economy: History and Prospects* (Austin: Univ. of Texas Press, 1978), p. 219; U.S. Bureau of Economic Analysis, *Long-Term Economic Growth*, p. 102.

during the initial years, its effects were more severe and developed more rapidly in the U.S. than in most of the other imperialist countries. In 1932-33, at the bottom of the trough, virtually a quarter of the U.S. labor force was unemployed. The cumulative loss of potential output in the U.S. during the years 1930-39 was of the order of $715 billion in 1972 prices, or about double the annual potential output the economy would have been capable of producing at four percent unemployment at the end of the 1930s.[47] Between its high point in 1929 and the low point in 1932, the index of industrial production declined more than 25 percent in Great Britain and 47 percent in France.[48] The total volume of world trade dropped from a 1929 peak of $68.6 billion to $26.9 billion in 1932; even the subsequent "recovery" only brought the aggregate to $46.1 billion.[49] The Great Depression wiped out the expansion of the 1920s, which had been so prodigious in the U.S. There had been no comparable setback in the history of capitalism.

In such a situation of economic and political stress, significant mass struggles erupted in the advanced countries. Had they not been steered into economist and reformist channels, some certainly had the potential for posing an all-around and revolutionary challenge to the established order. The existence of that possibility was integral to the installation of "popular front," or New Deal-type, and fascist regimes.

Compared with the advanced countries, the effects of the world economic crisis were even more ruinous in many of the oppressed countries. Coffee, cotton, rubber, and wheat prices declined more than 50 percent between September 1929 and December 1930; this had devastating consequences for the exports, income, and central bank reserves of countries like Brazil, Colombia, the then Dutch East Indies, and Argentina.[50] When the Depression began in the United States, it rippled and ripped through the economies of those oppressed countries most directly dependent on U.S. imperialism. Exports from Chile, for example, plummeted by over 80 percent;

[47] Robert Aaron Gordon, *Economic Instability and Growth: The American Record* (New York: Harper and Row, 1974), p. 46.

[48] Maurice Flamant and Jeanne Singer-Kérel, *Modern Economic Crisis and Recessions* (New York: Harper and Row, 1970), pp. 69, 72.

[49] William Woodruff, *Impact of Western Man: A Study of Europe's Role in the World Economy 1750-1960*, 2nd ed. (Washington, D.C.: University Press of America, 1982), p. 276; See also Landes, *Unbound Prometheus*, p. 366.

[50] Kindleberger, *World in Depression*, pp. 142-44.

from Bolivia, Peru, El Salvador, and Cuba by over 70 percent.[51] These countries were so tied to the imperialists that when their export markets shrank due to the stagnation in the imperialist centers, their entire economies faced collapse. And this in turn limited the ability of the imperialists to profitably export capital and goods to them. The problems were even more acute in those countries with relatively larger urban centers and larger concentrations of capital (including foreign capital). In Latin America, the most developed region of the Third World and the one most directly tied to the United States, unemployment ran as high as 50 to 75 percent at times between 1929 and 1933.

The international crisis brought with it an escalation in the resistance of the oppressed peoples. In Latin America, for instance, the struggle against U.S. and British imperialism mounted, notably in Cuba, Chile, Brazil, Mexico, Argentina, and Nicaragua. There was unrest as well in Asia, Africa, and the Middle East. As the 1930s proceeded, however, these struggles were increasingly affected by the heightening of interimperialist contradictions. In 1935, Italy invaded Abyssinia (Ethiopia). In 1937, Japan raised the ante, moving out of areas already held in the north of China in order to militarily occupy the key cities in the rest of the country. By the mid-1930s, the lines had been drawn between two rival imperialist blocs, and the developing struggle between them interpenetrated with colonial unrest. In China, for example, an antagonistic split developed between different sections of the Chinese big bourgeoisie: those tied to Anglo-U.S. interests versus those tied to Japan. In several other countries, the conflict between the internal allies of rival imperialists both contributed to social ferment and often diverted that ferment to the service of one or the other rival imperialist force.

In Latin America, U.S. imperialism faced a complex situation. It was unable to maintain the level of capital exports to the region reached in the 1920s; in fact, between 1929 and 1940 U.S. direct investment assets actually declined.[52] As a result, the U.S. imperialists were forced to intensify the exploitation of the Latin American peoples. Meeting increasing resistance from the masses, however, the U.S. had to modify its approach to Latin American politics. This

---

[51] Kindleberger, *World in Depression,* p. 191.

[52] U.S. direct investment assets in Latin America had declined from $3.5 billion in 1929 to $2.8 billion in 1940 (U.S. Bureau of the Census, *Historical Statistics of the United States, Colonial Times to 1957* [GPO, 1960], p. 566).

new approach, formulated in 1933, was called the "Good Neighbor Policy." Not unlike the Carter rhetoric of the late 1970s, Franklin Delano Roosevelt launched this campaign as an appeal for the observance of "human rights." The policy had its roots, as well, in the recognition (already operative in the late 1920s) that the movement "from adventure to permanent investment" necessitated more enduring and stable institutions of control than the mere stationing of U.S. troops in the dominated countries. As Roosevelt's Secretary of State Cordell Hull later remarked: "In the past we, too, stationed some soldiers in Central America and left them there as long as ten years, but the results were bad, and we brought them out. Since then we have found it more profitable to practice the 'Good Neighbor Policy.' "[53]

But no matter what the changes of policy, U.S. imperial dominance still rested on armed force. Nicaragua provided a clear example of how the new policy worked. No sooner had the U.S. withdrawn the Marines, following years of mass resistance to direct occupation, than, as a "good neighbor" of course, it organized, equipped, and advised a new Nicaraguan National Guard — with a "commander-in-chief" picked by the U.S. ambassador — to take the Marines' place. This National Guard then helped their U.S. "good neighbors" by continuing to prosecute the war against nationalist guerrillas led by Sandino, whom they managed to murder in 1934.[54]

With the important exception of the Philippines, most of the oppressed nations controlled by U.S. imperialism were not to become the ground on which the ensuing world war was fought. The most bitterly contested colonial preserves were in Asia, where both the United States and Japan sought to carve out new empires, and in the arc formed by North Africa and the Middle East, which occupied a strategic position with respect to the European theater.

[53] Cordell Hull to the Japanese ambassador in 1941, quoted in Lloyd C. Gardner, *Economic Aspects of New Deal Diplomacy* (Boston: Beacon Press, 1971), p. 47.

[54] For discussion of the more general application of New Deal diplomacy in the oppressed countries, see Gardner, *New Deal Diplomacy*, Chaps. 3, 6; and Eduardo Galeano, *Open Veins of Latin America: Five Centuries of the Pillage of a Continent* (New York: Monthly Review Press, 1973), pp. 124-26. Under the "Good Neighbor" policy, the U.S. imperialists backed the Machado regime in Cuba against revolt, supported attempts to undermine the Cardenas regime of Mexico (which, pushed by nationalist forces, was nationalizing U.S. oil interests), and carried out many other acts of interference. Needless to say, they continued to carry their big stick for use when deception and intrigue proved inadequate to the task.

Only in some areas of Latin America, most notably Argentina, did the imperialists of the German bloc gain significant influence through comprador elements and "fifth column" political factions. In these cases, the U.S. imperialists paid special attention to employing the deception of "good neighborliness" in "assisting" the resistance against the political influence of the rival bloc. In Brazil, for instance, they helped thwart an attempt by the Hitler-inspired Integralists to infiltrate the U.S. lackey government of President Vargas. Needless to say, the U.S. first had to pave the way by making the country safe from revolution, backing Vargas in arresting and torturing thousands and in killing hundreds of national liberation fighters, among whom numbered many members of the Brazilian Communist Party.[55] On the whole, the new tactics of the U.S. were incapable of eliminating the resistance to its brand of imperialism during these years, yet it had an altogether easier go of it than the other imperialists.

Meanwhile, in the realm of more direct relations between the vying empire builders, a complex pattern of rivalry was resolving itself into a more definite bipolar arrangement, although not without a certain measure of fluidity. On the surface, the United States seemed like the "wildcard." For instance, U.S. assistance was essential to keeping the British afloat. And this in turn served the larger interests of U.S. imperialism: "the stabilization of the pound was seen to be in America's interest because it was a major step toward the stabilization of the general European monetary situation, a prerequisite for the attainment of American financial and trading ambitions."[56] Thus in 1925, the Federal Reserve Bank of New York and a syndicate headed by J.P. Morgan & Co. negotiated loans of $200 million and $100 million, respectively, to restore the pound sterling to prewar parity.[57] But the U.S. was not only bolstering Britain. Beginning in 1928 (and more markedly after the crash of 1929) Germany, Britain's rival, found it difficult to meet even the reduced payments mandated by the aforementioned Young Plan. The Hoover administration proposed and brought about a moratorium on German repayments, much to the chagrin of the British and French.[58] The U.S. was clearly

---

[55] Whitaker, *Americas to the South,* pp. 195-96.

[56] Block, *Origins of International Economic Disorder,* p. 16.

[57] Block, *Origins of International Economic Disorder,* p. 16.

[58] Such actions, viewed as challenges to British leadership, often led observers of the time to erroneously conclude, as did Stalin, that the struggle between Britain and the U.S. for world domination had become the chief interimperialist contradiction.

(continued next page)

playing the field, and manipulating the weaknesses of the central antagonists in the global power struggle.

Escalating economic difficulties and political crises were leading to intensified rivalry among all the imperialist powers. But these tensions also created an objective basis for specific alignments. Thus, while the United States continued to implement the strategy of "sitting on the mountaintop," it had an enormous stake in any major shift in interimperialist strength among its rivals and itself operated according to the need to seek a redivision. For reasons which will become clearer in the later discussion of World War 2, this dictated a strategy based mainly on alliance with Great Britain.

Real material and strategic antagonisms separated the United States from what would later become the Axis powers, especially Japan. Both the U.S. and Japan coveted huge stretches of Asia. In 1933, the Japanese imperialists proclaimed their own functional equivalent to the Monroe Doctrine, warning other imperialist powers to steer clear of entanglements in China. The "Open Door" met its most serious challenge, with long-term U.S. interests threatened in China and Southeast Asia. As the Japanese consolidated control in Manchuria, the U.S. reaffirmed its claim to "Open Door" rights and its intention to enforce them. That the Japanese were prepared to expend vast amounts of weaponry and manpower in the Pacific theater galvanized the U.S. alliance with Britain, which was in fact the principal "status quo" power in Asia. This alliance served the broader interests of U.S. imperialism: on the one hand, the U.S. could more potently counter the German and Japanese challenge to its own global aims; on the other, and very much related, through the process of alliance with Britain the U.S. could more deeply penetrate the empire of its weaker, yet planet-straddling, ally.

It is often argued that the U.S. retreated from the prospect of world leadership into isolationism in the 1920s and 1930s by, for instance, rejecting membership in the League of Nations. But the U.S.

In 1930 Stalin wrote: "Both in the sphere of the export of manufactured goods and in the sphere of the export of capital, the struggle is raging chiefly between the United States and Britain. It is enough to read any journal dealing with economics, any document concerning exports of goods and capital, to be convinced of this" (J.V. Stalin, "Political Report of the Central Committee to the Sixteenth Congress of the CPSU[B]," *Works* [Moscow: Foreign Languages Publishing House, 1955], Volume 12, p. 255).

hardly turned its back on the world during this period. We have already reviewed some of its activities in Latin America. Beyond this, it even took the lead in certain diplomatic convocations. In 1921-22, for example, the U.S. managed to bring several imperialist powers to the Washington Conference, at which a number of agreements were concluded considerably strengthening the U.S. position. Among these was the famous fixing of a 5/5/3 ratio for larger classes of warships belonging to the U.S., Britain, and Japan, respectively. (Japan did not abrogate this agreement for over a decade.) Japan was also compelled to restore Shantung to joint imperialist plunder. The U.S. decision to stay out of the League of Nations was based on unwillingness to subordinate its power to a broader group, even in the limited sense implied by League membership. This unwillingness was echoed by both Germany and Japan when they withdrew from the League in 1933. The apparent isolationism of the U.S. was not prompted by any lack of desire to play an international role. It stemmed from the contradiction between the economic dynamism of U.S. imperialism, relative to other powers, and the fact that the U.S. rulers were not yet fully capable of seizing political and military leadership of the imperialist world and imposing upon it a Pax Americana similar to the Pax Britannica of the prewar era.

This raises the issue of the relative importance of a dominant and leading power among the imperialists, a question alluded to earlier. Before World War 1, Britain's nonpareil strength provided the conditions for relatively stable international monetary and trade relations. This was facilitated by an international monetary system pegged to the stabilizing role of the British pound, British gold, and London's position as the world financial center, as well as the relatively "free trading" framework conforming to British commercial supremacy. Following World War 2, the strength of the American behemoth, nearly uncontested by rival imperialisms, underlay an even stronger orchestration of relatively orderly interimperialist trade, financial, and monetary arrangements. In contrast to each of these situations, the period between the First and Second World Wars was characterized by the absence of any single power center capable of establishing and overseeing rational, integrated trade and monetary relations on a global level. Because of this, the inherent anarchy in relations within and between the formations of capital which underlay the world economy came more abruptly to the surface. By the 1930s, interimperialist trade and monetary relations were in a virtual shambles as each power erected high protectionist barriers against every other imperialist country.

Although the degree of world imperialist reorganization was the most important factor establishing the terms of the spiral following World War 1, an important secondary factor was that no imperialist power emerged from the First World War capable of playing an organizing or stabilizing role. This must be seen as a particular feature of the overall redivision effected by World War 1. Had either Germany been victorious and clearly established its leadership over the imperialist world or had Britain been able to fully hold on to its previous power through World War 1, the dynamic would have been different. However, due to the increasingly moribund nature of imperialism as a whole and to the anarchic forward motion of capital, a new crisis and war would still have erupted, even though the spiral from World War 1 to World War 2 would have unfolded with different alignments of imperialist power; different, and perhaps more coherent, economic conventions; and, quite possibly, a longer trajectory before the next imperialist war.

The existence of a "hegemonic" power is not by itself a defining feature of the imperialist spirals (any more than is its absence), though where such a factor exists it can significantly influence their course of development. Nevertheless, it was that redivision in its totality (and the shift in strength between the international proletariat and imperialism) that most determined the character of imperialist accumulation in the ensuing period, just as the Second World War set the initial and general parameters and possibilities of the post-World War 2 period.[59]

---

[59] Charles Kindleberger, whose study of the 1930s Depression has been cited in this work, is perhaps the most prominent exponent of the view that a single dominant power is the sine qua non of economic stability and growth. In his explanation of the origins of the collapse of the 1930s, he writes: "The world economic system was unstable unless some country stabilized it, as Britain had done in the nineteenth century and up to 1913. In 1929 the British couldn't and the United States wouldn't" (Kindleberger, *World in Depression,* p. 292). Kindleberger errs seriously in the direction of voluntarism. It was not a case of the U.S. simply failing to step forward; the U.S. also *couldn't,* given the depth of world contradictions and the relative strength of U.S. imperialism. More important, the nature and duration of expansion, as stressed above, is principally a function of the overall scope of reorganization, the factors influencing the volume and composition of capital exports (particularly to the Third World), and the long-term development of imperialism. In this larger context, and only in this context, does the question of an "organizing power" take on significance. But, as we see today, even an "activist" and "internationalist" U.S. imperialism can in no fundamental way reverse the crisis that grips the world capitalist system, that is, short of a total redivision.

The collapse of the 1930s sent shock waves through all the imperialist powers, and the financial crisis was felt acutely in Germany. The pathetic upswing of 1934-37, in which some countries, notably France, did not even participate, resolved nothing. In 1938, total real output in the U.S. was no higher than in 1929 and, in France, considerably below the 1929 level.[60] The situation in the United States was scarcely encouraging for its rulers. In 1925, machines more than ten years old made up only 44 percent of the total in use in industry, but by 1940 this proportion had risen to 70 percent. And as late as 1939, one of six employable workers was unable to find work.[61] Thus, the New Deal did not rescue capitalism from crisis, much less represent a moment of popular rule. The New Deal was symptomatic of what was occurring in all the imperialist countries: the further refinement of the imperialist state as an instrument of economic rationalization and social control and the mobilization of people and resources for global conquest (tailored to the requirements of U.S. monopoly capital).

The Depression intensified the rivalries leading to war, and hence the pace of militarization grew more feverish. In 1930, the armaments expenditures of 62 nations totalled $4.13 billion; by 1936, these expenditures had climbed to nearly $11 billion, and the larger imperialist powers were appropriating as much as 70 percent of their national budgets to pay off past war debts and to underwrite their arsenals.[62] The imperialist world was poised for the most destructive war yet in human history.

World War 2: U.S. Ascendance

World War 2 has been sanctified by all manner of patriotic and democratic cant as a just war waged by the Allied powers to save the world from fascist barbarism. The utter cynicism and hypocrisy of these self-serving claims is revealed, in an odd kind of way, in the popular movie *Casablanca*. Patriotic French nationals gather in Rick's Cafe and in one "touching" scene sing the Marseillaise in tribute to the glorious struggle to reclaim "la France" from the evil clutches of the Germans. But there is one curious element here. All

---

[60] U.S. Bureau of Economic Analysis, *Long-Term Economic Growth*, p. 275.

[61] Flamant, *Modern Economic Crisis and Recessions*, p. 75.

[62] Richard Krooth, *Arms and Empire: Imperial Patterns Before World War II* (Santa Barbara, California: Harvest Publishers, 1980), p. 126.

the romance and existential musing, brought to a head by a French resistance fighter in transit through the city, take place on the soil of a French colony — Morocco! A willing "political" suspension of disbelief is demanded of the viewer: forget the fact that the French imperialists have brought untold suffering to the peoples of Africa, including press-ganging them into the world wars, and that after World War 2 they would be applying electrodes to the genitals of Algerian freedom fighters.

The existing imperialist partition of Africa in 1939, particularly the holdings of Britain and France, put this holy crusade against fascism in some perspective (see Figure 2.1). Indeed, on the eve of World War 2, of the entire area controlled by imperialism (with about 90 percent of the world's population — that is everyone save those in the U.S.S.R. and a few liberated areas, as in China), the Allied imperialists (the "good guys") controlled the greatest part, namely all of the neocolonies of Latin America, the overwhelming bulk of Africa, and most of Asia, with the exception of China, which was contested, though largely in the hands of the Japanese. Put differently, fewer than one out of twenty persons in the colonial world (excluding China) saluted the flags of the Axis powers.[63] Imperialist cynicism runs both ways, and with figures such as these (and the same basic logic as the "antifascist" imperialists) one could perhaps make an argument that "right" was on the side of the Axis powers, potential "liberators" of the Third World — which, indeed, they frequently claimed to be. (For example, the Japanese raised the slogan "Asia for the Asians" in the 1930s and early 1940s.)

World War 2, like World War 1, was in its principal aspect and essentially a conflict between rival imperialist blocs to determine who would have the "right" to reshape and dominate the imperialist world order and rule over the lion's share of colonies. The international communist movement tended to mask that reality (and departed significantly from Leninism on this question) by preoccupying itself with the specter of fascism in Europe, as concentrated in the strategy of the united front against fascism. Bob Avakian has commented:

> [T]he focus was overwhelmingly on Europe. And I think that that's not entirely accidental, for two reasons. One, because it reflects the

---

[63] Calculated from League of Nations, Economic Intelligence Service, *Statistical Yearbook, 1939/40* (Geneva, 1940), pp. 14-22.

FIGURE 2.1
The Imperialist Division of Africa, 1939

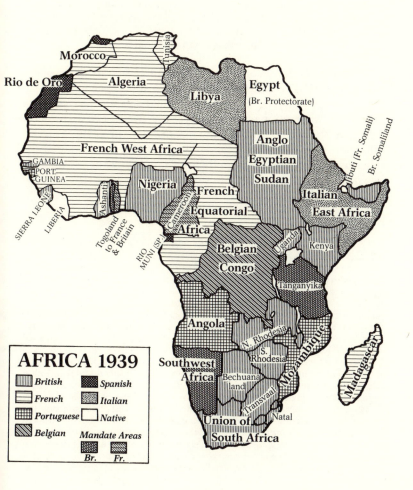

Source: Henry W. Littlefield, *History of Europe Since 1815* (New York: Barnes & Noble, 1961), p. 147.

exigencies of Soviet foreign policy at the time and their attempts to deal with the Western imperialist democracies; and on the other hand, if you were going to make a case about how much more terrible the fascist states were than the democracies, you'd make it better in Europe where there was more democracy than you would if you went in some of the colonial countries and started arguing about how great British imperialism was for India, for example, as compared with Japanese imperialism and its colonies.[64]

The roots of the Second World War lay in the redivision of the world in 1918. The interwar period was just that — a truce which would, of necessity, be broken. Britain had defeated its rivals, but found its international position greatly weakened. The U.S. emerged stronger, consolidating its position in Latin America where the most developed colonies were located. But dislodging the other imperialist powers from their most profitable or strategically key positions in Asia and Africa still required arduous struggle. The U.S. had designs on Britain's Far East colonies and spheres of influence — designs which became imperative with the onset and con-

---

[64] Bob Avakian, *Conquer the World? The International Proletariat Must and Will* (Chicago: RCP Publications, 1981), published as *Revolution*, No. 50, p. 25. One pertinent example of this is afforded by comparing British wartime agricultural policy "at home" with that applied in India. At home, the British aimed at lessening the country's dependence on international supply sources; as a result, the total area of tilled land increased by 66 percent. This expanded production, in conjunction with a comprehensive system of rationing, resulted in a diet for the population which was, on the whole, adequate in relation to prewar levels. On the other hand, in India, though a prize colony and an important field of operations against Japan, the British pursued a quite different policy — one with entirely different objectives. No serious or adequate attempts were made to head off a war-induced famine and to develop a self-sufficient agriculture. British policy was designed only to insure that rice and other critical supplies reached those working directly in the British war effort. Prices spiraled upward due to wartime inflation (the effects of the expansion of mainly British wartime industry and the fact that the British Raj was printing money at a ratio of two-and-a-half to one over its sterling reserves). With the fall of Burma to Japan, prices rose still further as rice and other food imports were cut off. Tremendous hoarding and price gouging ensued (in anticipation of still higher prices). As a consequence, starvation and the scourges of cholera, malaria, and smallpox exacted a devastating toll. British policy insisted that "the maintenance of essential food supplies to the industrial area of Calcutta [a principal base of British operations] must be ranked on a very high priority among their [the British controlled Raj's] wartime obligations." The deaths resulting from this policy were termed the "Great Bengal Famine" of 1943, and have been estimated at three million! Another glorious episode in the struggle against *German* and *Japanese* barbarism (see Amartya K. Sen, "Starvation and exchange entitlements: a general approach and its application to the Great Bengal Famine," in *Cambridge Journal of Economics* [1977], Volume 1, pp. 33-59; and also Alan S. Milward, *War, Economy, and Society, 1939-45* [Berkeley: Univ. of California Press, 1977], pp. 249-53, 280-81).

tinuation of profound crisis throughout the 1930s. Japan's need to expand its empire had been met only partially as a result of the first interimperialist war and reasserted itself more powerfully. The German bourgeoisie could not break out of the strangling vise of defeat in the last war and gain new spheres of influence without coming into direct confrontation with both Britain and, especially, France.[65]

On its western border, Germany faced France and Belgium; in the east it faced a set of defense alliances among smaller states, most of which were backed by France; at sea in the European theater, Germany faced a still-dominant British navy. The opening stages of the war saw Germany attack Poland in order to smash one flank of the Anglo-French imperialist front and turn it to their advantage in the larger contest to follow. British and French aid to Poland was extended to fortify that flank as part of their contention with Germany. As for the U.S., some sections of the bourgeoisie (Henry Ford, for one) favored joining their fortunes with the German and Japanese imperialists. But most were committed to siding with the British, both as the most efficacious means of advancing their international interests vis-à-vis other imperialist powers and in support of British efforts to encourage German ambitions eastward in the direction of the then socialist Soviet Union.

In order to understand U.S. maneuvers and advances through the Second World War, it is necessary to consider the positions, goals, and strategies of the other great powers. The British strategy for dealing with Germany found initial expression in Prime Minister Neville Chamberlain's "appeasement" policy. The purpose of Chamberlain's 1938 Munich agreement to give the

---

[65] The controversy surrounding the analysis of the British historian A.J.P. Taylor in his study, *The Origins of the Second World War,* is of some interest to Marxists. Pared to its essentials, Taylor's thesis is that, far from being a madman out to conquer the world, Hitler was in fact a "traditional German statesman" defending traditional German goals. War, according to Taylor, developed out of the inability of the diplomats of both sides to accommodate these goals to the international power equation. Thus, in Taylor's account, the outbreak of armed conflict cannot be blamed solely on the German tyrant's maniacal expansionism, but on actions taken on both sides. Not surprisingly, Taylor has been widely accused of being an apologist for appeasement, though actually he is more a nationalist who bemoans the leniency allegedly shown Germany after the First World War. As he concludes: "In international affairs there was nothing wrong with Hitler except that he was a German" (Taylor, *Origins of the Second World War,* p. 293). Despite Taylor's rather narrow focus on diplomacy — he even argues that some other diplomatic course could have prevented the war — his work serves in many ways as a useful tool for dispelling much of the self-righteous and patriotic fog surrounding other bourgeois accounts of the war's origin and nature.

Sudetenland to Germany was, in fact, to push the Germans to the east and into confrontation with the Soviet Union. One reason for this, of course, was the imperialists' fond dream of smashing the socialist Soviet Union, something which the British (along with the Americans, French, and other imperialists) had already attempted immediately after World War 1. But Britain's more immediate goal was to prepare better military and political ground for its own direct confrontation with Germany, hopefully by weakening it in a war with the Soviets. The U.S. imperialists went along with this as part of their own strategy of moving in later to "pick up the pieces." There was, however, never any question, either on the part of Britain or the U.S., of letting the German imperialists swallow the Soviet Union: they wanted the Germans to choke on it. The Soviet Union, quite rightly, was determined neither to be swallowed nor to be shattered. Owing to the Soviet need to buy time and the German need to first establish a tenable western periphery before it lay siege to the Soviet Union, the two countries signed a mutual non-aggression pact in August 1939.

When the war broke out, the immediate tack of the U.S. imperialists was to sit it out as long as possible, primarily to protect their own economic base as the combatants of the two sides mutually weakened one another, and, secondarily, to reap huge war-related profits as suppliers of war materiel. This had its intended long-run effect of strengthening the international position of the U.S. From 1934 to 1937, the stock of gold at Fort Knox rose from $7.4 billion to $11.3 billion, which represented more than half of the world's monetary reserves.[66] This was due largely to the influx of gold from Europe. The British, for example, were forced to pay "on the barrelhead" for U.S. arms. More generally, the precariousness of European conditions made the U.S. an attractive haven for investment capital. At the same time, U.S. corporate profits jumped from $4.0 billion in 1938 to $17.7 billion in 1941 (almost tripling their share of national income) and then, once the U.S. became an active combatant, they rose further to $25 billion in 1943.[67]

When the U.S. entered the war at the end of 1941, it did so with clearly formulated goals. As early as 1940, study groups set up by the U.S. Council on Foreign Relations were laying plans for a new global order dominated by the U.S. The Council, which col-

---

[66] Michael Hudson, *Super Imperialism: The Economic Strategy of American Empire* (New York: Holt, Rinehart and Winston, 1972), p. 35.

[67] U.S. Bureau of Economic Analysis, *Long-Term Economic Growth*, p. 227.

laborated with the government, produced high-level memoranda examining prospects for the consolidation and integration of trade and investment within the Western Hemisphere and the Pacific. By 1942, ideas for an international monetary fund, a world bank, and a new league of nations were germinating in the State Department.[68] U.S. war aims were perhaps best summed up by Henry Luce, owner of the Time-Life propaganda empire, who, in his 1941 book, *The American Century,* lamented that at the close of World War 1 the U.S. bourgeoisie had let slip a "golden opportunity, an opportunity unprecedented in all history, to assume the leadership of the world...."[69] Such an opportunity, he and many others in the bourgeoisie argued, should not be missed again. Of course, in reality the opportunity had not yet fully developed after World War 1, but Luce's point was obvious nonetheless. Though the principal concern of U.S. leaders was the defeat of the Axis powers, they were also dedicated to the subordination of their erstwhile allies, especially after the tide of battle turned in 1943. Indeed, for the U.S., the Second World War was a multifront conflict: not just against Japan and Germany but, in a different way, against the British as well, and, in still another way, against the Soviet Union.

For its part, Germany recognized that bursting through the confines of the existing division of the world and displacing Britain as the dominant imperialist power (and ultimately absorbing its colonial empire) could not be accomplished without obtaining overwhelming political and military superiority over Britain. As far as the German imperialists were concerned, the key to forcing Britain to its knees was the defeat of the Soviet Union. The plunder of the USSR's industry, agriculture, and abundant mineral resources, such as its southern oil fields, while valuable in itself, was essential in order to prepare Germany for further battle. Germany could then once again shift the bulk of its military weight toward the West, now backed by the resources of all of continental Europe.[70]

---

[68] See Laurence H. Shoup and William Minter, *Imperial Brain Trust: The Council on Foreign Relations and United States Foreign Policy* (New York: Monthly Review Press, 1977), Chap. 4.

[69] Henry R. Luce, *The American Century* (New York: Farrar & Rinehart, 1941), p. 26.

[70] For an overall assessment of Nazi war aims, see Norman Rich, *Hitler's War Aims,* Volume 1: *Ideology, the Nazi State and the Course of Expansion* (New York: W.W. Norton, 1973). See also Hitler's statement on how the Axis forces would shatter the British colonial empire, quoted in Gordon A. Craig, *Germany: 1866-1945* (New York: Oxford Univ. Press, 1980), p. 753.

On June 22, 1941, the German armies crossed into the Soviet Union.

The Allied imperialists' objective role in relation to the USSR thus changed. They were unable to directly attack it or work for its defeat at the hands of others; they even had a stake — albeit a limited and temporary one — in the Soviet capacity to put up a substantial fight against Germany. A German walkover of the Soviet Union and the consolidation of a strong eastern flank would pose a serious danger to the Allied imperialists' own interests. But their underlying imperialist nature and their specific aims in this war, as well as the nature of the main objective interests in conflict from one end of the globe to the other, had not changed. As it turned out, the main way that the U.S. and British allies worked to defeat Germany was through the Soviet Red Army. Military history here is very clear. Even Winston Churchill admitted in March 1943 that for the next six months Great Britain and the United States would be "playing about" with half a dozen German divisions while Stalin was facing 185 divisions.[71] Overall, the Soviet Union suffered 20 million war-related deaths, including 7.5 million who died directly in battle. By contrast, the combined British, French, and U.S. battle deaths totalled under 750,000 — less than 10 percent of the Soviet figure.[72] Simply put, the Soviet Union was responsible for the defeat of Germany. What neither the Germans nor, for that matter, the U.S. imperialists banked on was the force and tenacity with which, once the initial German advance was halted at Stalingrad, the Soviet army would push back the German invaders; nor, of course, had they anticipated the political reverberations this would have.

The German invasion of the Soviet Union was an extremely im-

---

[71] Winston Churchill, *The Second World War*, Vol. 4: *The Hinge of Fate* (Boston: Houghton Mifflin, 1950), Appendix A, Book Two: "Prime Minister's Personal Minutes" (July 1942-May 1943), p. 935. Another account of the war summarizes the disposition of forces this way: "Until the summer of 1944 the majority of American divisions actually in combat were waging war against Japan.... From early 1941... [until] the cross-Channel invasion in June 1944, the entire strength of the British Empire and Commonwealth intermittently fought between two and eight divisions of the principal Axis power, Germany. On the other hand, during all but the first six months of this same period the Russians contained an average of about one hundred and eighty German divisions in more or less continuous action" (Trumbull Higgins, *Winston Churchill and the Second Front* [New York: Oxford Univ. Press, 1957], p. 186).

[72] *Encyclopedia Americana* (1983), s.v. "World War II: Costs, Casualties, and Other Data."

portant component of World War 2. Unlike the international situation existing at the time of World War 1, the workers of the world now had a socialist base area, the USSR, and the imperialists of the whole world were maneuvering to crush it. As crucial to the international proletariat as this was, the interimperialist contradiction more determined the course of the conflict between German imperialism and the socialist USSR than that conflict influenced the interimperialist struggles, although these two conflicts clearly affected each other. The interimperialist contradiction was also more determining than were the national liberation struggles in the colonial and semicolonial countries, although they played a significantly greater role in World War 2 than in World War 1.

The view of the international communist movement was that the Allied cause during World War 2 was a progressive one. It is beyond the scope of this work to do more than outline the reasons why this notion is erroneous.[73] In brief, our view is this: even though progressive and revolutionary aspects, especially the defense of socialism and the revolutionary liberation struggles in the colonies, were major factors in the war, the basic conflict both arose out of interimperialist rivalry and had as its principal outcome a second imperialist redivision of the world.

That the U.S. alliance with the Soviet Union was at best an uncomfortable marriage of convenience on both sides is, of course, obvious. The U.S. remained hostile to the Soviets and sought from the outset to limit the growth of Soviet influence in Europe and elsewhere. Though Roosevelt was not averse to tactically uniting with Stalin against Churchill in particular instances in the delicate tripartite maneuvering at Teheran and Yalta, strategically the two imperialist allies shared a more fundamental interest in opposing and ultimately seeking to dispense with their socialist ally. All this, however, was for the time being secondary in the context of the immediate necessity of defeating the Axis powers, and was conditioned by it.

Roosevelt and Churchill met right after Pearl Harbor and agreed

---

[73] The Comintern's line that the Allied cause during World War 2 was a just and progressive one served as a rationalization for raising the state interests of the Soviet Union above the advance of world revolution, although there was an important task of defending the only socialist state in the world. How the relationship between the defense of a socialist country and the promotion of world revolution during the conjunctural period of World War 2 was mishandled and what its ramifications were for the international class struggle are issues addressed in Bob Avakian, *Conquer the World*, and *Revolution*, No. 49 (June 1981), which contains several important articles on these themes.

that defeat of Germany was their first aim. But the U.S. imperialists made no effort or plans to do this directly, and actually made the defeat of their Japanese rivals the first priority, while maneuvering to gobble up the empires of the British and other European imperialists in the Far East and Pacific. Ultimately the strategic aims and requirements of U.S. imperialism could only be met through decisive victory in the European theater — Europe remained the pivot of imperialist power relations. In the immediate period, however, the U.S. imperialists relied on the Soviet Union to combat and tie down the Germans on the Eastern front and let the British be bombed. While both the U.S. and Britain delayed the opening of a second front, they were particularly active in North Africa and the Pacific, fighting principally to protect and expand their respective colonial and neocolonial empires.[74] The much ballyhooed U.S. lend-lease assistance made only a limited contribution to the Soviet campaign against the German armies. Up through the spring of 1943, by which time the Red Army had turned the tide of the war against Germany, U.S. lend-lease deliveries were more than a million tons short of what had been promised, and had played no part in the most perilous days of the Eastern front. Even the official historians of the U.S. Army, speaking of the war up until this point, concluded: "The impact of U.S. aid to the Soviet Union was as yet insignificant and played no role in the repulse of the German attack before Moscow."[75]

The U.S. shared information with the British concerning development of the atomic bomb (selectively and judiciously, of course), but kept it a tightly guarded secret from the Soviets. As General

[74] Guided by its own imperialist interests, Japan moved toward the south and west of Asia and the rich prizes of the British, French, Dutch, and U.S. colonies. The Japanese strategy was to knock out U.S. naval power and quickly consolidate an impregnable position in the Pacific. The imperialist war in the Pacific was mainly a battle of navies and air forces, and not of massed troops, as was the land war in Europe. However, the anti-Japanese war in China (and also the guerrilla movements in such places as Malaya and the Philippines) played a significant role in the overall war, insuring that large numbers of Japanese troops could not be used to defend the Pacific islands against U.S. attack. The vast bulk of the Japanese forces were stationed in China, well poised to control the Asian land mass.

[75] Leon Martel, *Lend-Lease, Loans and the Coming of the Cold War: A Study of the Implementation of Foreign Policy* (Boulder, Colorado: Westview Press, 1979), pp. 46, 38. Lend-lease was the aid program during World War 2 through which the United States provided food, munitions, and other goods to countries whose defense against Germany and Italy was considered vital to U.S. strategic interests. The Lend-Lease Act was passed on March 11, 1941, before the U.S. became directly involved in the fighting.

Leslie Groves, director of the Manhattan Project for research on the bomb, later put it, "there was never from about two weeks from the time I took charge of this project any illusion on my part but that Russia was our enemy and that the project was conducted on that basis."[76] In fact, the detonation of atomic bombs in Hiroshima and Nagasaki was aimed more at trying (unsuccessfully) to intimidate the Soviet Union, as well as powerful revolutionary movements in China and elsewhere, than at defeating Japan, which was ready to surrender anyway.[77]

Common opposition to socialism and revolution, concentrated in opposition to the Soviet Union, also conditioned and somewhat tempered the often sharp rivalry — even conflict — between the U.S. and Britain. As Foreign Minister Anthony Eden expressed it for the British: "If it came to a direct conflict of policies and we had to choose between the United States of America and the Soviet Union, we should no doubt decide that Anglo-American cooperation is more indispensable and the more natural. . . ."[78] For the Americans, presidential aide Harry Hopkins put it this way: "It was vital for the United States to have a strong Britain because we must be realistic enough to understand that in any future war England would be on America's side and America on England's. It was no use having a weak ally."[79]

---

[76] Testimony of Groves in United States Atomic Energy Commission, *In the Matter of J. Robert Oppenheimer,* Transcript of Hearing Before Personnel Security Board, Washington, D.C., April 12, 1954-May 6, 1954 (GPO, 1954), p. 173.

[77] See Gar Alperovitz, *Atomic Diplomacy: Hiroshima and Potsdam — The Use of the Atomic Bomb and the American Confrontation with Soviet Power* (New York: Vintage, 1967). The U.S. also, in an immediate sense, used the bomb to force a quick Japanese surrender before the USSR could consolidate a position in China (where the Soviet army had just begun to fight the Japanese in Manchuria) or claim a share in the occupation of Japan (Alperovitz, Chap. 4 and pp. 176-94, 239; see also Gardner, *Economic Aspects of New Deal Diplomacy,* pp. 258-59). According to one account, just after the Trinity explosion (the first successful test of the A-bomb): "Truman now knew that he no longer needed the Russians to help in finishing the war in the Far East. They might decide to join the war against Japan of their own accord, but Truman was 'still hoping for time, believing after the atomic bomb Japan will surrender and Russia will not get in so much on the kill. . . .' Thus a speedy and successful outcome for the first use of the bomb was of the greatest importance to him" (Peter Goodchild, *J. Robert Oppenheimer: Shatterer of Worlds* [Boston: Houghton Mifflin Co., 1981], p. 163).

[78] Anthony Eden, *The Reckoning: Memoirs* (Boston: Houghton Mifflin Co., 1965), p. 371.

[79] Quoted in Martin J. Sherwin, *A World Destroyed: The Atomic Bomb and the Grand Alliance* (New York: Knopf, 1975), p. 113.

Nevertheless, the U.S. did not hesitate to take advantage of Britain's wartime desperation. Alliance with Britain, both during and after the war, served the dual strategic aim of whittling away at British strength while, at the same time, bolstering Britain as a key flank in the construction of a new, U.S.-dominated imperial order — what we describe as the dialectic of "edging out" and "propping up." As a first step in penetrating the British empire, on September 2, 1940, the U.S. signed an agreement with the British under which fifty largely obsolete U.S. destroyers were transferred to the British fleet in exchange for 99-year leases granted to the U.S. for military bases in British possessions in the Americas. Indeed, lend-lease operations in general were often treated by the U.S. imperialists as "investments" in the future. All told, U.S. lend-lease aid amounted to $48.4 billion, of which nearly two-thirds went to Britain.[80]

In the master lend-lease agreement of February 1942, the U.S. insisted the British agree to Article VII, which committed the signatories "to the elimination of all forms of discriminatory treatment in international commerce."[81] The British quickly recognized in this an effort by the Americans to break down the remaining barriers to U.S. penetration of the sterling currency bloc (especially access to investment and trade in Britain's colonies) and to establish a postwar economic system dominated by the U.S., much as the world economy of the nineteenth century had been overseen by the British themselves. As one American official baldly expressed it, the British would be "giving us as a quid pro quo or a partial quid pro quo the right to exploit some of her Crown colonies."[82]

In the end, Britain managed to obtain an imprecise and vague rephrasing of Article VII, but the lend-lease program's actual implementation was designed as much to keep the British in line as to defeat the Germans. On January 1, 1943, the State, Treasury, and War Departments, with the endorsement of Roosevelt and Vice-President Wallace, defined U.S. policy on lend-lease aid as designed to insure "that the United Kingdom's gold and dollar balances should not be permitted to be less than about $600 million nor above about $1 billion."[83] In other words, "the United States

---

[80] U.S. Treasury, Bureau of Accounts, *Cumulative Report on Lend-Lease Fiscal Operation, 1941/47* (GPO, 1947), pp. 5-7.

[81] Richard N. Gardner, *Sterling-Dollar Diplomacy in Current Perspective*, 3rd ed. (New York: Columbia Univ. Press, 1980), p. 59.

[82] Quoted in Gabriel Kolko, *The Politics of War* (New York: Vintage, 1970), p. 293.

[83] Quoted in Kolko, *Politics of War*, p. 283.

manipulated the flow of lend-lease aid to prevent Britain's currency reserves from rising too high. American officials feared that, if Britain's reserves became too substantial, it would be possible for the British to formulate an independent policy that might conflict with U.S. aims."[84] Moreover, Washington adopted a secret wartime policy of using lend-lease as a lever to influence Britain's trade policies.

U.S. wartime policy toward Britain thus aimed at maintaining the British as a reliable ally, first against the Axis powers and then against the Soviet Union, while at the same time subordinating British interests to those of U.S. imperialism and battering down obstacles to deeper U.S. penetration of the British Empire — in a word, to clear the way for ascension to the former British position on top of the imperialist world. This led to several sharp conflicts between the two allies in Latin America and the Middle East. For instance, a minor crisis developed in Argentina which had long been a center of British, as opposed to U.S., influence. During the war, the U.S. treated the Argentine government as pro-fascist and instituted wartime trade controls. These were, however, summarily ignored by the British who traded extensively there, as Argentina piled up over $1 billion in gold and foreign exchange reserves. In 1944, the British prepared to sign a meat contract with Argentina which was blocked by U.S. interference. The U.S. Ambassador to Mexico complained that all over Latin America the British were "definitely tending toward the disruption of inter-American unity," a euphemistic phrase which meant that the British were "disrupting" U.S. plans for a tighter hemispheric hold.[85]

In Latin America, the British were conducting a mainly rearguard action against U.S. economic and political advance, since even before the war the U.S. had definitely overtaken them as the dominant power in that region. But in the Middle East the struggle was sharper and more intricate: hanging in the balance was control of the world's largest oil reserves. Moreover, as a State Department trade analyst wrote in 1945, "petroleum has historically played a larger part in the external relations of the United States than any other commodity."[86] The twisting and complex series of developments whereby the U.S. supplanted the British as the rul-

[84] Block, *Origins of International Economic Disorder*, p. 57.

[85] Kolko, *Politics of War*, p. 292.

[86] Quoted in Kolko, *Politics of War*, p. 294.

ing power in Iran, Iraq, Egypt, and Palestine, extending well into the postwar period and, to some extent, to the Suez crisis in 1956, is beyond the scope of this chapter (and will be covered in the next volume). However, the story of how in 1943-44 the U.S. squeezed out Britain in Saudi Arabia, as told by the historian Gabriel Kolko in his important study of U.S. wartime policy, can be mentioned as a brief illustration of the wartime rivalry between the two allies.[87]

Before the war, American oil interests had a monopoly in Saudi Arabia, although U.S. domestic consumption had not yet become dependent upon the resources of the region. The sale of Saudi oil to Europe was highly profitable for the U.S. companies and had the added advantage of giving the U.S. bourgeoisie more leverage with the increasingly oil-dependent European powers. Until 1941, the California-Arabian Standard Oil Company handled all U.S. relations with Saudi Arabia; Washington did not even bother to send a diplomatic representative. In early 1941, through the mediation of California-Arabian Standard, the Saudis appealed for a loan to cover losses incurred by wartime disruptions of oil production (and the interruptions of pilgrimages to Mecca). The U.S. decided to let Britain assume responsibility for Saudi Arabia's immediate difficulties, including the demands of King Saud's widely acknowledged lavish and decadent lifestyle, and Britain eagerly grabbed at this opportunity to strengthen its position in what had hitherto been a U.S. stronghold.

By 1943, however, the U.S. was increasingly concerned with growing British influence in the region. In January of that year the U.S. representative in Egypt reported that the U.S. had "lost considerable prestige in the eyes of Saudi Arabians who have been

---

[87] The following account is drawn from Kolko, *Politics of War*, Chap. 12: "Planning for Peace," Sec. 2: "Great Britain in Theory and Practice." The quotations are from pages 295, 298, 306, and again 306, respectively. Another aspect of wartime jockeying between the United States and Great Britain is chronicled in Wm. Roger Louis' important study, *Imperialism at Bay: The United States and the Decolonization of the British Empire,* 1941-45 (New York: Oxford Univ. Press, 1978). Louis surveys American and British wartime planning for the postwar colonial world through an examination of recently released archival material and private papers. Both powers haggled over the scope and timetable of postwar "decolonization." The U.S. had developed a very definite strategy according to which colonial regimes would become accountable to an international organization (with the U.S., naturally, to play a major role in any such organization). Hence, the U.S. embrace of the concept of "international trusteeship." The rub was that the U.S., under the cloak of "anti-colonialism," wanted to make trusteeship regimes out of British colonies. For their part, the British sought to defend and extend the prerogatives of "formal" empire.

given increasingly to feel that the British were their only friends in need." Secretary of the Navy Forrestal put it more bluntly in a telephone call to Defense Secretary Byrnes in December: "the main thing is that stack of oil is something that this country damn well ought to have and we've lost, in the last ninety days, a good deal of our position with this Sheik — Eben Sihudo, whatever his name is — and we are losing more every day. The British have now sent, under the guise of naturalists to prevent a locust plague, have got 500 people in Saudi, Arabia, for no other reason than to see what the hell we are doing and what we've got."

King Ibn Saud was quick to take advantage of U.S.-British rivalry over Saudi oil. Perhaps getting wind of the fact that high American officials did not know or could not pronounce his name, in February 1944 the King initiated a long series of complaints to American representatives over inadequate support and began to increase purchases from the British. Throughout 1944, both sides lavished the opportunistic ruler with lend-lease aid far beyond any rational wartime needs. In June, the U.S. proposed to build an air base in Saudi Arabia "so that we, particularly our Navy, would have access to some of King Ibn Saud's oil." But the British managed to get the King to delay construction, which the U.S. branded an "unfriendly act." "There was no law in heaven or earth," blustered Assistant Secretary of State Berle to the British counselor in Washington, "which entitled anybody to interfere with our building an airfield for legitimate purposes in Saudi Arabia." By the end of 1944, a long-range U.S. assistance program to Saudi Arabia had been inaugurated and an Aramco (the new name for American oil interests in Saudi Arabia after a 1944 reorganization) pipeline to the Mediterranean was under construction — the British had been squeezed out. The British imperialists, for all their experience in colonial relations, were simply not in a position to go toe-to-toe with the U.S. imperialists over the latter's vital interests in the oppressed countries.

World War 2: The Aftermath

The Second World War thus saw not only the decisive defeat of the German-Japanese-Italian bid to redivide the world but the relative eclipse of British and French power as well. This war and its aftermath, with the U.S. now clearly on top among the imperialists, resulted in a more extensive redivision of the world and a more radical restructuring of capital on an international scale than did the previous world war. This imperialist spiral whose basic origins lay in the resolution of World War 1 had essentially come to an end: the roots of a new spiral had been planted.

The U.S. emerged from World War 2 as an unprecedentedly dominant and organizing power (even taking into account Britain's late nineteenth century role). Its military superstructure and productive base dwarfed those of its battered rivals (allies and enemies alike). Removed from the devastation of the battle zones, the U.S. sustained less than three percent of Allied battle deaths.[88] By the end of the war, the United States had acquired a string of bases that stretched from Korea in Northeast Asia around to Iceland in the North Atlantic; by 1949, the United States flag flew over some 400 overseas military bases.[89] The U.S. enjoyed global naval supremacy (for a short period in 1947, the British navy, the traditional "lord" of the seas, was down to a total active strength of one cruiser and four destroyers),[90] deployed a modern airforce, and possessed a weapon of awesome destruction. The island territories captured by U.S. forces from the Japanese empire in the Pacific basin became strategic bases for the American colossus. Indeed, the U.S. ranged over the Pacific as undisputed master, with the communication lines of a commercial and military network in that part of the world clearly drawn.

The expansion of industrial production in the United States during the 1940-44 period had no parallel in U.S. history: the total output of manufactured goods increased 300 percent and that of raw materials by about 60 percent.[91] Investment in new plant and equipment, most of it in the form of direct investment by the government, led to an increase in productive capacity of more than 50 percent between 1939 and 1945.[92] The superior productivity of

[88] *Encyclopedia Americana*, (1983), s.v. "World War II: Costs, Casualties, and Other Data." We use battle deaths because they are the best documented, but it should be noted that in any comparison of civilian casualties or war-caused deaths broadly, the U.S. percentage would be even lower — certainly less than 2 percent (see the rather conservative figures in Alan S. Milward, *War, Economy, and Society*, pp. 210-11).

[89] "Introduction," David Horowitz, ed., *Corporations and the Cold War* (New York: Monthly Review Press, 1969), p. 17.

[90] Felix Greene, *The Enemy* (New York: Vintage, 1971), p. 64.

[91] Milward, *War, Economy, and Society*, p. 65.

[92] U.S. Senate, Report of the Smaller War Plants Corporation to the Senate Special Committee to Study Problems of American Small Businesses, *Economic Concentration and World War II*, 79th Cong., 2d Sess., (GPO, 1946), Doc. 206, p. 37.

the U.S. war effort and the absence of any destruction to its internal industrial base left U.S. imperialism in a position of overwhelming economic strength at the war's end.

With industrial capacity seriously crippled in Europe and Japan, the U.S. produced more than 60 percent of the world's output of manufactures in the late 1940s.[93] The U.S. share of the world production of motor vehicles and steel in 1950 was 76 percent and 46 percent, respectively.[94] At the same time, and very much related to the war-ravaged state of these economies, U.S. export trade soared. For every year from 1925 to 1937, the U.S. was a net importer of consumer goods; but in 1946 the U.S. emerged from the war as a net exporter, and in 1947 the surplus on consumer goods trade was nearly $1 billion.[95] Exports in general rose from $4.6 billion in 1939 to $20.2 billion in 1947.[96] The U.S. share of world export trade increased from 13.7 percent in 1938 to 21.6 percent in 1948.[97] Its share of world gold reserves rose from about one-third in 1934 to 72 percent by 1948, and by 1950 it held 50 percent of the world's total supply of international reserves.[98]

The U.S. not only had the resources and reserves to oversee reconstruction but the political leadership to see to it that such reconstruction conformed first and foremost to the needs of a new imperialist order, as defined by U.S. imperialism. New global institutions reflecting this dominance were established: the World Bank, the International Monetary Fund, and the United Nations. The U.S. was well situated to consolidate many of the advances it had made in the interwar period and during the war itself, particularly in the colonies. Moreover, it was favorably positioned to displace the traditional colonial powers in areas where it was historically weak — notably Africa and portions of Asia.[99] The settlement of the

---

[93] William H. Branson, "Trends in United States International Trade and Investment since World War II," in Martin Feldstein, ed., *The American Economy in Transition* (Chicago: Univ. of Chicago Press, 1980), p. 183.

[94] Peter G. Peterson, *The United States in the Changing World Economy,* Volume 2 (GPO, n.d.), Chart 9.

[95] Branson, "Trends in U.S. Trade," Table 3.19, p. 209.

[96] "Economic Report of the President," January 1981 (GPO), p. 233.

[97] U.S. Dept. of State, *The Trade Debate* (GPO, 1979), p. 6. U.S. exports as tabulated here include military grant-aid.

[98] Hudson, *Super Imperialism,* pp. 35, 63; Peterson, *The United States,* Chart 11. This 1950 figure includes foreign exchange and reserve position in the International Monetary Fund, in addition to gold.

[99] In Africa, where many of the old colonial holdings and empires were left intact, the U.S. was able to consolidate strategic investments. Before World War 2 the U.S.

previous world war had seen the formal redistribution of colonies. The U.S., however, was now amassing and consolidating a more "informal" (neocolonial) empire; but it was far more powerful and extensive than any that had preceded it. Having successfully penetrated the old European empires in the closing years of the war and having played the dominant role in drafting the UN conventions governing "trusteeship" and "self-government," the U.S. would seek to turn the process of "decolonization" to its advantage, although it never banked on the ferocity of the liberation struggles that would follow the war.[100]

In sum, the gains of the U.S. in expanding its colonial empire vis-à-vis other imperialisms and the vastly greater freedom to restructure relations of capital internationally opened up new possibilities for profitable accumulation. Here we might consider one striking measure of overseas expansion. In 1930, the U.S. held about 35 percent of the total stock of foreign investment; by 1960, it held just under 60 percent of the total foreign investment stock.[101] But these postwar advantages must be understood against a broader canvas.

The world as a whole had changed dramatically. Most decisively, a socialist camp had emerged from the turbulence and struggle of the war and its aftermath; indeed, the postwar world was principally a bipolar one, pitting this socialist camp against the imperialists. The Soviet Union had not only survived the war, with all its devastation, but was now joined by new allies in Eastern Europe. The Chinese Revolution would soon claim monumental victory; as Mao exclaimed in 1949, one-quarter of humanity had "stood up." At the same time, and closely related, the Third World, especially Asia, was seething with liberation struggles. And in Europe itself, particularly France and Italy, the situation was volatile in the immediate postwar years.

True, the U.S. imperialists were much stronger, but the imperialist system as a whole was not. The very fact that even their

---

controlled 43 percent of all manganese mining operations in Africa, by 1946 it expanded its control to 76.8 percent; for copper mining the percentage rose from 7.1 to 29.2. Similar advances in the U.S. share of control over key raw materials were recorded for chromium, cobalt, and rubber (E.A. Tarabrin, *The New Scramble for Africa* [Moscow: Progress Publishers, 1974], p. 33).

[100] See Louis, *Imperialism at Bay*, Part IV.

[101] U.S. Senate, Report to the Subcomittee on Multinational Corporations of the Committee on Foreign Relations, Richard S. Newfarmer and Willard F. Mueller, *Multinational Corporations in Brazil and Mexico* (GPO, 1975), Table 2-1, p. 31.

allies were weakened and that only one imperialist power could even hope to hold the imperialist order together, while this order itself faced the challenge of an expanded socialist camp and rising revolutionary struggles, especially the movements for national liberation in the colonies, revealed the long-term direction of history — the motion of the imperialist system towards its final extinction. All this had immediate and profound consequences for the policies and actions of U.S. imperialism. The dialectics of the situation were this: the most pressing problem facing the United States was the political and economic stabilization of war-torn Europe, but the logic and modalities of reconstruction and a new hierarchical arrangement among imperialisms were inseparable from and predicated upon the existence of the Soviet Union and a socialist camp.

What was this socialist camp? It was a grouping of states (in various stages of political transition) headed by the socialist Soviet Union and oriented toward serving its state interests. This camp soon came to include another, major socialist country, China. As for the Soviet Union itself, capitalism had not yet been restored. (The new bourgeoisie, centered in the leadership of the Communist Party itself, had not consolidated supreme power, but was firmly entrenched and poised to do so.) The socialist camp embraced one-third of the world's land mass and nearly that proportion of its people. It possessed not inconsiderable military strength. It had come to represent the internationally recognized anti-imperialist pole, becoming a force of attraction for some bourgeois as well as many revolutionary-led liberation movements in the Third World. And it even commanded influence in the imperialist world itself, largely through the organizational strength of the Communist Parties in Western Europe. Thus, despite its complex internal configuration, despite the fact that the Soviet Union could scarcely be said to have assumed a consistently revolutionary stance in the world, and despite the fact that this camp would disintegrate not long thereafter with the rise to power of revisionism in the Soviet Union in the mid-1950s, this grouping of states had enough cohesiveness and combined strength to coalesce into a front objectively opposed to imperialism in the immediate postwar period.

Consequently, U.S. strategy had to aim for the breakup of this powerful socialist camp. Franz Schurmann has described the Soviet challenge this way:

It was the only power capable of matching the United States militarily. The world's major trouble spots — Berlin, Greece, Iran, and Korea — were in areas where Russia collided with the newly emerging American empire. And the most threatening form of "chaos" came from communist revolutionary movements in such countries as Greece, Azerbaijan, the Philippines, Malaya, Korea, Indochina, and, of course, China. Cultivated gentlemen like Acheson and Kennan, machine politicians like Truman, tough lawyers like Forrestal and Dulles, all shared an overwhelming fear born of two world wars and a great depression. The only way to banish that fear was to have total security or, as James Forrestal said in December 1947: "We are dealing with a deadly force and nothing less than 100 percent security will do."[102]

Thus, the U.S. implemented coercive economic measures and exerted military pressure against the socialist camp. The efforts to limit the spread and influence of the socialist camp fell under the rubric of the "containment strategy." Its first major application was heralded by the proclamation of the Truman Doctrine in 1947; U.S. national security interests were explicitly linked to the suppression of a revolutionary movement in Greece and to the encirclement of the Soviet Union and its allies in Eastern Europe. The idea of drawing an imperial line of demarcation was of course nothing new; only now, the "inviolate" frontiers of empire, previously consecrated by such manifestos as the Monroe Doctrine and the Roosevelt Corollary, were pushed outward. That the encirclement of the Soviet Union was never intended as mere "containment" is borne out by newly declassified U.S. government documents which reveal that U.S. military planners had by 1948 begun to develop workable contingency plans for atomic war against the Soviet Union.[103] The U.S. reinstituted the draft and later embarked on a massive rearmament program. The decision to rebuild both Germany and Japan, the wartime enemies of the U.S., is understandable only in this larger strategic context.

The contradiction between the two camps was the principal contradiction in the immediate postwar world, the contradiction which more than any other conditioned the unfolding of world

---

[102] Franz Schurmann, *The Logic of World Power* (New York: Pantheon, 1974), p. 100.

[103] The evolution of U.S. plans for atomic war between 1945 and 1949 is discussed in David Alan Rosenberg, "American Atomic Strategy and the Hydrogen Bomb Decision," *The Journal of American History,* Volume 66, No. 1 (June 1979).

events in general and of the secondary contradictions in particular, even though an all-out war was not imminent. This contradiction conditioned and helped shape the U.S. relationship with its own imperialist allies; and, if only by "tying down" the U.S. militarily, politically, and diplomatically in the task of "containment," the socialist camp also conditioned and somewhat limited the U.S. imperialists' ability to act as decisively as necessary in the Third World. While the existence of the Soviet Union and the socialist camp gave the U.S. rulers a convenient target for their campaigns of demagoguery, that camp also stood objectively as an obstacle to the achievement of their goals. In everything they did, it was essential for the imperialists to take into account the existence and potential responses of the Soviet Union (even where it was in the short run largely incapable of directly affecting the course of events) and the other states of the socialist camp, especially, after 1949, the People's Republic of China.

Had the complex class struggle in the Soviet Union and most of the other countries of the former socialist camp not turned out unfavorably for the proletariat, as indeed it did in the mid-1950s, then the imperialists under the leadership of the United States would almost certainly have been forced to go to war against these countries. The latitude the U.S. enjoyed elsewhere in the world to consolidate and extend its empire would have been ever more constricted. In other words, the current spiral would have reached an earlier nodal point, one that need not necessarily have involved economic crisis and explosive interimperialist rivalry (although a collision between a socialist camp and imperialism would be ultimately grounded in the expand-or-die nature of imperialism).

During the first postwar decade, an imperialist bloc, understood both as a political alliance and a broader but highly integrated economic sphere, was forged on the basis of the commanding economic and political-military supremacy of the United States, on the one hand, and the political challenge of the socialist camp, particularly the Soviet Union, on the other. This was the initial dynamic of the new spiral that began at the close of the Second World War, and this is why it was essential for the U.S. to both edge out and prop up the British and why a similar course of action proved necessary with respect to the other imperialists, including the two main defeated powers, Germany and Japan.

Let's look briefly at the example of Japan. The U.S. achieved a resounding military victory over Japanese imperialism and enjoyed considerably more freedom of movement there than it did in

Europe. During the early postwar period, Japan was a captive market for the U.S., which provided nearly two-thirds of all Japanese imports.[104] In particular, Japan was an important outlet for the American agricultural surplus.[105] The U.S. also came to exercise a stranglehold over the supply of oil to Japan, control which continues to the present day. But in a totally prostrate condition Japan would be a drain on U.S. capital since injections of U.S. aid would be continually needed to prevent total collapse. And of critical importance in the calculations of the U.S. imperialists was the imminent victory of the Chinese Revolution and the tremendous strengthening of the socialist camp that this represented, especially in Asia. Thus, by 1947 the U.S. began to shift its policy.

During a visit that year to the Japanese islands, George Kennan outlined the new situation on behalf of the State Department: "The changes in occupation policy that were now required were ones relating to an objective — namely, the economic rehabilitation of Japan and the restoration of her ability to contribute constructively to the stability and prosperity of the Far Eastern region. . . ."[106] Moves were taken to strengthen the apparatus of repression, weaken the trade unions and the Left, boost the position of the capitalist class, and generally consolidate Japan as an imperialist ally of the U.S. Japan was also set in a new triangular system of trade "whereby the United States would sell, say, cotton, to Japan to be made into textiles, which Japan would then export to the East Indies, from which the United States would then purchase tin and other raw materials. Where necessary, Washington would provide the loans to lubricate such triangular operations."[107] This arrangement, in which the U.S. as the leading imperialist power directed the division of the imperialist spoils between itself and Japan, proved especially irksome to the British who found themselves increasingly squeezed out of Asia, especially after the revolution in China diverted Japanese exports and investments into formerly British territories to the southeast.

---

[104] Jon Halliday, *A Political History of Japanese Capitalism* (New York: Pantheon, 1975), p. 186.

[105] In fact, the U.S. enjoyed a substantial trade surplus with Japan between 1945 and 1964 and, despite "buy American" jingoism, Japan remains today the single largest foreign market for U.S. agricultural products ("Trade War Feared Over Food Export Issue," *New York Times*, 21 Feb. 1983).

[106] Quoted in Halliday, *Japanese Capitalism*, pp. 187-88.

[107] Halliday, *Japanese Capitalism*, p. 186.

Nevertheless, by 1947, even before enactment of the Marshall Plan, U.S. imperialism had effectively begun and basically shaped its favorable redivision of the postwar world and had firmly established economic and political leadership, although such restructuring could not obliterate interimperialist rivalry. But U.S. leadership was also conditioned by its relationship to the peoples of the colonial and neocolonial countries. The ability of the U.S. imperialists to "seize the time," so to speak, at the close of the war rested on the immediate economic advantages they enjoyed. But for these advantages to become the basis for a longer-term expansion, the U.S. had to secure not only the subordination of rival imperialisms but its own access to their former colonial empires. Indeed, the capacity of the U.S. imperialists to export capital to the colonial world was the single most important factor underlying their postwar economic expansion.

This control, however, was not achieved without continual struggle, not only against other imperialists but against the peoples of the colonial world as well. What is important to note by way of backdrop is that World War 2 was much more of a global conflict than was World War 1. A greater number of countries were active belligerents in this war and its direct and indirect impact on the oppressed countries was devastating and far-reaching. In Asia, damage to land and livestock was extensive; in China, yarn, cotton cloth, coal, and electric power output declined sharply; in many African countries the rupture of trade with Europe (which was the principal market for many primary commodity exports) caused extreme privation.[108] While war-induced demand led to the expansion of some industries in certain colonial countries, nothing commensurate with the expansion of industrial capacity and technological upgrading that took place in the advanced countries occurred in the colonial world.

The destruction and dislocation caused by the war not only wreaked devastation in Asia but also triggered explosive struggles for national liberation. As the most powerful and thoroughgoing of these, the Chinese Revolution symbolized, to imperialists and revolutionaries alike, the close ties uniting the powerful upsurge in the colonial world with the camp of socialism. In the earliest days after victory over Japan, the U.S. viewed the defeat of the Chinese Revolution as crucial to its ability to consolidate control in the rest

---

[108] See Milward, *War, Economy, and Society*, pp. 355-57.

of Asia. Billions of dollars in weaponry, credits, aid, military advisors, and logistics support were poured into the Kuomintang effort to crush the red base areas. As it turned out, the U.S. watched as the communist-led armies ate up the 45 KMT divisions equipped by the U.S. and the 540,000 KMT troops the U.S. transported to the frontlines, and forced out the 90,000 U.S. Marines stationed in key cities and along communication lines.[109]

In a certain sense, the struggle in Korea epitomized how tightly interwoven with the existence of the socialist camp were both the movements for national liberation and the U.S. imperialists' efforts to suppress these movements. Clearly, the U.S. invasion of Korea was less a response to the imperialists' own weakening grip on that country (the South Korean government was on the verge of collapse just prior to the outbreak of the war) than it was their answer to the Chinese Revolution and the formation of the Sino-Soviet alliance. Moreover, it was, as one history put it, "The War for Both Asia and Europe."[110] The conflict erupted in 1950, following five years of intrigues and maneuvers by the U.S. imperialists to maintain pro-U.S. forces in power and block national unification and independence. Having acquired a UN cover, the U.S. imperialists launched a savage campaign against the popular forces. Among other weapons, napalm was experimented with for the first time. The leveling of industrial and population centers was awesome. The head of the U.S. Bomber Command in the Far East explained: "I would say that the entire, almost the entire Korean peninsula is just a terrible mess. Everything is destroyed. There is nothing standing worthy of the name. . . . Just before the Chinese came in we were grounded. There were no more targets in Korea."[111] When the U.S.-led forces pushed toward the Yalu frontier, the Chinese people's volunteers entered the war. Soviet military aid poured into China; that the U.S. did not expand the war into China was very much conditioned by the prospect of Soviet intervention. The U.S. could only salvage a settlement at the 38th parallel, its self-proclaimed myth of invincibility punctured.

Other national liberation struggles raged in Asia. At the end of

[109] Mao, "Talk with the American Correspondent Anna Louise Strong," *Selected Works,* Volume 4, p. 101n.

[110] Walter LaFeber, *America, Russia and the Cold War, 1945-1971,* 2d ed. (New York: Wiley, 1976), p. 95.

[111] Quoted in I.F. Stone, *The Hidden History of the Korean War* (New York: Monthly Review Press, 1971), p. 312.

the war, the U.S. returned to the Philippines to reimpose colonial rule on this, its key strategic flank in Southeast Asia. It rebuilt its bases and organized local reactionary forces under its military command. A bloody counterguerrilla campaign continued through the early '50s. The British faced their "Malayan emergency" starting in 1948. French troops reoccupied Saigon in 1945 and carried out shellings of Haiphong, causing 6,000 deaths, the following year.[112] The Vietnamese war had begun in earnest. Gaining in strength, the guerrillas, who were now welded into mobile regular units, drove the colonialists southward. By 1954, the U.S. was financing about 80 percent of the costs of the war, the same year the French met ignominious defeat at Dien Bien Phu.[113] Anticolonial struggles erupted elsewhere: in Indonesia as well as in North Africa and the Middle East. In Africa, insurgencies broke out in Nigeria, Ghana, and Kenya. But these struggles were, for the most part, either quashed or neutralized through a combination of brutal suppression of the masses and concessions to sections of the bourgeoisies.

The U.S. has never been able to fully subdue resistance to imperialist domination in the Third World. In the direct aftermath of the war, and throughout the postwar period, national liberation struggles pounded away at imperialism. These movements, however, did not all proceed along the same path. Some went forward to socialism — here China was the outstanding example. Others, while striking real blows against imperialism, stopped half way and their impact was blunted. In fact, not a few of these struggles were absorbed into a larger neocolonial strategy of the U.S. imperialists. In some cases, they encouraged resistance against the traditional colonialism — although only within certain bounds — and then moved to take control of the newly independent states, through political subsidization of "new leaders" and a web of financial and political entanglements. In Indonesia, the Dutch bore the initial brunt of the liberation struggle while the U.S. managed to use its overall strength to edge out Dutch-British interests in the area (although it never allowed these interimperialist contradictions to seriously jeopardize its common counterrevolutionary cause). The pattern varied in its particulars, but this neocolonial strategy and the blocking and parrying by the U.S. with its alliance

---

[112] Fernando Claudin, *The Communist Movement: From Comintern to Cominform* (Middlesex, England: Penguin, 1975), p. 742, note 40.

[113] The course and impact of the war in Vietnam will be a major subject of analysis in a subsequent volume.

partners were key elements in the postwar period.

As noted, at the war's end the most immediate problem facing the U.S. was the political and economic stabilization of war-torn Europe. This was an indispensable component of a new, coherent international economic order, both for the investment and trade opportunities that Europe afforded in its own right and because of the continent's historical ties and economic relationships with the oppressed nations — which is to say that U.S. capital could penetrate the oppressed nations in significant ways through the medium of European-based investments and larger alliance interrelationships. At the same time, Europe was at the center of the confrontation with the Soviet Union. But the European political situation was precarious. In a late 1945 BBC broadcast, historian A.J.P. Taylor went so far as to tell his listeners: "Nobody in Europe believes in the American way of life — that is, in private enterprise; or rather, those who believe in it are a defeated party...."[114]

In this situation, a pressing task was to isolate, suppress, and — where these were not feasible — co-opt revolutionary forces or forces in opposition to U.S. imperialism, especially pro-Soviet opposition. The U.S. was greatly concerned about the spread of such tendencies once the tide of the war turned in the Allies' favor, and this conditioned the way the U.S. fought the closing phases of the war. Everywhere the U.S. occupation armies went, a major concern was to undercut the influence of Communist-led resistance movements. As U.S. troops marched up the Italian peninsula, for example, Eisenhower decreed that "no political activity whatsoever shall be countenanced...."[115] Unfortunately, in carrying out this policy the U.S. imperialists were all too often assisted by the leaders of the Communist Parties themselves who committed serious class-collaborationist errors, and worse. Carrying its prewar and wartime stand and policies to their logical conclusion, the French Communist Party, for instance, organized the dismantling of the popular armed resistance forces and encouraged the working class to submerge its political (and even economic) struggle beneath the "battle for production." As CP head Maurice Thorez stated in his report to the Tenth Party Congress in June 1948: "Today the extent and quality of our material production and

[114] A.J.P. Taylor, "The European Revolution," *The Listener*, 22 November 1945, p. 576.

[115] Harry Coles and Albert K. Weinberg, eds., *Civil Affairs: Soldiers Become Governors* (Washington, D.C.: Office of the Chief of Military History, Dept. of the Army, 1964), Part 6, p. 435.

our place in the world market are the measure of the greatness of France. [The people must] steel themselves for the battle for production as they steeled themselves for the battle of the liberation. The task is to rebuild the greatness of France, to secure in more than words the material conditions of French independence."[116]

This sentiment was fully in line with another major concern of the imperialists in the immediate postwar period — the reconstruction of the European economy. In Europe, the war ended with a shortage of goods, a paralysis of trade, and a dangerously expanded money supply due to the wartime monetization of debt to meet war costs. There was as yet no coherent monetary or trade system established. In 1945, industrial production was less than a third of its prewar (1937) level in the Netherlands, Belgium , Italy, and the occupied zones of Germany, and was only half of its prewar level in France, Austria, and Norway. Only Denmark, Sweden, and Britain came out of the conflict with over three-fourths of their 1937 level of production.[117] Sent abroad to survey the food situation, Herbert Hoover concluded: "It is now 11:59 o'clock on the clock of starvation." Most Europeans were living on less than 1,500 calories per day as compared to 3,500 in the U.S.[118]

To stabilize the situation, and, ultimately, to establish its unchallenged supremacy, the U.S. released some $20 billion in "foreign assistance" from July 1945 to June 1947. Of this, $16 billion went through channels such as the United Nations Relief and Rehabilitation Administration (UNRRA), lend-lease, surplus property sales on credit, Export-Import Bank loans, and direct loans authorized by Congress. About $9 billion went to Europe and $7 billion elsewhere.[119] Private capital exports also increased, but capital export through the state was the principal means by which U.S. imperialist reserves helped prop up and penetrate other imperialist powers during this postwar transition period.

Actually, the recovery in Europe turned out to be remarkably rapid. What underlay this was the *total* reorganization of international capital in the war's aftermath. Moreover, wartime destruction, great as it was, had not been so severe as initially feared. This was due, first, to the capitulation of the French bourgeoisie — that

[116] Quoted in Claudin, *The Communist Movement,* p. 331.

[117] Sidney S. Alexander, *The Marshall Plan* (Washington, D.C.: National Planning Association, 1948), p. 17.

[118] Morison and Commager, *Growth of the American Republic,* Volume 2, p. 895.

[119] Alexander, *The Marshall Plan,* p. 7.

is, its accommodation to German domination in France — which spared most of that country from actual battle. Second, it was the result of the cynical Allied policy of "area bombing," that is, carpet bombings of mainly civilian-populated areas, the result and partial purpose of which was to leave certain major industrial installations and concentrations intact.[120]

During 1945-46, considerable reorganization of production took place in Europe. By 1947, most of the continent was already restored to 1937 levels. This is borne out by United Nations statistics which reveal that by mid-1947, France, Denmark, and Sweden, for example, were functioning at about 100 percent of their 1937 level of industrial production and could boast of employment increases of 6, 29, and 21 percent, respectively, over 1937 levels.[121] By 1950, gross investment as a share of GNP stood at record high levels for Great Britain, Italy, and Germany.[122]

Of course, certain caveats must be introduced. First of all, levels of production and capital formation indicate neither what the new production was geared to nor its exact technical composition. A great deal of the growth of this period was simply the replacement of productive forces destroyed by the war. What is most significant, however, is that even when it did represent just the restoration of prewar investments, the capital formation which took place generally resulted in substantial hikes in productivity. Moreover, while a country like West Germany experienced a high rate of capital formation, average real wages did not reach their 1938 level until 1956.[123]

In this initial reconstruction of the European economies, U.S. capital was injected into a situation where capital was scarce relative to investment opportunities, unlike the situation before the war or at present where overproduction of capital is the prevalent state of affairs (and where any correct concept of capital shortage

---

[120] See Milward, *War, Economy, and Society,* pp. 301-4. In the final stages of the war, as well, the U.S. took care to avoid damage in the Ruhr (Germany's main industrial center), so important, as it was put, to "the economic future of Europe" (see Kolko, *Politics of War,* p. 375).

[121] Alexander, *The Marshall Plan,* p. 20.

[122] W.W. Rostow, *The World Economy: History and Prospects* (Austin: Univ. of Texas Press, 1978), pp. 375, 443, 396, 404.

[123] Günter Minnerup, "West Germany Since the War," *New Left Review,* September/October 1976, p. 15.

indicates insufficient capital to overcome the lack of profitable investment conditions). In the immediate postwar environment, the injection of U.S. capital was complementary and stimulative to the self-expansion of the European imperialists' own capital. Further, owing to the power, size, and technical level of the U.S. economy, to the magnitude of U.S. trade with Europe, and to the fact that U.S. capital flowed into the most modern and advanced sectors, the U.S. imperialists played a key role in shaping the pattern of European economic reconstruction.

In general, the economic activity of the U.S. paralleled and served its political interests. U.S. aid, investment, and monetary policies in the postwar transition period were not mainly defined by short-term profit interests. In an ultimate and overall sense, U.S. policy had its foundation in imperialist economics, but economic interests were and had to be defined broadly and strategically, not narrowly in terms of immediate return. In contributing to the economic recovery of Europe, the U.S. imperialists were most concerned with two things: first, restoring the economic vitality of the other imperialist powers so that these states might play the role of lesser partners in a new U.S.-led world imperialist order; and second, subduing the masses and, intimately linked to this — and, beyond the immediate situation, of greater importance — containing and, if possible, disrupting and even destroying the socialist camp.

Overall, the second concern was more important, but right after the war the first held greater immediacy. Without forging a new political and economic order, it would be impossible for the imperialist camp to successfully face the challenge of the growing socialist camp. And here again the tasks were twofold. On the one hand, it was necessary to assist the recovery of the rival imperialists, both those who had been allies and those who had been enemies during the war. On the other, it was essential to channel recovery in a way which would break down the exclusivities of the old prewar empires, with their monetary and trading blocs, and bring them into a more rational and, of course, U.S.-led economic arrangement. This was what lay behind all the pious rhetoric of the time calling for the establishment of a liberal trading system and the attainment of an expanding world economy.

Thus, there was a definite and clear link between expanding the U.S. empire and restoring the economies of the other imperialist powers. Charles S. Dewey of the Chase National Bank expressed it quite clearly in the U.S. bourgeoisie's language of the time:

There are three business ideologies existent in the world today, the Soviet system, our own free-enterprise system, and a third which is neither one nor the other.... I am extremely troubled about the future of free enterprise [read: the freedom of U.S. enterprise to be heads and tails above the rest of the imperialist world]. To put it bluntly, are we going to let this third group [i.e., the imperialists who had reason in the immediate situation to favor some protectionist policies against the U.S.] abandon the policy of free enterprise and open competition and become state trading nations or are we going to take a smart gamble and back our own future by advancing funds [i.e., such as those advanced through the Marshall Plan] that may tide them over their difficult period and permit them to play the game under the rules we adhere to.[124]

There are of course only two ideologies: that of the bourgeoisie and that of the proletariat. The point was that under the conditions of the day the U.S. bourgeoisie was the only imperialist ruling class with an immediate interest in relatively laissez-faire economic relations in certain spheres (due to the enormous advantages in scale, technology, growth potential, and, most decisively, its widened, and widening, access to the oppressed countries). Given its overall strength and strategically advantageous position in the division of the world, the American colossus was for the time spouting a rhetorical admixture of (1) "free trade" and "multilateralism," meaning mainly the breaking up of bilateral relations between the European imperialists and their colonial preserves as well as "free" access to those colonies; and (2) "international cooperation" and "economic stabilization," meaning planning and rationalization of monetary, financial, trade, and other economic arrangements in accord with a U.S. orchestration of the imperialist world economy (quite *un*-laissez faire).

This dynamic can be seen clearly in the key case of Britain. The U.S. rulers were, of course, very much aware that the British were in dire straits. Although it suffered only a third as many "manpower casualties" as it had in the First World War, Britain incurred over $70 billion in debts, used up $750 million in gold reserves, liquidated $6 billion in overseas investment to finance the war effort, suffered $3.5 billion in shipping losses, and faced the need of rebuilding almost one-fifth of its housing.[125] Despite a formal

---

[124] Quoted in Joyce and Gabriel Kolko, *The Limits of Power* (New York: Harper and Row, 1972), p. 24 (bracketed comments added by R.L. and F.S.).

[125] Felix Greene, *The Enemy,* p. 97.

understanding that lend-lease would be reduced gradually and in a manner calculated to encourage orderly reconversion, on August 21, 1945, Truman abruptly terminated all aid. "It was a great shock," British Prime Minister Attlee later recalled. "The tap was turned off at a moment's notice. It made quite an impossible situation. That's why we had to go and ask for an American loan right away."[126] Which was exactly what Washington had been banking on. The final agreement gave the British $3.75 billion in return for their termination of the so-called "dollar pool," which had sent all sterling bloc members' dollar earnings to London, and for the free convertibility of all sterling currency and a British obligation not to reduce imports from the U.S. In a separate statement the two parties pledged themselves to "the elimination of tariff preferences" and "adequate measures for the substantial reduction of barriers to world trade."[127]

Alliance with British imperialism was an integral and crucial component of the U.S. leadership's vision of the postwar world. As Fred Block, a student of Western monetary policy, has concluded:

> In general, Britain was seen as a kind of bridge between the United States and the rest of the world. If the United States could count on British economic, political, and military resources in the pursuit of U.S. global aims, it was thought that it would then be infinitely easier to gain the acquiescence of other countries. It was precisely U.S. dependence on British cooperation in a variety of areas that made U.S. policy toward Britain so complicated. On the one hand, if Britain were too strong. . .it would be difficult to force her to act according to American wishes. On the other hand, if Britain were too weak. . .she would be of little help in financing European trade, in working to eliminate trade and exchange controls, and in a whole variety of other tasks. The trick, then, was to keep Britain weak and dependent, but not too weak. . . .[128]

Coming into being was an imperialist system in which rivalries and competition among differing national capitals would still continue,

---

[126] Francis Williams, *A Prime Minister Remembers: The War and Post-War Memoirs of the Rt Hon. Earl Attlee* (London: Heinemann Publishers, 1961), pp. 129-30. The abrupt lend-lease cut-off was also designed to bring pressure on the USSR in the postwar negotiations on Europe and to slow the pace of Soviet reconstruction.

[127] Gardner, *Sterling-Dollar Diplomacy*, Appendix: "Financial Agreement Between the Governments of the United States and the United Kingdom," and pp. 152, 225.

[128] Block, *Origins of International Economic Disorder*, p. 59.

but where a single power played the orchestrating role.

The preceding pages represent an application of our spiral/ conjuncture thesis and serve as an overview of the rise of U.S. imperialism. We have shown how the outcome of World War 1 established a certain framework for imperialist expansion and how the U.S. maneuvered within it. We have seen how new contradictions erupted within and eventually destroyed that framework. Yet out of the carnage of World War 2 emerged a new imperial order. There are of course other analytic approaches to both the history and political economy of the period. But unable to apprehend the movement and contradictions of imperialism as a concrete stage of world history, these approaches can neither explain the underlying causes and overriding significance of the first two world wars nor can they furnish an understanding of why we are in a prewar period today. Unfortunately, the dynamics of the postwar period were, to put it generously, misread by prominent spokesmen within the international communist movement. The fantastically disequilibrated relations of economic strength between the United States and the other imperialist economies and the removal of large stretches of the world from the imperialist orbit fed predictions of imminent breakdown and collapse. The dominant view in the international communist movement was that with the conclusion of the war, the capitalist economies would lapse into depression, or, more accurately, the Great Depression of the 1930s would resurface.

William Z. Foster, Chairman of the Communist Party, USA, argued in 1949 in his book *The Twilight of World Capitalism*:

> The next and inevitable economic collapse, which will center in the United States, will have its basis in the fact that war-swollen production in the U.S. has far outrun the consuming capacity of the lagging capitalist domestic and foreign markets. It will be much more terrible in its effects than the last crisis. [129]

Throughout the Western bloc, demobilization and the problems and complexities of reconstruction led to real difficulties. But they were essentially by-products of the preliminary phase of reorganization and restructuring of capital, that is, they were bound up with a brief period of adjustment. The 1945-47 period, far from being the end of a cycle of war-induced growth (which was how, in the main,

---

[129] William Z. Foster, *The Twilight of World Capitalism* (New York: International Publishers, 1949), p. 10.

TABLE 2.6

Economic Performance of the O.E.C.D. Countries,*1950-60
(at 1963 prices and exchange rates, in U.S. dollars)

Year	Gross National Product	Gross Domestic Fixed Asset Formation
1950	665.6	122.7
1951	715.5	123.7
1952	741.5	124.0
1953	776.2	132.8
1954	784.8	140.1
1955	841.3	154.9
1956	868.9	162.9
1957	893.0	166.9
1958	899.2	165.0
1959	949.3	178.4
1960	991.3	188.4
Average annual increase 1950-60	4.1%	4.4%

*The O.E.C.D. (Organization for Economic Cooperation and Development) countries include Canada, U.S., Japan, Austria, Belgium, Luxembourg, Denmark, Finland, France, Germany (F.R.), Greece, Iceland, Ireland, Italy, Netherlands, Norway, Portugal, Sweden, Switzerland, Turkey, and United Kingdom.

Source: Organization for Economic Cooperation and Development, *National Accounts of O.E.C.D. Countries, 1950-68* (Paris: O.E.C.D.), Table d, p. 21.

it was understood by revisionists and many genuine Marxists too), was actually the starting point of a whole new spiral, which included a rather prolonged period of development and expansion.

The proletariat, it is true, did make significant advances internationally through the war, but the imperialist order was also temporarily buoyed by the war's outcome and, in particular, by the magnitude of the U.S. victory over all its rivals. In point of fact, there was at the time no basis for a worldwide depression. And it was possible then, in basic terms, to analyze the concrete conditions of that time, especially as compared with those of the prewar period, and to actually discern the very real maneuvering room enjoyed by the imperialists. The essence of the matter is that the U.S.

TABLE 2.7
Growth of Total Real Output, Leading Imperialist Countries
(annual average percent increase)

	1900-1955	1947-1955*
U.S.	3.3	4.4
Japan	2.9	8.9
Germany	2.4	12.0
U.K.	1.3	2.9
France	1.1	6.0

*France and Germany averages are for 1948-55. After World War 2 the category "Germany" comprises only the Federal Republic of Germany.

Source: U.S. Bureau of Economic Analysis, *Long-Term Economic Growth, 1860-1970* (Washington, D.C.: GPO, 1973), D1-D5, pp. 274-75.

imperialists were not fundamentally stymied by interimperialist rivalries, economic difficulties, and other challenges, as they and the others had been before the war (and as they are again today). The problems were secondary to the more propitious framework that had been established.

The international communist movement held a view of crisis and war diametrically opposed to that of Lenin and to what has been argued in this work. That official orthodoxy was the theory of "general crisis." The theory of general crisis postulated the evolutionary descent of capitalism, based on the somewhat mechanical notion that the ground was being cut out and cut away from imperialism (even almost literally in a geographic sense). In the era of imperialism and proletarian revolution, according to this theory, capitalism could no longer fundamentally reorganize itself. A passage from *Economic Problems of Socialism in the U.S.S.R.*, written by Stalin in 1951-52, encapsulates much of this thinking. In it he wrote:

> Can it be affirmed that the thesis expounded by Lenin in the spring of 1916 – namely, that, in spite of the decay of capitalism, "on the whole capitalism is growing far more rapidly than before" – is still valid?
> I think that it cannot.

As he observed:

> . . . [T]he sphere of exploitation of the world's resources by the major capitalist countries (U.S.A., Britain, France) will not expand,

FIGURE 2.2
The Growth of World Trade: Value of Exports of Western Imperialist and Oppressed Countries, 1948 and 1958
(in billions of constant U.S. dollars)

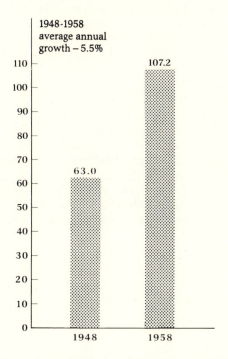

Source: *United Nations, Statistical Yearbook, 1977* (New York: 1978), Table 14, p. 55.

but contract; . . . their opportunities for sale in the world market will deteriorate, and . . . their industries will be operating more and more below capacity. That, in fact, is what is meant by the deepening of the general crisis of the world capitalist system in connection with the disintegration of the world market.[130]

[130] J.V. Stalin, *Economic Problems of Socialism in the U.S.S.R.* (Peking: Foreign Languages Press, 1972), pp. 32, 31.

History has surely rendered its verdict on that assessment. The experience of the 1950s alone (before capitalism was restored in the USSR itself and the victory of capitalism consolidated in most of the other countries of the Soviet-led socialist camp) shows that Lenin's thesis was indeed "still valid." Table 2.6 demonstrates capitalist expansion between 1950 and 1960 as measured by two useful indices. Overall growth is reflected in the index of Gross National Product. One can also note the increase in gross domestic fixed-asset formation. Table 2.7 compares the annual average growth rate of total real output of five leading imperialist countries over the period 1900-55 with that achieved during the 1947-55 period. The latter period was markedly higher. As for trade per se, the substantial (and, according to Stalin's prognostications, thoroughly unexpected) expansion of trade by the West and its colonial spheres of influence in the decade following the war (at a time when trade contact between the Western and Eastern bloc countries was minimal) is illustrated in the accompanying bar graph (see Figure 2.2). Since this theory sought to explain many of the same phenomena that have been examined in this chapter and denied the possibility of international reorganization of capital, the subject of the next volume, we shall conclude this volume with a critique of the theory of general crisis.

The Comintern Legacy: The Theory of General Crisis

Marxism-Leninism holds that capitalism is a doomed system. But how is this to be understood? The charge of "chicken-little"-ism is frequently leveled at Marxist political economy. At any given moment, some communist, it is alleged, will be shouting "the sky is falling" and prophesying impending capitalist economic collapse...only to put the predictions into cold storage when the vaunted breakdown fails to materialize. Unfortunately, the caricature rings of some truth, and much of the basis for it is to be found in the theory of general crisis, as promulgated by the Comintern. The damage inflicted by general crisis theory has been enormous: not only was Lenin's groundbreaking theoretical work on the political economy of the epoch not carried forward by the international communist movement, but in many crucial respects it was effectively overturned.

The influence of this has been far-reaching. Soviet political economy today makes use of the general crisis model, tailored to the shifting needs of social-imperialism. Major premises of general crisis theory have also been the fountainhead of analyses of imperialism produced outside the communist movement, even by neo-Marxists explicitly disavowing the Comintern tradition.[1] The persistent influence of general crisis theory, both as a unified explanation of the "limits" of capitalism since the Bolshevik Revolution and as a gloss on the texts of Marx and Lenin, calls for some

---

[1] Paul Sweezy and Paul Baran's highly influential *Monopoly Capital,* published in the 1960s, is a prominent case in point.

critical dissection based on what has been learned about the nature of imperialism in the first half of the twentieth century. It is perhaps ironic that a species of doomsday logic should be subjected to criticism in a work arguing that imperialism faces its most serious crisis. But if we are to truly comprehend the origins of this crisis and grasp its implications for revolutionary struggle, it is necessary to sharply differentiate the theory of general crisis from Marxism-Leninism, to settle accounts with a profoundly erroneous view of the imperialist epoch.

Notions of general crisis were bandied about by Soviet theoreticians in the early 1920s, but it was in the authoritative statements of Stalin at the Fifteenth and Sixteenth Congresses of the Communist Party of the Soviet Union in 1927 and 1930 that the idea of a general crisis of world capitalism received more specific formulation and was held to be vindicated by world events.[2] In the works of Eugen Varga, the leading Soviet political economist of the 1930s, it would be more fully spelled out in terms of basic categories of Marxist political economy; an accompanying picture of socioeconomic atavism in the capitalist countries would be drawn as well in *Fascism and Social Revolution* by R. Palme Dutt of the British Communist Party. The term general crisis was used at times to describe the post-World War 1 period, that is, an apparently new, disequilibrated state of affairs brought on by the Bolshevik Revolution's breach of the world imperialist front and the political and economic dislocations of the war. At other times, the term was used interchangeably with the imperialist era; in still other usages, it was a characterization of an allegedly new stage of imperialism. In the period of expansion following World War 2, the methodological legacy of general crisis theory led to a dizzying flip-flopping by Communist Party theorists between dire predictions of wholesale capitalist collapse and visions of a new, powerfully resilient and adaptable capitalism.

To put the matter bluntly, the theoreticians of the international communist movement neither understood Marxist political economy very well — that is, they failed to grasp the essence of capitalist crisis, falling instead into neo-Sismondian and neo-Luxemburgian underconsumption and market theories — nor did they really

[2] J.V. Stalin, "Political Report of the Central Committee to the Fifteenth Congress of the CPSU(B)" (2-19 December 1927), *Works* (Moscow: Foreign Languages Publishing House, 1954-1955), Volume 10, pp. 277-98; and "Political Report of the Central Committee to the Sixteenth Congress of the CPSU(B)" (27 June 1930), *Works*, Volume 12, pp. 242-69.

understand Leninism and the role of wars of redivision in temporarily and partially resolving the contradictions of imperialist accumulation. Indeed, general crisis theory downplayed and mis-
construed the global dynamics of imperialist accumulation, and the
world was viewed from a country-by-country and Eurocentric
perspective. Running through the various expositions and applica-
tions of this theory were three erroneous and interrelated explanations of crisis. First, stagnation was imperialism's normal state.
Capitalism had entered into an irreversible systemic crisis in which
periods of revival and boom were exceptional and bound to be
short-lived. Owing to universal impoverishment of the masses and
shrinking market opportunities, capitalism lacked the incentive to
develop the productive forces and to advance science and
technology. Second, and as the preceding point suggests, this
chronic crisis was rooted in a widening gap between producing and
consuming power. Finally, the world market was conceived in
terms of global consumer demand, and this world market itself was
constricting and nearing complete collapse. Viewed historically,
capitalism was reaching the absolute limits of internal and external
expansion. The general crisis was its slow dance of death. These
themes are the main targets of the critique that follows.

Capitalism, according to the Comintern theorists, no longer
developed through thrusts of expansion and crisis, the one dialectically related to the other. Rather, capitalism was passing through
stages of development of a prolonged, basically unrelieved crisis.
The Great Depression of the 1930s was viewed as paradigmatic of
capitalism's future. R. Palme Dutt, writing in 1934, argued that no
substantive recovery was possible:

> The general crisis of capitalism should not be confused with the
> old cyclical crises of capitalism which, although demonstrating the
> inherent contradictions of capitalist relations, nevertheless con-
> stituted an integral part and direct factor in the ascent of
> capitalism....
> ... Their characteristic feature was to *solve* the contradictions, al-
> beit by anarchically violent and destructive means, to *restore the
> equilibrium*, and permit of the resumption of production on a *higher*
> plane....
> Elements of this character can also be traced in the postwar world
> economic crisis; but these "progressive" elements are overshadow-
> ed by the major, negative effects of the whole process of the develop-
> ment of the cyclical crisis on the basis of the general crisis of
> capitalism, in the consequent destruction of stabilization and

hastening of revolutionizing processes.
For the general crisis of capitalism admits of no such solution.[3]

The Comintern theorists took note of the rather obvious deformation of the industrial cycle in the imperialist era and the undeniable fact that the crisis/recovery dialectic of classical capitalism no longer operated in the same way. While they correctly observed that the industrial cycles in themselves could not establish a new framework for growth, they were unable to grasp the internationalization of capital's circuits and how that dialectic played itself out in the international arena. Capitalism's inner mechanisms, they concluded, no longer sufficed to push it forward and out of crisis. The Great Depression could thus be expected to last indefinitely, punctuated by brief upward movements and revolutionary storms.

Here we might single out two notorious theorizations of this stagnationism. In many of the oppressed countries, the received Comintern tradition held that imperialism could not or would not promote the development of the productive forces, that imperialism was indissolubly linked to backward and stagnant modes of precapitalist superexploitation and incapable of spurring any significant industrialization.[4] But when both the possibilities and requirements of imperialist accumulation dictated diversification and modernization, as in the post-World War 2 period, then we find many of the Latin American Communist Parties jumping on the imperialist bandwagon. These parties were now seeking alliance with "progressive" bourgeois sectors, who, it was claimed, were doing battle with feudalism and backwardness. In actuality, these "progressive" sectors were tied to the imperialists and these ostensible battles amounted to imperialist-sponsored land reforms, infrastructure development, and other efforts on the part of the imperialists to restructure capital in the colonies (albeit, in some respects, at the expense of vested landed interests).

Dutt took the stagnationist argument to its logical conclusion: capitalism was in revolt against the machine and science, restrict-

---

[3] R. Palme Dutt, *Fascism and Social Revolution: A Study of the Economics and Politics of the Extreme Stages of Capitalism in Decay* (New York: International Publishers, 1934), p. 10.

[4] For some of the early Comintern debate around this question, see "Extracts from the Theses on the Revolutionary Movement in Colonial and Semicolonial Countries, Adopted by the Sixth Comintern Congress" (1 September 1928), in Jane Degras, ed., *The Communist International 1919-1943: Documents* (New York: Oxford Univ. Press, 1960), Volume 2, pp. 526-28.

ing instead of increasing production, and destroying productive forces (his central observation was that the post-World War 1 period had witnessed the first large-scale absolute setback of capitalist production). Society was actually being hurtled back in time to a lower stage of technical development; this retrogression and decay would continue until, according to Dutt, the working class, the real champion of technical progress, comes to power.[5] The main indictment of imperialism was thus its supposed inability to develop the productive forces. Moreover, it was argued that fascism would become the necessary and inescapable form of political rule since the bourgeoisie could only maintain control over an ever more impoverished proletariat through unmitigated terror (imperialism and democracy were held to be incompatible). And, again, when the imperialists showed themselves capable of unleashing productive and technical development, it was not too great a leap in theory (and practice) to now embrace the "progressive" and "antifascist" wings of the bourgeoisie.

General crisis theory correctly recognized that one inter-imperialist war would lead to another and that imperialism was heading towards extinction. But the latter was conceptualized as a secular decline, as the evanescing of a system that had lost its dynamism. Figure 3.1 shows the growth of total real output in five major capitalist countries during a period ostensibly gripped by a general crisis. What stands out is both the precipitous decline of the 1930s depression and the boom of the post-World War 2 decades. The theory of general crisis could not explain such phenomena.

This vision of decline represented a departure from the Leninist analysis of simultaneous growth and decay, of an internally dynamic system which can only develop through breakneck leaps, of a throbbing and convulsive capitalism which is like a stumbling runner — lurching forward but never capable of regaining any smooth stride. In essence, it denied that imperialism represented a development and a continuation of the fundamental characteristics of capitalism. Hence, instead of development through explosive intensification of captalism's contradictions — and with it the strengthening of the material basis for proletarian revolution and the ultimate goal of classless society — we get a gradualistic slide into the abyss, a kind of prescribed endgame. While capitalism cannot in the long run overcome its contradictions, there is no such

---

[5] See Dutt, *Fascism and Social Revolution*, pp. 12, 24-25, 42-58.

FIGURE 3.1
Indices of Total Real Output for
Five Leading Imperialist Countries, Selected Years
(1913 = 100 for each country)

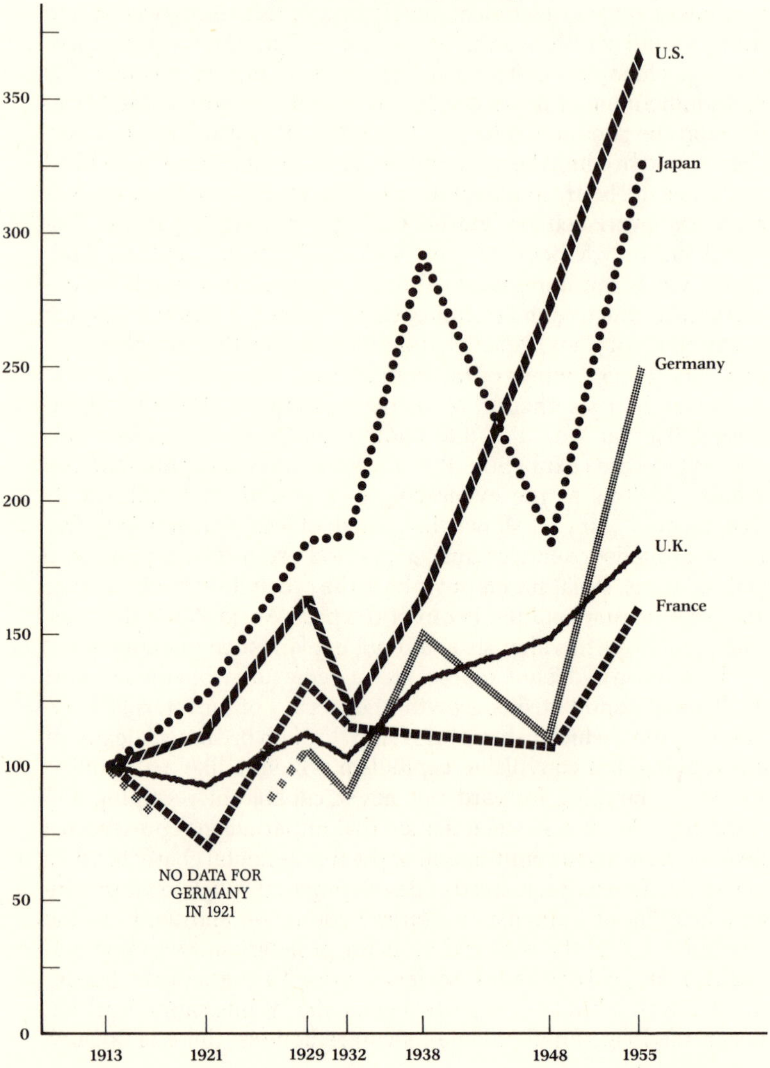

Source: U.S. Bureau of Economic Analysis, *Long-Term Economic Growth, 1860-1970* (Washington, D.C.: GPO, 1973), D1-D5, pp. 274-275.

thing as a permanent crisis.[6] To put it differently: *capitalism cannot endlessly expand, but it cannot, as capitalism, stop expanding.*

The conceptual underpinning of the stagnationist perspective was underconsumptionism. Varga's *The Great Crisis and Its Political Consequences*, completed in 1934, posited as its theoretical point of departure the distinction between "purchasing power," which was defined as constant capital, variable capital, and surplus value, and "consuming power," which was defined as the sum available for the purchase of commodities for individual consumption. The relative diminution of the latter, particularly that component represented by wages, was held to be the Achilles' heel of capitalist reproduction:

> The constant relative diminution of consuming power (disregarding the cyclic course of production) compared to the development of the productive forces leads to a chronic accentuation of the contradiction between the productive power and the consuming power of capitalist society, since the individual capitalists, driven by the necessity of winning in the competitive struggle, develop the productive forces without taking the relative diminution of consuming power into consideration. This is *the economic basis for the general crisis of capitalism,* for the chronic idleness of a large part of the productive apparatus, for chronic mass unemployment.[7]

The significance of monopoly was also analyzed through the underconsumptionist lens: the growing power of the financial oligarchy, the resort to monopoly price, the practice of wage-cutting, and monopoly-induced rationalization were factors exacerbating this lagging absorptive capacity. In A. Leontiev's *Political Economy*, the standard primer circulated by the Comintern, we find this typical passage in the chapter on crisis:

> Thus, inherent in capitalism, there is the deepest contradiction between the colossal growth of production possibilities and the relatively reduced purchasing power of the working masses. . . . This tendency towards an *unlimited expansion of industry* inevitably comes into conflict with the *limited powers of consumption* of the broad masses of workers. The growth of exploitation does not only

---

[6] Karl Marx, *Theories of Surplus Value,* Part II (Moscow: Progress Publishers, 1968), p. 497n.

[7] Eugen Varga, *The Great Crisis and Its Political Consequences* (New York: International Publishers, 1934), p. 20.

mean the growth of production. It also means a reduction in the purchasing power of the masses, a curtailment of the possibility of selling commodities. The purchasing power of the masses of workers
and peasants remains at a low level. Hence the *inevitability of overproduction crises* under capitalism.[8]

This approach was dead wrong and not at all Marxist.

Lenin contrasted two different approaches to crisis, the one,
Sismondian, and the other, Marxist:

> The first theory explains crises by the contradiction between pro-
> duction and consumption by the working class; the second explains
> them by the contradiction between the social character of produc-
> tion and the private character of appropriation. Consequently, the
> former sees the root of the phenomenon *outside of* production
> (hence, for example, Sismondi's general attacks on the classical
> economists for ignoring consumption and occupying themselves on-
> ly with production); the latter sees it precisely in the conditions of
> production. To put it more briefly, the former [Sismondian] explains
> crisis by underconsumption . . . the latter [Marxist] by the anarchy
> of production.[9]

The Comintern theorists basically operated within a Sismondian
mold. They ritualistically asserted that the contradiction between
socialized production and private appropriation was the fundamental contradiction of the capitalist mode of production. But this
was reduced to the contradiction between the bourgeoisie and the
proletariat and that contradiction itself was narrowly defined. The
problem, they argued — and we should recall Leontiev's description of the "deepest contradiction" — was that the working class
could not consume its social product, since capitalism did not produce for use. Thus, lack of consuming power was the cause of
crisis. The argument required a theoretical sleight of hand. The
contradiction between socialized production and private appropriation was essentially transformed into the contradiction between the level of production and the level of effective demand.
And the contradiction between production and consumption was
equated with increasing immiseration of the masses. Pride of

[8] A. Leontiev, *Political Economy* (New York: International Publishers, n.d.), p.
184.

[9] V.I. Lenin, "A Characterization of Economic Romanticism," *Collected Works*
(*LCW*) (Moscow: Progress Publishers), 2, p. 167.

place in this schema was implicitly accorded the realm of consumption and the production of wage goods. In effect, the consuming capacity of society was considered the independent variable of accumulation.

A brief discussion of these points is necessary. To begin with, the restricted consumption of the masses is hardly a new phenomenon. As Engels pointed out:

> It has existed as long as there have been exploiting and exploited classes. . . . The underconsumption of the masses is a necessary condition of all forms of society based on exploitation, consequently also of the capitalist form; but it is the capitalist form of production which first gives rise to crises. The underconsumption of the masses is therefore also a prerequisite condition of crises, and plays in them a role which has long been recognized. But it tells us just as little why crises exist today as why they did not exist before.[10]

What, then, is the specificity of consumption under capitalism? " 'Consumption,' " Lenin wrote, "develops *after* 'accumulation,' or *after* 'production'; strange though it may seem, it cannot be otherwise in capitalist society."[11] It is the demand of capital for labor power that sets the productive process in motion. While the value represented by wages is created by the labor of the workers themselves in the overall process of capitalist production, these wages in fact form part of the expenses of the capitalists. Wages are an element, variable capital, of the total investment bill.[12] Hence, even though the demand for consumer goods comes preponderantly from the wage-earning population, this demand is a *derivative* one — it has its source in the investment outlays of the capitalist class, and these correspond to the needs of the self-expansion of capital. Wages and consumption are not separable from investment nor is consumption the goad of capitalist production. Actually, it is the ability of capital to *profitably* accumulate surplus value which is the deepest determinant of the level of social purchasing power and, *a fortiori*, it is the labor process as a value-creation process that defines the historically limited character of capitalist production.

[10] Frederick Engels, *Anti-Dühring* (Moscow: Progress Publishers, 1969), pp. 340-41.

[11] "A Characterization of Economic Romanticism," *LCW*, 2, p. 155.

[12] This is a point stressed and developed by Anwar Shaikh in his "An Introduction to the History of Crisis Theories," *U.S. Capitalism in Crisis* (Union for Radical Political Economy, 1978).

Grasping this makes it possible to understand both why lower production costs and accelerated accumulation may be accompanied by higher wages, as was the case for an extended period after World War 2, and why Marx could also observe (with respect to the accumulation cycle of premonopoly capitalism) that "crises are always prepared by precisely a period in which wages rise generally and the working class actually gets a larger share of that part of the annual product which is intended for consumption."[13]

The advance of capitalist production is not simply a matter of the growth of the consumer goods industries. Given the decisive importance of mechanization and technical innovation to the expanded and profitable reproduction of capital, the producer goods industries must undergo extensive development. Further, personal consumption does not represent the totality of consumption in capitalist society. The *productive* consumption of the capitalists, i.e., demand for and use of machine tools, steel, etc., will augment social purchasing power: both directly, in the form of the demand for means of production, and indirectly, in the form of greater demand for consumer goods coming from workers employed in producer goods industries. To be sure, constant capital is not "produced for its own sake."[14] Through a complex series of interrelationships, production of means of production is connected to production of means of consumption. But there is no one-to-one relationship between, let's say, so many tons of aluminum and so many commodities for personal consumption. Some of this aluminum is purchased by automakers and other producers in department 2 who manufacture consumer goods. But some of it goes into department 1, the sector producing means of production — either to branches producing machines that would be used by the consumer goods industries (and thus eventually expand consumer goods output) or into branches producing machines and equipment to produce machines and equipment. The point is that the production of means of production is relatively independent of production of articles of consumption (and some output, like military hardware, is never even indirectly destined for personal consumption). Mass consumption neither regulates the interrelation between or the growth of the two departments of social production, nor does it represent the absolute bound of capitalist production as a whole.

[13] Marx, *Capital,* II (Moscow: Progress Publishers, 1971), p. 415.
[14] *Capital,* III, p. 305.

There is indeed a contradiction between the unlimited drive to expand the productive forces and the limits to consumption, and it is a contradiction which intensifies economic disorder. But there is no intrinsic or widening "demand gap" that represents capitalism's fatal flaw.[15] The accumulation of surplus value is also a process of the creation of markets. Through the extension of the capitalist mode of production and a more complex division of labor, the demand for means of production and, via demand for labor power, for means of consumption, increases. Nonetheless, it remains true that the conditions of production and realization are not identical and the existence of separate and unevenly developing commodity producers, in competition with each other and working for an unknown market, makes the realization of the aggregate social product anything but a smooth process. But, as Marx emphasized, "crisis arises out of the special aspects of capital which are *peculiar* to it as capital, and not merely comprised in its existence as commodity and money."[16] It is the overall (deteriorating) conditions of profitability which result in declining demand for both means of production and means of consumption, and it is the anarchic interrelations of an overaccumulating capital that impede and undermine its profitable reproduction. The resolution of crisis resides neither in the restriction of output nor in the stimulation of demand as such; rather, it involves the overall restructuring of capital, which is fundamentally a matter of its value relations. Expanded consumption is a result of such restructuring, not its cause.

The Comintern theorists sought to buttress their underconsumptionist case by arguing that "the *absolute impoverishment of the working class* comes to the fore more and more strikingly in the period of the general crisis of capitalism."[17] By this they meant that the numbers of unemployed must increase while the wages of the employed would invariably be pushed below the value of their labor power. During the late 1920s and early 1930s, Varga set out to demonstrate that capitalist development had finally led to an absolute decline in the number of productive workers, and that this was the trend of the future; thus capitalism's absorptive capacity

---

[15] The reformist implications of many underconsumptionist positions are none too mysterious: a redistribution of income (higher wages or transfer payments) would be to the mutual advantage of both workers and capitalists since the increased consumption of workers would result in a greater volume of sales for capital.

[16] *Theories of Surplus Value*, II, pp. 512-13.

[17] Varga, *The Great Crisis*, p. 20.

would be permanently impaired.[18] Dutt picked up the cudgel. Correctly stating that the accumulation process displaces workers and creates an industrial reserve army which both serves the fluctuating requirements of production and helps maintain the proletariat in subjection, he then went on to argue:

> But this industrial reserve army was a part of the machinery of expanding capitalist production; the absolute number of productive workers successively grew. It is only since the war that the new phenomenon appeared of a permanent unemployed army, grudgingly kept just alive at the lowest level of subsistence by the bourgeoisie, while the absolute number of productive workers employed has directly decreased.[19]

The explanations for this phenomenon of a permanent diminution of employment possibilities ranged from technological revolutions in the twenties and rationalization schemes during the crisis years to the complete absorption of noncapitalist modes of production.

The experience of the ensuing four decades certainly does not sustain this thesis. Although a permanent reserve army of the unemployed (into which has been crowded many oppressed nationalities, immigrants, youth, etc.) is an important feature of the imperialist economies, the total volume of employment has not secularly declined in any of them. Now if a case were being made for reduced demand stemming from the decline of productive or industrial employment, it overlooked the demand stimulated by the increase in nonindustrial employment.[20] More to the point, the argument sidestepped the significance of the internationalization of capital. The structure of production and employment in particular imperialist countries is influenced by the division of the world, including, very decisively, the distribution of colonies. In this spiral, for instance, a tremendous shift of industrial employment out of the imperialist countries to certain Third World countries has taken place. If one were to compare the total level of industrial employment in the world in the period of the 1920s with that of any decade since World War 2, it was certainly higher in the latter period; at

---

[18] For an account of the debate around Varga's theorem, see Richard B. Day, *The "Crisis" and the "Crash": Soviet Studies of the West (1917-1939)* (London: New Left Books, 1981), pp. 146-70.

[19] Dutt, *Fascism and Social Revolution*, pp. 16-17.

[20] See Day, *"Crisis" and "Crash,"* pp. 154-55.

the same time, the level of nonindustrial employment relative to total employment has also been higher during these recent decades. The Marxian view, that the displacement of human labor by machines is accompanied by a declining rate of growth of variable capital in relation to total capital, holds.

The real crux of this issue is the international framework and determinants of accumulation. Based on the overall structure of international capital, the profitability of capital, the unemployment rate, and the living standards in the imperialist countries can go up or down. There are several imperialist countries, notably West Germany and Japan, that sustained economic growth for decades — with rising living standards and negligible unemployment. Indeed, one pernicious legacy of general crisis theory has been a tendency to assume that the central manifestation of crisis is economic collapse, mass unemployment, and widespread impoverishment within the imperialist countries themselves. Actually, for the Comintern, mass unemployment in the advanced countries was seen as the elixir of revolution. Apart from underestimating the degree to which the imperialists can make economic concessions (even in crisis), such thinking denies that the greatest unemployment and immiseration is centered in the Third World. Not grasping the dialectical connection between these phenomena in the imperialist and colonial countries is yet another legacy of the theory — which raises a related issue.

There was a definite Eurocentric bent to general crisis theory. The importance of the colonial world to the successful accumulation of imperialist capital was downplayed and seen, in the main, in relation to the overproduction of commodities in the advanced countries. The privileges of the imperialist nations were papered over and the theory cut against one of Lenin's principal insights into class relations in the imperialist countries: "the split in the working class." The parasitic position of the imperialist countries results in the corruption of significant sections of the working class; the revolutionary vanguard, Lenin emphasized, must "go down *lower* and *deeper*, to the real masses. . . ."[21] The Comintern tended to treat the working class as a monolithic bloc, an approach which nurtured voluntarism and opportunism. In the twenties and early thirties, the Communist Parties blamed the social democrats for the backwardness and reformism of various sections of the working

---

[21] "Imperialism and the Split in Socialism," *LCW*, 23, p. 120.

class. By the mid-thirties, they were conciliating these same social democrats and sections of the bourgeoisie in order to "win the majority" of workers — with a program of democracy and antifascism. Not only was their political economy dubious, but (besides the evident chauvinism) it led to an arrantly incorrect view of the preparatory tasks of revolution in the advanced countries.[22]

Lenin conceptualized imperialism as a world system; the Comintern theoreticians conceived it as the mere aggregate of individual national economies. Conspicuously missing from their analytic framework was an understanding of a new international dynamic in the imperialist era — in short, that national economies are integrated into a single world process which is linked with the qualitatively heightened socialization of production, the internationalization of capital, and the complete partition of the world among the imperialist powers. The Comintern theorists did not operate with an understanding that the world market is an integral and determining whole. In general crisis theory, imperialism was largely approached from the perspective of the national formation looking out into the world.

Expansion was seen as a response to the pressure for markets, specifically in relation to shrinking domestic markets. In many important respects, the view more closely resembled that of Lenin's contemporary, the British liberal economist Hobson, who regarded the foreign market as a safety valve for an excess of goods that could not be sold at home on account of high monopoly prices. The role of capital export was consistently minimized and generally presented as a means to climb tariff walls to facilitate the sale of goods. Rather than proceeding from the reproduction and contradictions of an internationalized mode of production which is rooted in national

---

[22] It is beyond the scope of this work to fully trace out the political implications of the general crisis line. Suffice it to say that lack of clarity on Lenin's theory of imperialism reinforced tendencies to cast *What Is To Be Done?* to the winds. The "struggle for bread" in the imperialist countries was held to have become an intrinsically revolutionary one: if imperialism were incapable of meeting the barest needs of survival of the laboring masses, then the demands that these needs be met would of necessity pose a direct challenge to the entire imperialist order. Lenin's verdicts on economic struggle were reversed, his struggle against economism abandoned. On these and related points, see J.P., "Some Notes on the Study of *What Is To Be Done?*" *The Communist*, No. 5 (May 1979); "Slipping Into Darkness: 'Left' Economism, the CPUSA, and the Trade Union Unity League," *Revolution*, Volume 5, No. 2-3 (February/March 1980); Revolutionary Communist Party, "Imperialist Economism, or the European Disease," *A World To Win*, No. 2 (May 1982).

markets, an attempt was made to explain the crisis of the 1930s from the standpoint of the market problems of relatively self-contained national formations. It was argued that a fundamental tendency of the epoch was the increasing isolation of states from one another[23] — when any real analysis shows just the opposite tendency to be principal. The Comintern theorists were extrapolating, of course, from the protectionism of the 1930s. But in point of fact, the international arena was not any less of a determining whole; there was simply more disorder within it.

Speaking of the course of the crisis of the 1930s, Varga wrote:

> The inner mechanism of capitalism was effective enough to overcome the lowest point of the crisis, to bring about the transition to a depression, and in some countries to create a limited revival; but it does not prove to be effective enough to produce a real boom, a prosperity phase.[24]

The depression of the 1930s did not in itself generate the conditions for recovery. But to conclude from this that capital cannot undergo any fundamental or thoroughgoing reorganization which would furnish the basis for accumulation on a renewed and higher level is to deny the very nature of capital. The inner mechanism of capital accumulation, the destruction/restructuring dialectic, continues to operate in the imperialist era. This has been extensively analyzed in terms of international conjunctures, the role of interimperialist war, and the restructuring that follows in the aftermath of major changes in international alignments.

General crisis theory focused on depression (of a "special kind"), as opposed to interimperialist war. And war itself was sundered from the real dynamics of imperialist accumulation and rivalry. Consequently, the two imperialist world wars were often regarded as wholly dysfunctional, in no substantial way thrusting accumulation forward — hence the routine predictions of postwar collapse. And world war was treated as an expression of the realization and market difficulties of a capitalism which, having passed its historic apogee of development, could only utilize productive forces for destruction. To wit, Dutt on the specter of a second world war: "In the face of these facts increasing doubts begin to assail the capitalists whether there can ever be full-scale employment again. . . . As

[23] See Varga, *The Great Crisis*, p. 26.
[24] Varga, *The Great Crisis*, p. 74.

this new situation begins to be realized, the beckoning phantom of a new world war as the only 'solution' to utilize the productive forces and wipe off the 'superfluous' population begins to exercise a visibly increasing attraction on capitalist thought and policy as the final gamble.''[25]

The dialectic of imperialist expansion and crisis works itself out through the overall reorganization of capital on a world scale, within which the colonies play a central role. If the Comintern theorists did not grasp this, still, they recognized that capitalism must extend and reorganize itself. The problem, as they saw it, was that this was no longer possible:

> In the present depression the following change has taken place: the process of "depeasantizing," as Lenin calls it, i.e., drawing the agricultural producers into the capitalist market is essentially completed in the most highly developed capitalist countries: the U.S.A., England, and Germany. In the present agrarian crisis the process of differentiation develops into the wholesale ruin of the small and middle peasants.[26]

These assertions scarcely comport with the factual evidence. To take a striking example, one of the most extraordinary social transformations in the history of U.S. capitalism took place during and in the aftermath of World War 2: the large-scale proletarianization and urbanization of millions of Black people, the bulk of whom were previously engaged in sharecropping agriculture.[27] Similar processes occurred in the other imperialist countries, especially Japan and Italy. On the other hand, precapitalist relations in the advanced countries were largely of the order of remnants and in the above discussion Varga barely touched on the potential for transforming production relations in the Third World, a process which was extensive and pivotal to expanded reproduction in the post-World War 2 period. In general, the colonial countries were viewed mainly in stagnationist terms. Mired in backwater modes, their capacity for absorbing goods from the advanced countries was chronically impaired.

---

[25] Dutt, *Fascism and Social Revolution*, pp. 22-23.

[26] Varga, *The Great Crisis*, p. 76.

[27] The Comintern also argued, in keeping with its stagnationist orientation, that Black people would remain, in their vast majority, sharecroppers in the southern United States.

The Comintern theorists constructed a logical argument, focusing in the realm of circulation, as to why capitalism could no longer profitably reproduce and extend itself. In the advanced countries, the nonproletarian reserves were well-nigh exhausted, overproduction and low wages put a brake on the renewal of fixed capital, and these same low wages and permanent unemployment undercut the market for consumer goods. In the colonies, the pricing "scissors" (high prices charged by the imperialists for their manufactured goods and low prices forced on the colonies for their marketed output), the one-crop and highly agrarian character of their economies, competition to the imperialists from local consumer manufacturers, and the existence of a large and impoverished peasantry — all militated against imperialist expansion. This overall analysis was at once an accounting of a specific, concrete crisis of imperialism and a projection of imperialism's trend-line. In other words, the crisis was so severe and the systemic and structural obstacles to the generation of new markets so complete (and to these factors would later be added the existence of a socialist camp), that capitalism could not extricate itself from crisis. The future held out long-term stagnation or self-destructive war.

A theoretician from an earlier period reached similar conclusions which bear directly on the discussion. This was Rosa Luxemburg, a founder of the Communist Party of Germany, who was murdered in 1919 by the military authorities acting under the auspices of the Social Democratic Party. Luxemburg failed to comprehend the specificity of the imperialist stage of capitalist development, in particular the contradiction between monopoly and competition. For Luxemburg, capitalism's international thrust was mainly a question of increasing and extending the scope of its trade with the rest of the world. Closely related, she, like the Comintern thinkers, posited a unilinear approach by capitalism to its final limit. And, like the Comintern again, she posed this in the realm of realization. In this sense, the Comintern's position was just a warmed-over variant of Luxemburgism. The difference — and this was her virtue in a certain way — was that Luxemburg associated that limit precisely with the Third World, with the depeasantizing process there.

In 1913, Luxemburg published her major theoretical work, *The Accumulation of Capital*. There and in her subsequent *Anti-Critique* she put forward a schema based on a chronic shortfall in demand. How was the total commodity product to be realized when workers' consumption was confined to the narrow limits of their wages and when the capitalists had to defer spending (outside their own personal consumption and replacement expenditures to maintain the current level of production) in order to accumulate the money reserves to finance future investments? Closing this demand gap required, according to Luxemburg, a class of buyers outside of capitalist society who could absorb this output without adding to it — and these consumers were to be found in pre- or noncapitalist sectors, mainly in the colonies. Eventually, however, these layers would be incorporated into the process of capitalist production and no one would be left to realize this commodity product. Hence, the capitalists would not be able to realize surplus value and underwrite further expansion.

Luxemburg tended to view the total capital as a single and indissoluble unit.[28] She incorrectly assumed that all capitals are simultaneously hoarding money capital for future investments — when in fact this process goes on unevenly, with some saving and others borrowing idle funds and investing. She implicitly assumed that the total social product streams into the market simultaneously, requiring that it be realized all at once — when in fact realization, like investment, is a continuous, if anarchic, process. More important, she failed to see how investment, premised on profitability or the prospect of it, could stimulate expanded consumption within the orbit of capitalist society. The expansion of capital requires the continual perfecting of the division of labor and generates its own demand and markets. In short, Luxemburg's central thesis is wrong, capitalism's fate does not rest on "outside" buyers.

But what of the "eating up" of the noncapitalist milieu by capitalist production relations? Lenin put great emphasis on the spread of commodity production and the differentiation of the peasantry — some becoming proletarians and others becoming capitalists — in the process of market creation. Colonial superprofits play a decisive part in the process of imperialist accumulation. It is also true, on the other hand, that there is a dynamic of heightened contradiction as the world is consumed by capitalist production relations. Is there a sense, then, in which neo-Luxemburgism — at least to the degree that it takes into account the critical role of the Third World — can be said to be accurate? The answer is no.

---

[28] This point is made by Michal Kalecki in connection with Luxemburg's view of investment in his *Selected Essays on the Dynamics of the Capitalist Economy* (London: Cambridge Univ. Press, 1971), pp. 151-52.

Even if all production relations in the world were to become capitalist — and assuming that even were there a socialist camp it would almost certainly exist for some time in a world dominated by the capitalist mode of production — the theory of general crisis and stagnationism would still not be valid. While the Third World is a crucial reserve of imperialism — as well as a crucial arena of revolutionary struggle — it would be incorrect to identify the transformation of the noncapitalist regions of the world as the driving force of capitalist expansion. The Third World, even understood scientifically in terms of the export of capital and the internationalization of production, is not the ultimate limit to imperialist expansion. Capital must and can restructure itself, though ever more spasmodically and violently, in an increasingly capitalized world environment; theoretically, it can do so even in one in which precapitalist relations have been totally dissolved. Capital is driven to break through the barriers that hem in the development of the productive forces, even though in doing this it only strengthens the basis for its destruction.

In *Capital*, Marx had provocatively posed that the problem for analysis was to explain why the capitalist mode of production had not already fallen apart, given all its contradictions.[29] This was in the context of his exposition of the countertendencies to the tendency of the rate of profit to fall. Marx's point was that capitalism is capable of expansion, but that this is a "moving contradiction." There are boundaries to accumulation coterminous with the very determination of value. The foundation of capital is the appropriation of surplus value, which is produced by living labor. In the *Grundrisse*, Marx wrote:

> Thus the more developed capital already is, the more surplus labor it has created, the more terribly must it develop the productive force in order to realize itself in only smaller proportion.... It can move only within these boundaries. The smaller already the fractional part falling to *necessary labor*, the greater the *surplus labor*, the less can any increase in productive force perceptibly diminish necessary labor....
>
>   ... Capital itself is the moving contradiction, in that it presses to reduce labor time to a minimum, while it posits labor time, on the other side, as sole measure and source of wealth.[30]

[29] See *Capital*, III, p. 232.

[30] Marx, *Grundrisse*, translated with a foreword by Martin Nicolaus (Middlesex, England: Penguin, 1973), pp. 340, 706.

The end of capitalism, however, is not a predetermined point in time and space when an absolute limit to the production (or realization) of surplus value will be reached. "Production," Marx wrote, "moves in contradictions which are constantly overcome but just as constantly posited,"[31] and his image of capital's ever more "terrible" exertions to maintain and extend itself is graphically to the point in this epoch and takes on special meaning. This mode of production is driven to displace its contradictions to wider spheres and to intensively restructure itself. More rapid growth, more pervasive parasitism; accumulation thrust forward, only to turn into its explosive opposite — this is a system which in straining against its limits produces upheavals and transformations. The dialectics of these spirals are the dialectics of the extinction of imperialism.

The theory of general crisis sought to locate certain limits which would, to borrow a phrase from Lenin, signify the impossibility of capitalism. Between here and there growth would decelerate. But the destruction of imperialism is not a process of secular economic decline, much less the product of intensifying economic struggle. For imperialism and all exploiting classes must be consciously overthrown. And as Mao brilliantly analyzed and showed through the Cultural Revolution, they must be ever more consciously overthrown *again and again* until the soil from which grow commodity production and antagonistic social divisions is cleared away through revolutionary transformation in all spheres of society. This is the process of worldwide and continuing proletarian revolution: the final limit to capitalism.

For all its apocalyptic trappings and soundings, the theory of general crisis posited a kind of moving equilibrium of crisis. There was no dynamism left in capitalism, only a crisis that would progressively worsen. This fed an evolutionist (and economist) political strategy; the forces for revolution would gradually accumulate against the backdrop of a static environment, the general crisis. The system would break down and the working class would more or less "step into the breach." Thus the question of leaps in the objective situation, including unexpected political jolts, was negated. Thus the importance of all-around revolutionary work and the role of revolutionary political consciousness were denigrated. And thus the disorientation when the economic collapse did not materialize. Let us return to Soviet political economy in the immediate post-World War 2 period.

---

[31] *Grundrisse*, p. 410.

FIGURE 3.2
Trends in World Trade, 1928-1958
(volume of world trade exports in billions of U.S. dollars)*

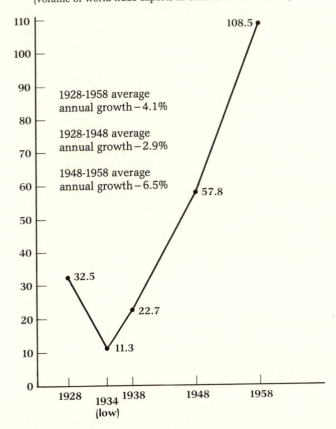

*Since this graph is calibrated in *current dollars* and the graph in Figure 2.2 is calibrated in *constant dollars*, neither the dollar figures nor the growth rates are directly comparable between the two graphs.

Source: U.S. State Department, *The Trade Debate* (Washington: GPO, January, 1979), p. 6

Each time the cycle in the imperialist countries, especially the United States, turned downward, official Soviet political economy was quick to pronounce this the beginning of the end, the onset of a real and "final" crisis of overproduction. And, of course, each time the cycle resumed an upward climb, the same economists spouting this conventional wisdom would make a self-criticism, explaining why, after all, the previous recession had not been the "real" crisis, but how the next one surely would be. Which brings us back to Stalin's views, cited at the end of Chapter 2, on the postwar period. Capitalism, he argued, would grow less rapidly than before since a large portion of the world now formed part of the socialist world market; hence, the opportunities for sale must deteriorate and industry stagnate. The picture that emerged from his postwar pronouncements was that of a world imperialist system closing in on itself.

In keeping with the Comintern problematic, Stalin regarded capital expansion only in extensive terms, i.e., new markets and territories. He overlooked the ability of the capitalists to more thoroughly, that is, more intensively, exploit existing markets through the further development of capitalism in the colonies, for instance, and the further restructuring of capital in the advanced countries. The fact of the matter was that the imperialist bloc headed by the U.S. could expand trade well beyond previous levels, even though this was within a geographically smaller part of the world than it had controlled before the war. Capitalism's ability to do this hinges on the wholesale reorganization of the imperialist world within which these territories and markets reside, precisely what war serves to accomplish. As for the overall growth of world trade, a possibility Stalin effectively denied, see Figure 3.2.

Stalin was in part waging a rearguard struggle against those political economists (among whom now numbered none other than Varga) who were arguing that the capitalist countries could manipulate and stimulate demand through the right mix of state expenditure and planning, and thus ameliorate crisis indefinitely. This was a new wrinkle, but, in a very significant sense, a logical continuation of the general crisis formulation. Confronted by the reality of post-World War 2 capitalist growth, economists like Varga could only explain the situation by turning to an "external" agent, like state planning. This was facilitated as well by their developing view of socialism as the combination of technical progress and a state plan. Hence, the roots of "peaceful competition," "peaceful transition," and other revisionist theories of the 1950s and 1960s.[32]

---

[32] On Varga's theoretical ambivalence towards the New Deal and his postwar prognostications, see Day, *"Crisis" and "Crash,"* Chap. 8. Varga's fusion of general crisis theory with the tenets of Khrushchevite revisionism can be found in his last major work, *Twentieth-Century Capitalism* (1964. Reprint. New York: Arno Press, 1972).

Just as in the case of the struggle he waged in the late 1920s against the rightists, who had suggested that capitalism could stabilize itself — a struggle out of which came the general crisis theory — Stalin was again countering revisionist formulations with incorrect methodology and theory, with indeed *the same* incorrect methodology and theory that he had held twenty-five years earlier. Only in the late 1920s the imperialist system was entering into a deep crisis which, on the surface, seemed to confirm the theory, or at least lent it credence. Now, however, the imperialist system was at the starting point of a whole new wave of expansion.

General crisis theory could neither explain the underpinnings and parameters of that expansion nor refute the claims of those political economists intoxicated by the seeming "success" of capitalism. Its methodological weaknesses stood out the more as the floodgates opened to all variety of revisionist junk: notions of a capitalism more responsive to social need; obsessions with "technological revolutions"; fascination with state intervention; and arguments that imperialist states could peacefully coexist with each other and with socialism. Either imperialism faced impending collapse and war or it had become something more benign and rational: such a debate could not comprehend the dialectics of the new situation, because its protagonists could not comprehend the dialectics of the epoch. With the triumph of revisionism in the Soviet Union in the mid-1950s, a theory marred by economism and Eurocentrism underwent a qualitative transformation. With a self-serving fluidity of formulation, a now wholly social-chauvinist version of general crisis has been pressed into the service of a new imperialist class.

U.S. military and political dominance fostered the reorganization of the structure of imperialist power (principally on the basis of counterrevolutionary imperialist unity). This created a new framework for the conflict among capitals and made possible, based on the settlement of the war — and, in particular, the more thorough penetration of U.S. capital into the colonies this facilitated — a relatively long period of expansion. This process of restructuring was accomplished chiefly through the political reorganization of the world and the concomitant possibilities this opened up for the export of capital. Widespread areas of the world were drawn into a new imperialist network of relations headed by the U.S. The global structure of capital was recast. How the world economy was reorganized and the U.S.-led bloc forged and how the existence of a socialist camp which would later emerge as a rival imperialist bloc influenced that process is the subject of the next volume of this work.

Index

About Raymond Lotta

Raymond Lotta has written extensively on international relations, the current world crisis, and problems of the socialist transition period. He edited and wrote the introductory essay to *And Mao Makes 5* (Banner, 1978), which chronicles the struggle within the Chinese Communist Party in the early and mid-1970s culminating in the defeat of the revolutionary forces. In 1983, he represented the viewpoint that the Soviet Union is imperialist at an international conference and debate on the nature of the Soviet Union held in New York City. His presentation and the text of the entire debate appear in *The Soviet Union: Socialist or Social-Imperialist? Part 2: The Question is Joined* (RCP Publications, 1983). Lotta has traveled widely, including to China. He has been a frequent lecturer at universities and has made numerous appearances on television and radio public affairs programs. At present, he is completing research on the concluding volumes of *America in Decline*.